Are you in need of urgent help with your finances? Do you feel trapped by a critical shortage of money to pay bills, buy food, pay your rent or mortgage, and cover other living expenses? Do you believe it's God's will for you to take a vow of poverty (whether you really want to or not)? Or are you just starting out in life and wondering how to avoid making colossal blunders in your financial plan? Whatever your situation may be, here's all the help you've been looking for. In this lively and informative book, Harold Hill presents the Master's plan for money management, drawn from "The Manufacturer's Handbook," the Bible. Practical and easy-to-follow, **The Money Book for King's Kids** is packed with biblical wisdom concerning financial matters and hearty exhortations for creating the proper attitude for prosperity. With spirited discussion, Harold Hill gives you an effective plan for applying these principles in specific areas, including:

- **savings and investments**
- **debt reduction**
- **groceries, utilities, and medical expenses**
- **giving and tithing**
- **credit cards**
- **insurance and wills**

If you don't have enough time for all the Bible reading you need to do, neither do I. That's why everywhere I go, I listen to Bible tapes on a little cassette player. For ordering information about my favorite version, as well as about the books and teaching tapes that will help you with attitude control for victorious living, send a self-addressed, stamped envelope to:

Harold E. Hill
King's Kids' Korner
P.O. Box 8655
Baltimore, MD 21240
Phone (301) 636-4518

I'm also available for success seminars and workshops, television and radio appearances, and speaking engagements, both religious and secular. Contact me at the above address.

The Money Book for King's Kids

Harold Hill
with Irene Burk Harrell

Power Books

Fleming H. Revell Company
Old Tappan, New Jersey

Unless otherwise identified, Scripture quotations are from the King James Version of the Bible.

Scripture quotations identified AMP are from AMPLIFIED BIBLE, OLD TESTAMENT. Copyright 1962, 1964 by Zondervan Publishing House, and are used by permission.

Scripture quotations identified NIV are from Holy Bible, New International Version, copyright © 1978, New York International Bible Society. Used by permission of Zondervan Bible Publishers.

Scripture quotations identified NKJB-NT are from The New King James Bible-New Testament. Copyright © 1979. Thomas Nelson, Inc., Publishers.

Scripture quotations identified RSV are from the Revised Standard Version of the Bible, copyrighted 1946, 1952, © 1971 and 1973.

Scripture quotations identified TLB are taken from *The Living Bible*, Copyright © 1971 by Tyndale House Publishers, Wheaton, Ill. Used by permission.

Scripture quotations identified AMPLIFIED are from the Amplified New Testament, © The Lockman Foundation 1954, 1958, and are used by permission.

Scripture quotations identified WUEST are from AN EXPANDED TRANSLATION OF THE GREEK NEW TESTAMENT by Kenneth S. Wuest, published by William B. Eerdmans Publishing Company.

Excerpts from *Your Money and How to Make the Most of It* are used by permission of the First National Bank of Maryland.

Thank you, Mary Elizabeth Rogers, for research done on this book.

Library of Congress Cataloging in Publication Data

Hill, Harold, 1905-
    The money book for King's kids.

    1. Finance, Personal—Religious aspects—Christianity.
I. Harrell, Irene Burk.   II. Title.
HG179.H47   1984   332.024′2   84-2086
ISBN 0-8007-5160-4

C⊛NTENTS

-1-
MONEY TROUBLES?
THEY CAN BE
SOLVED!

Is your money—or lack of it—your number-one problem? Are your finances going from bad to worse? Does getting out of debt seem completely beyond hope?

Is bankruptcy staring you in the face—or almost? Are you fearful the dollar will die? Is your marriage tottering because of money problems?

Are you telling everyone, "I'm at the end of my rope—I'll never make it"?

Today, more marriages are wrecked, more lives ruined, and more suffering results from the lack of a good money plan than from almost any other cause. Is it true for you, too?

If you have answered yes to one or more of these questions, this book is designed for you.

"Oh, no, not another dying-dollar and money-failure treatise!" I hear someone moan. That's right, this *isn't* one of them. No indeed. This money book is for King's kids, so it's different. It's all about success instead of failure in the pocketbook area of your life. Before you have finished reading it, you will have discovered ways to improve your finances by learning how to make your money behave, using the principles God spells out in His Holy Bible—I call it the *Manufacturer's Handbook*—which tells His people how to live for best results on planet earth.

In these pages, instead of learning about financial failure, you will learn how to do better with what you have— how to plan for success. While others are wailing over their dying dollar, you'll be soaking up principles for pumping new life into yours. Instead of throwing a pity party and blaming someone for the "failing economy," you will be experiencing resurrection life in your money matters.

You will be delighted to find out how *good* things can be, right now, in your own money department, as you begin to apply the principles of success, starting today.

In *The Money Book for King's Kids,* I will give you the benefit of my lifetime of experience, covering over sixty years of success in applying the secular principles of good management, *and* the principles of a higher order— God's Master Plan for financial security and prosperity this side of heaven.

Read on, and you will find answers to questions like these:

- Is poverty God's perfect plan for holy living?

- What is money, where does it come from, and whose is it?

- Is money the root of all evil, as some claim?

- Should believers have insurance?

- What about working wives?

- Should you have a personal last will and testament?

- How can you
    get out of debt and stay out?
    get rid of your home mortgage?
    make money on credit cards?
    get a refund on your income tax?
    help your kids get on the right track with
        their financial affairs?
    make your money work for you?
    deal with the WOLO thief?
    plug money leaks that may be robbing you
        of 20 percent of your money?
    remove the roadblocks to success in your
        financial affairs?
    start saving?

The answers that have worked for me will work for you as soon as you start applying the right principles. Then you will be able to join me in answering a reverberating NO! to all the bad-news questions with which I began this chapter.

At this point some of you are probably asking, "But Hill, just why do you feel qualified to speak to these questions when our best thinkers have failed to solve them—including my very godly pastor, who is always just about as broke as anyone could ever be?"

I'm glad you brought that up. There are three reasons why I am qualified to offer you these guaranteed-to-work answers to money questions.

1. Qualification number one. I received my academic training in engineering, economics, banking, business law, and administration in four of our finest institutions of higher education.

You're not impressed with all that head training? I don't

blame you. I wouldn't be impressed either—if that's all there was to it. Both of us know that many of our "best thinkers," *and* our most dismal financial failures, have also made high marks in the classrooms of academe. It was some of them who came up with that disastrous principle called *deficit spending,* where you spend more and more of what you don't have, to buy something you don't need, leaving it to your grandbabies to sweat out the debt somewhere down the line.

Deficit spending never makes sense; it's like trying to come back from where you've never been. But some politicians have seized upon it as a means of buying votes from their gullible and unsuspecting followers. Poor voters. They never dream that the funds for the "free benefits" always come right out of their own pockets.

No indeed, secular education by itself simply doesn't qualify me or anyone else for anything but eggheaditis. But I have much more to offer than that!

"And just what would that be?" some kibitzer's asking. Read on. . . .

2. Qualification number two. Until my recent retirement, I was president of a group of four highly successful multi-million-dollar corporations showing a continuous profit— which is, after all, the bottom line in the world of business.

That second qualification is much more impressive, isn't it? One that really means something in today's rat-race economy. One that really qualifies me to tell you how you too can make *your* money behave so *you* can prosper as I have.

In case you have a lingering suspicion in your mind, no, I did not inherit a fortune from rich Uncle Charlie. I began at the bottom, with an investment of a few hundred dollars, and built it into those four multimillion-dollar corporations by simply applying the principles of success.

If all that wealth had produced inner peace and satisfaction, I would probably not be a King's kid today. But what the Bible calls "the deceitfulness of riches" finally got to me. I had about as much zest for living as a dead slug, and that's when I arrived at—

3. *Qualification number three, the only one that really matters.* When I was at the top of the heap financially and at the bottom of the pile in every other way, I met the Author of the *Manufacturer's Handbook,* the One who made everything there is, including you and your money. His name is Jesus, and He changed my worldly successes into a new career of money management for the Kingdom of God. While He was at it, He also gave me God's Master Plan, with guaranteed results of prosperity every time. Follow it, and you can't miss. As a matter of fact, I learned that certain principles of His Master Plan were behind the success I had experienced even before I knew Him.

Now I'm picking up vibes that tell me some of you are still quibbling. Maybe you're saying, "Well, that's all well and good from a *business* standpoint, but what I'm interested in is improving my *personal* finances. Do you have any expertise in that area?"

Again, I'm glad you asked the question.

For the past twenty-nine years, ever since I began applying God's Master Plan for financial success to my life:

1. I have not had a mortgage on any of my homes. I have paid cash for all three of them.

2. I have paid cash for every car I've owned.

3. I have not had a single loan from any bank or financial institution—so I've paid them no interest. I've not been at the mercy of the prime rate or the fluctuating economy.

11

4. I have had no unpaid overdue bills of any kind.

Instead of any of the above, I have been the lender, not the borrower.

"But I'm retired and living on a fixed income," someone squawks. "There's no possibility of *my* lending to banks—frankly, they're getting more and more uncomfortable about lending to *me*. I'm really worried about what to do about inflation, the failing dollar, and the eroding economy."

You think I don't understand your predicament? Think again. I too am retired and living on the same sick spacecraft called planet earth as you are. I don't blame you for being worried. Admittedly, things look bad from a pagan standpoint. But you don't have to be stuck with a pagan standpoint. You can live like a King's kid, entitled to the success guaranteed by God's Master Plan. It has been carefully designed to solve even such "biggies" as the ones facing retirees, young marrieds, college kids, and middle-agers. It can give you victory in the face of world conditions that baffle the wizards of the financial world.

"But I'll bet you've never faced the problems I've faced with *my* finances!" someone's still wailing.

Don't be too sure, brother. Don't be too sure.

Here are just a few samples of some of the woe-is-me financial circumstances that have confronted me over the years:

A fellow Christian robbed me of a large sum of money. Should I have hired a lawyer and taken him to court—an action practically guaranteed to give the attorneys a chance to run giggling all the way to the bank with their fees from my pocket? Or should I have eaten my heart out when he refused to pay loans of many years' standing? Or was there a better way?

How about the close friend to whom I entrusted a large part of my retirement fund, who made off with it forever without even a thank you? Or the relatives who got more than their fair share of an inheritance through a sneaky legal maneuver?

And how about the Great Depression? I was a young family man in the midst of folks diving from windowsills into pools of hardened cement. How about the investments I've made without checking the research carefully enough?

In every situation, God's Master Plan has proved more than adequate to handle all my money messes. I'm satisfied that what He has done for me, He will do for you.

Simply put, the twofold purpose of *The Money Book for King's Kids* is to show you:

1. that prosperity is God's will for all His people, including you;
2. how to get it by uncorking the principles of God's Master Plan
   that will cure your present financial distress and keep you out of further ailments forever in the pocketbook area of your life, God being your helper.

Sounds like a tough assignment for a book, you think? It is. But I'm not bragging on myself or my superior ability in these matters. I'm bragging on the unmatchable excellence of God's Master Plan for success and prosperity. Once you get that plan in gear for you, you too will begin proving to the pagan world that things are really different for anyone who puts God first in his life.

"But I've never exactly *put* God in first place in my life," an apologetic voice pipes up from the balcony. "Will God's Master Plan work for me too?"

Yes, I've observed in my own experience that the principles in the *Manufacturer's Handbook* often "work" temporarily even for folks who haven't put God in charge. But it's impossible for anyone to experience the *full* benefits without becoming a member of His family. And, of course, family membership is the only way to have the benefits *forever* in your financial affairs and in other areas of your life. Otherwise, the benefits expire when you do.

But there's no reason for you to remain an outsider— there's good reason for you to come into the Kingdom yourself. God's "recipe" for turning you into a full-fledged King's kid, entitled forever to all the rights and privileges thereunto appertaining, as the legal beagles like to say, is so easy that most folks miss it. There's nothing to memorize, nothing to sign, no sponsor required, no initiation fee. . . . In fact, becoming a son of God is a whole lot less trouble than becoming a citizen of the United States of America, and far more beneficial. Instructions are found in several places in the *Manufacturer's Handbook*. If you miss it one place, you'll come across it in another. Here are a few to feast your eyes on:

> For God so loved the world, that he gave his only begotten Son, that whosoever believeth on him should not perish, but have everlasting life. (*John 3:16*)

> Repent, and be baptized, every one of you in the name of Jesus Christ for the remission of sins, and ye shall receive the gift of the Holy Ghost. (*Acts 2:38*)

Believe on the Lord Jesus Christ, and thou shalt be saved, and thy house. (*Acts 16:31*)

If you confess with your mouth the Lord Jesus and believe in your heart that God has raised Him from the dead, you will be saved. (*Romans 10:9* NKJB-NT)

If we confess our sins, he is faithful and just to forgive us our sins, and to cleanse us from all unrighteousness. (*1 John 1:9*)

But as many as received him, to them gave he power to become the sons of God, even to them that believe on his name. (*John 1:12*)

Are you ready now for your life to be lived under new management—to enter into a new dimension of living, free from all the "iffies" of the old way, with all its emptiness and the frustrations of uncertainty? If so, whether you're an up-and-outer or a down-and-outer, whether you're from jail or Yale, you can now meet Jesus Christ in person and begin living the life of prosperity and satisfaction available in no other way.

I hear someone saying, "But I tried all that a while back and have gotten myself way out in left field. Do you think God has given up on me?"

You can settle that right now, by consulting Jesus on the subject. His answer to you is already written: "I will never leave you nor forsake you" (Hebrews 13:5 NKJB-NT).

In other words, He was there all the time. That means you can settle everything right now and get on with King's kid living. And just in case you're not much good at putting together a prayer of your own, here's one of mine that you can borrow:

Lord Jesus Christ, I'm sorry for the mess I've made of my life. I'm really sorry I have left You out of my life and affairs. Please forgive me for all my yukky past, and let me know that I'm forgiven. Thank You for washing away all that black filthiness, guilt, fear, and anxiety down inside me by Your death on the cross. I now receive it with gratitude.

Thank You, Jesus, that I am now a King's kid. I am turning my life and affairs over to You the best I know how, and I now trust You for taking over the management of everything about me.

Thank You for coming into my heart, Lord Jesus, and making Yourself real inside me and filling that awful emptiness. I've been told You have the power to change my life and affairs as well as my appetites and desires. That sounds like a tough assignment, and I don't see how You can do it. In fact, I'm not sure I want all that to happen to me. I'm not even sure I'm being sincere in all this. But whether I am or not, You just go ahead and do it anyhow.

And now, Lord, help Yourself to me completely and keep on doing it. The results are entirely up to You. I rejoice now that I am a born-again King's kid, with Your Holy Spirit living in me and guiding my life and affairs from now on.

[While you have Him on the line, it might be good to unload on Him all the burdens—financial and otherwise—you've been carrying that are just too heavy for you. He'll be delighted to take them over and give you rest. Also, toss in anything else you can't handle. He'll keep on listening even after you've stopped praying.]

I ask all these blessings in the name of Jesus. Thank You for hearing me. Amen.

Feel any different? Some people do, some don't. Feelings either way are unimportant. The important thing is that you have met the requirements of God's Master Plan. You have His Word for it now that you are saved, born again, a full-fledged member of God's own family, and subject to all the rights and privileges thereof. Here's Bible for it: "Now, therefore, you are no longer strangers and foreigners, but fellow citizens with the saints and members of the household of God" (Ephesians 2:19 NKJB-NT).

That's all there is to it. I can absolutely guarantee from my own personal experience that your life will never be the same again. It will get better and better. That's the report of everyone who has ever tried Jesus Christ as "the Way, the Truth, and the Life," which is His own job rating of Himself in John 14:6 (AMPLIFIED).

"How about being baptized?" someone is asking. I asked that, too, right after I prayed that prayer and Jesus became real inside me. And I followed the first question with another: "Wasn't the sprinkling I received as a baby adequate?" And then I realized that, like a vaccination for smallpox I received once, "baby baptism" just "didn't take" in my case, and I might as well get it redone.

"But what method is best?" I wanted to know next. I had discovered folks recommending a wide variety of methods. Some said, "Sprinkling is superior." Others let

17

on that it wouldn't work any way except by "pouring from a pitcher." Still others claimed, "Spattering is superlative." Since *folks* had such varied opinions about these things, I decided to check it out with Jesus and found that "dunking" was what John used on Him. Apparently Jesus was perfectly satisfied with that, claiming He was being baptized in order to "fulfill all righteousness—that is, to perform completely whatever is right" (Matthew 3:15 AMPLIFIED).

So I went ahead and got dunked in the dunk tank behind the altar in the little Baptist church where I had made a public profession of Jesus Christ as my Lord and Savior. Somehow, it helped to make my salvation experience more real to me. No wonder Jesus recommended it so highly.

Did I get an extra dose of salvation by being baptized? No indeed. I got all the salvation I could ever use by turning my life over to Jesus. But baptism really did do something beneficial to my faith and gave me an additional benefit I later discovered in Colossians 2:11, 12. You can read all about that in your own Bible.

So now you're a full-fledged King's kid, ready to go into action with life under New Management, and Jesus guiding all the way. For best results, you need to become knowledgeable about what you have going for you by spending a lot of time in the Heavenly Code Book, the Bible.

What's that I hear? You don't really *have* all the time for Bible reading that you need? Neither do I. But I've found that I can remedy that by listening to Bible tapes during the many hours a day I spend behind the wheel of a car. For details about my favorite listening version of the Bible on cassettes, send a stamped, self-addressed envelope to me—Harold Hill, King's Kids' Korner, P. O. Box 8655, Baltimore, MD 21240.

For more about my own experience in this whole area of God's "full power" in my life, see my first book, *How to Live Like a King's Kid,* available from your local bookstore. And let me hear from *you* about how things work under New Management, once you've turned it all over to Jesus.

And now, let's go into action!

-2-
THE ROYAL ROAD
TO SUCCESS
UNLIMITED

"So there you have it, folks—my formula for success unlimited. It has served me to the tune of several million dollars in my lifetime. Apply it faithfully, and you too may find that your first million is only the beginning."

With that, the speaker, a top-flight business executive turned college professor, concluded a series of graduate-school lectures.

Impressive indeed were those words of assurance from a living example of the effectiveness of what he had called "an unfailing success formula for success without excelling." I didn't know it then, but that formula would one day become the basis for a significant turning point in my life.

Having only recently graduated with a degree in electrical engineering, I had a science-oriented mind that struggled to grasp the things the professor was talking about. I was at that time basking in the rosy glow of my new position as a junior member of a prestigious, world-famous engineering firm. There in my "office," a drafting board in a drafty corner high above Manhattan's traffic tangles, I was the "poor country boy," making good in a big way, in the Big Town, in the Roaring Twenties. Recognizing that my engineering degree was insufficient by itself to equip me to progress up the ladder to the management level of any large company, I had enrolled for further graduate study.

No, Harold Hill wasn't born with a silver spoon in his mouth, with a head start on brains or bucks because of his earthly inheritance. On the contrary.

To begin with, my academic life had gotten off to a poor start. At age six I was enrolled in the first grade in a small two-room country schoolhouse in Brookside, Connecticut. Not long after the first bell rang, homesickness set in, and I bawled and squalled until the teacher sent for Mama to come and take me home.

That ended my formal education until a year later when I was enrolled again. This time it took. But I had already earned for myself such nicknames as "Mama's Boy" and "Crybaby," real ego busters for a kid who wasn't all that swift at learning. My self-image wasn't much to brag about.

We were literally "poor folks," a phrase seldom heard these days. The psychobabblers have changed it to a polite "moderate circumstances," but that doesn't alter the fact that we were living on the ragged edge of poverty.

My dad was a semi-invalid. As a young man in the construction business, he had gone to South Carolina to build a big textile mill. The water was polluted, full of mosquitoes, and he contracted malaria. About twice a year, it would hit him with raging fever. Quinine kept the recurring bouts under control, but he never got the malaria entirely out of his system. Furthermore, too much heavy lifting on the job had permanently weakened his back. But in spite of his physical handicaps, he and my mother did a remarkable job of raising three young'uns—my brother, my sister, and me—during the depression years of the first part of this century.

We had a truly no-frills life-style at our house. There was money for the barest necessities, but none for the luxuries deemed so necessary by modern standards of happiness and satisfaction in living.

If we didn't raise it, we didn't eat it. If we couldn't make it, we went without. Following Dad's example, I became an expert at making things by improvising. There was no such thing as getting something for nothing. No credit cards so you could buy now and cry later. Back in those days, it wasn't fashionable to try to avoid working for a living or to expect the world to give you a free ride. Dad would never have fallen for food stamps or deficit spending even if they had been readily available to him. Over and over again I heard him state two of the principles by which he lived: "Never buy something until you can pay for it," and "If you don't work, you don't eat."

My daddy was what was known as a country horse trader. He'd head downtown on Saturday afternoon with a horse and buggy and would come home the next day or later that night with a better horse and buggy and money in his pocket besides. "Boot money," he called it, and he advised me never to make a trade unless I could come out better on both ends—a better swap than the other fellow got and more cash in my pocket. Dad practiced what he preached. For me, it was good training in basic economics.

I vividly remember the day the doctor came to our house in a funny-looking red thing that made a lot of noise. My eyeballs nearly popped out of my head as the contraption chugged to a stop. Holding my breath like a kid confronted with a man from Mars, I ran lickety-split to Dad with a question: "What's *that*?"

"That's an au-to-mo-bile," he said, carefully pronouncing each syllable separately. I repeated the strange word after him and ran back to the front yard to stare some more. After the doctor left, I had another question for Dad: "Why can't we get one of those things?"

"Well, they cost a lot of money, son," he answered, rubbing his jaw thoughtfully. "But I'll tell you what. When the three of you children are all grown up, we'll all work and save our money and buy us an automobile."

Dad was as good as his word, as always. Years later, he took the horse and buggy and the second wagon with all the hay he could load aboard, and took off to town. He came back without them, driving a car. And there was "boot money" in his pocket.

Later, Dad gave me another rule for successful living in the financial realm: "Never live up to the level of your income, son. Then, if a decrease takes place, it won't make you too unhappy."

Training me along those lines, when I was only five years old, my daddy started a savings account at the bank for me. A "building for the future" fund, he called it. Then, when I reached the ripe old age of seven, he opened a building-and-loan account in my name.

Whenever I earned any money—no matter how small the amount—I put some of it in the bank. Little kids could earn pennies—maybe twenty cents a day—by feeding chickens for a neighbor, walking dogs for folks who lived in town, cutting grass, picking strawberries, weeding onions, carrying firewood, and hauling out stove ashes. Little by little, my "building for the future" fund grew.

The necessity to work didn't mean there was no time for fun. We made our own skis, barrel-stave canoes, rowboats, fishing poles, bobsleds, and later on, even our own radios—all of which was great training for me in developing manual skills.

The worst handicap of poverty, as it seemed to me then, was those awful hand-me-downs I had to wear—the cast-off clothing of friends and relatives. Hand-me-downs came in two sizes—too big or too small. As soon as I was old enough to notice that uncomfortable fact of life, my self-image took a nose dive. Discouragement became my attitude toward all of life. Developing a fear of classroom failure, I would awake in the night in panic over the low marks I was sure would be mine when the next report-card time rolled around.

My parents, bless 'em, tried to assure me that I was not the "dumb nobody" I was programming myself to be by adopting the tag given me by my peers. My mother, who was a devoted Christian, prayed with me every night when she tucked me in bed, assuring me that God loved me and that everything would come out all right for me if I trusted Him. Trouble was, I didn't know *how* to do that, and she died before I could find out.

The first positive turning point in my life came one day when I sat dejectedly on the bench at the ball game, hungrily watching the action. I had not been invited to take part because I was, in their words, "too big and too clumsy." Sitting down beside me, in a few minutes' time my dad gave me a new vision for living.

"Son," he began, "you can have anything in life you want—

IF you will work hard for it,
   IF you let nothing and no one interfere,
      IF you never expect to get something for nothing,
        and
        IF you never, never listen
           to those who want to tell you
              why you *can't* do it."

I could have anything I wanted? That sounded too good to be true. *"Anything* I want, Dad?"

There was no hemming and hawing, no trying to weasel out of it, just a matter-of-fact, "Yep. Anything you really want." I had learned long ago that my dad was a man of his word. If he said a trip to the woodshed was in the offing for me, it was. Lining my britches with extra padding to cushion the blows might do some good; trying to talk him out of what I had coming wouldn't help matters. What Dad said, I could count on, good or bad.

"Your word should be as good as your bond," he was fond of saying. I didn't know what a bond was, but I knew it meant I always had to tell the truth—or suffer the consequences when he found out that I had stretched it a little.

Another of Dad's favorite sayings was, "The best paper promise is no better than the words of the signer." That, I could understand.

One day I overheard him talking to a neighbor about me. "That boy of mine can do anything and be anything he makes up his mind to be, even president of the USA," he boasted. I remember standing up a little taller, wondering what I ought to pick as my goal in life.

"Never say no to a challenge," he drilled into me. "Say yes, and then learn to catch up with your answer."

Gradually, my attitude toward myself changed as Dad continued to literally brainwash me into thinking success. Somewhere down inside me, the seed of self-confidence began to grow, and I felt myself agreeing with an inner self-image that whispered, "I don't care what it is, I can do it." Before long, I made up my mind to believe I *could* be anything I chose.

When I was ten years old, I read a book on the laws of electricity and became fascinated with science in general and electricity in particular. Almost immediately there was born in me a burning desire to become an engineer—and that motivated me to become a study-holic. Let the other kids *have* their fun and games. I'd show 'em. I was on my way to becoming *somebody*.

Soon after my original decision to be an engineer, I tied it down to specifics: I would become an electrical engineer—eventually chief engineer and president of my own company—with a magnificent salary of one hundred dollars a week. I would get rid of those awful hand-me-down clothes, have plenty of money, a large home with an acre of lawn, and a beautiful family. By the time I was fifty years old, I told myself, I would have fifty thousand dollars saved, one thousand for every year of my life. I would travel the world and be the happiest person alive.

Quite a vision for a poor country kid who was a slow learner with no hope whatever of carrying out even a small sliver of it, wasn't it? But highly motivated, I buckled down to work, and the vision headed for reality.

I graduated from high school at age fourteen. No, I wasn't a genius, I was simply in a hurry to succeed.

But then what looked like a major hurdle loomed on the horizon. There was simply no money for me to go to college. My "building for the future" fund just wasn't big enough.

But the new vision for success Dad had given me that day on the bench, and nurtured at every opportunity, reminded me that I could *still* have what I wanted—*if* I didn't give up but kept on working for it. For the next four years, I tackled any honest labor that would produce income.

I harvested ice from local ponds, to be packed away in sawdust until folks wanted cold summer lemonade; I weeded the wild onions out of our neighbors' gardens; I got a bicycle milk-delivery route; I cut grass, picked strawberries, and worked as a helper in a boatyard and a machine shop. I was learning some of everything as I went along, all for the unofficial maximum wage of teenagers in those days—fifty cents for a ten-hour day no matter what you did.

"Even elephants start from a small seed," Dad would remind me whenever I was tempted to be discouraged. With that in mind, I kept on building that college-education fund on fifty cents a day.

When I got my first full-time job, working in a machine shop for sixty hours a week, a major part of every paycheck went into the building-and-loan savings account for my future education.

Many people thought I'd never make it. I can still hear the jeers of some of my peers as they made fun of my well-patched clothing and scuffed shoes. One of them had an unusual streak of boldness one day and told me to my face, "Hill, you're just about the least likely person to succeed that I have ever known in my entire life." I knew I fit the bill—except for the fact that I believed what my dad had told me, that I could be anything I chose.

By the time I was eighteen, my savings account held about half of what Dad and I figured I'd need for college. If I could only find a way to cut the expense in half, I could get on with it.

"You can do it, son," Dad kept telling me. Then he helped me find a college where I could earn a degree in electrical engineering in two years if I was willing to carry an extremely heavy work load. Was I willing? And how! Carrying a heavy load would be nothing new to me—I was already in practice!

And so I went to classes, did my homework, and earned the additional money I needed by clearing tables in the college cafeteria, playing in the college dance band, doing homework for the playboy rich guys, working weekends with the college maintenance crew, and picking up any other odd jobs I could find.

I pared expenses to the barest minimum by eating only two meager meals a day, cutting out all entertainment, and studying hard to complete the four-year course in two. It worked! In 1926, I graduated in my chosen profession.

A killer regimen? It certainly was. On graduation day I weighed a bare 160 pounds, which for my six-foot, two-and-a-half-inch height gave me string-bean proportions. Sideways, I hardly cast a shadow. Weak, anemic, worn-out, and run-down would have described the physical results of my workaholic program of self-discipline. But I had that coveted degree under my arm and was off and running to make my fortune and win the rat race of life, as one of my professors had termed it.

He didn't tell me that the winner of a rat race is number-one rat. I found out about that later.

Looking back, I'm glad for those lean years and for the feeling of accomplishment and success that comes through hard work. And I'll always be grateful for the encouraging words Dad spoke to me that turned my life around by making a change in my defeatist attitude.

So there I was, early in 1927, in a big office in New York City, launched into the burgeoning world of science and industry, associating in my first professional job with top-flight engineers. I was certain that, for me, there in the heart of the Roaring Twenties, the rat race was as good as won.

And so I set out to make it big all on my own, and temporarily forgot the formula for success unlimited. It sounded too easy for me to use in big business anyhow. "Overly simplistic" would be the modern terminology for how I judged it.

But as the months passed with no promotions, it became apparent to me that my "juniority" status wouldn't improve much until one of the senior engineers either dropped dead or retired. They all looked too young and healthy for that to happen any time soon. I could feel that old familiar discouragement coming up out of somewhere, about to poke its unwelcome head above the horizon. I knew it was headed my way. I had to do something.

Just how does a bottom-of-the-totem-pole member of a group of highly skilled professionals get ahead without waiting for someone to disappear? I wondered, with a feeling of growing frustration. In my lowly position as field engineer, starting from the bottom to learn industrial and utility engineering, I didn't rate a private office, and my corner drafting table was becoming monotonous.

Then one day I remembered what the success-unlimited professor had said in his final lecture.

"What do you have to lose?" he had asked the class. "Just try the simple formula I am about to give you, and you will leave the competition far behind——for the simple reason that very few have the courage to try it." Then he turned his back to the class and wrote on the blackboard the formula that was about to skyrocket me to success: "The person who does a little more than he is paid for will soon be paid for a little more than he does."

At the time, I had thought the words sounded silly. The professor had acknowledged that they probably did. "Folks, take my word for it," he said, "that principle may sound crazy to you in this dog-eat-dog world, but it has paid me millions of dollars over the years since I began putting it to work."

Yes, the principle still sounded crazy to me, all right. I mean, who in his right mind would give anyone more than he was paid for? But the man said it had worked for him.

29

And since I was getting nowhere fast with *my* methods, I decided to try *his* for a while.

And so I began applying his simple formula, using the three-point "implementation procedure" the man had given us:

1. Begin NOW.

2. Let nothing—and nobody—interfere, ever.

3. Don't become impatient. Try it for at least a year.

From then on, I quit daydreaming out the window about how to get ahead and started giving my boss a little more than I was paid for. Instead of clearing out in the midst of the traffic-jam rush when the five o'clock bell rang, I remained bent over my drafting table, designing power systems and electrical generating stations for the great millionaires of this country.

Those were the days before electrical power was widely available, and such well-known industrial giants as J. P. Morgan, the Vanderbilts, and their cronies looked to the company for which I worked to supply private utilities for the production of electricity for their country estates. In doing that work, I was seeing firsthand how the "biggies" in the world of finance enjoyed their vast fortunes.

People started noticing my overtime right away. And it didn't take long for the snickerers to come out in the open with their derision. What made it easier for them was that I was the most junior man on the staff, and all of them already regarded me with "you're still wet behind the ears" condescension. One day the office wise guy summed up their feelings loud enough for me to hear during the five o'clock mass exodus:

"There's young eager beaver at it again," he sneered. "That dumb country kid is trying to get in good with the boss by working overtime—making it tough on the rest of us who are struggling to make a living." I could read the silent agreement of condemnation in the eyes of my co-workers, but I remembered the second point of the professor's "how to do it" lecture. "Let nothing interfere," he had said, and so I pretended not to hear the criticism and ridicule.

Several weeks of harassment made me keenly aware that discouragement was still crowding in hard and threatening to take over, but I kept forcing myself to stick to the program.

After a few months of putting in extra work at the office with no tangible results other than my being the butt of many wisecracks from the rest of the organization, something happened.

One night after hours as I was bent over my drafting table in the deserted office, the big boss himself stopped by unexpectedly to pick up some papers for an early-morning meeting the next day. He looked the epitome of success, wth his half-glasses pinched over his nose and the black ribbon tucked behind his ear. He was plainly surprised to find me still working.

"Hill, what are you doing here at this late hour? Don't you know we don't pay overtime?"

"Yes, sir," I said, sitting up straight, but keeping my pencil in my hand. "I know that, sir, but I had some things to finish on a private power plant installation for Mr.—" I named a big New York banker—"for his estate in Bermuda. I find it easier to concentrate after the crowds have left. Besides, my boss, the chief engineer, needs this project completed in time for an early meeting tomorrow morning."

"How often do you do this sort of thing—working overtime?" he asked, looking over my shoulder to study the intricate drawing nearing completion on my board.

"Oh, once a week or so," I mumbled, shrugging my shoulders as if it was nothing, trying not to make a big deal of it.

"Very interesting," he mumbled back, "very interesting." His comment didn't tell me much about what he was thinking, but at least he had noticed me.

"See you in the morning," was his noncommittal parting word.

He went on his way without saying anything further, and the next day, the snickering from the office staff continued. Then, a few weeks later, I was summoned to the front office and promoted to the position of vice-president—over the heads of all the scoffers and snickerers, some of whom were engineers greatly superior to me in seniority and experience, but all of whom lacked the "secret weapon" that I had working for me.

The scoffing and snickering came to a screeching halt. I was now *Mr.* Hill, with my own private office. The office wise guy was closemouthed as a clam and red as a lobster whenever he caught me looking in his direction. I was the one who snickered then, all the way to the bank with my double pay raise and a bonus on all the company business, while visions of goodies—otherwise known as fringe benefits—danced in my head. Someone else was field engineer in my drafty drafting-board corner.

Several principles I later identified as straight out of the *Manufacturer's Handbook* had begun to produce fantastic results in my life. And that was only the beginning! In industry, workaholics are appreciated, and I was one of them. Seven days a week meant nothing to me. I was on my way to the top, and I was willing to spend full time at it.

Shortly after my promotion to vice-president, my immediate boss, the chief engineer, was transferred to our London office. Who got his job? Why, the "dumb country boy" who didn't know any better than to work overtime without pay, that's who. Still in my twenties, I had CHIEF ENGINEER added to my title in gold letters on the door to my own private office.

The youngest, least experienced engineer in that organization was rapidly on his way up, using principles God has designed into the world system. I was programmed for success. Nothing could stop me. I had a vision ahead of me for what I wanted out of life, and I was going for it with all I had.

What was it the professor had said? Something like, "Skyrocketing to the top can be your experience." It was certainly working out that way for me.

Years later, word reached the BIG, BIG boss, the managing director of the entire organization in England, that they had a real eager-beaver workaholic on their payroll in New York and that they had better consider him for greater things. That *him* was me! I was invited to spend a few weeks in England, at their expense, to discuss the plans the company had for my future.

I'd been with them now for eleven years, and I returned home from the trip with another fabulous promotion. Now I was officially director of operations for the entire North American continent for one of Europe's largest engineering firms.

And it all started when I gave the boss a little more than I was paid for. I was in the "big time," traveling with the nobility of Europe, no longer wearing hand-me-downs. My suits were custom-made by the best London tailors.

But then—

-3-
HOW TO SURVIVE TOUGH TIMES

"Whoa! Wait a minute!" someone's been hollering, trying to get my attention for the last ten minutes.

"Okay, what is it?" I'm asking. The rest of my success story can wait.

"Hill, I'm convinced that you had it made, but what about us young marrieds here in the middle of the eighties? The honeymoon is over, and now we're facing the very scary reality of the world of debtors, bill collectors, higher rent than expected, astronomical utility bills, and all the rest of the grim financial facts of life that inflation brings. We're setting up housekeeping under huge financial burdens and handicaps. We'll just *never* be able to reach financial security like you're talking about. You just don't understand how tough it is to make ends come even close to meeting in this day and age."

I don't? Hang on. I was about to get to that part of my story when you so rudely interrupted. Let me tell you all about it.

I was married late in 1928. Those were what are affectionately referred to as the Roaring Twenties, when just about everyone was making fortunes on paper and living high on the hog with a chicken in every pot and a car in every driveway. Social Security hadn't been invented yet, and income tax was only a relatively minor irritation.

Did you ever hear of the Crash and the Great Depression? I was right there in the midst of it all.

On that memorable Black Friday afternoon, the office boy came back from lunch with a glowing report of the thousands of dollars he had made that month speculating on the stock market. It was all on paper, of course, but could be converted into real cash *someday*. Almost all of my fellow employees had similar success stories to relate.

Then came the doomsday news—the Wall Street market had collapsed. Prices tumbled thousands of millions of dollars within a few hours, and all those paper profiteers were wiped out. Completely. Not long afterward, the banks closed their doors, and no one had any money except for the loose change jingling in his pockets. It was scary.

Some people walked the streets in a daze, all their holdings wiped out in the twinkling of an eye. Others rode the elevators to the topmost stories of the tallest skyscrapers, found an unoccupied windowsill, and provided temporary employment for the sidewalk-scraper-uppers.

The depression years following the Crash were tough for everyone. Top-flight executives, professional people, and blue-collar workers melted into one to sell apples on the street corners of New York so they could buy groceries for the wife and kids.

As a young family head, I was right in the midst of all that, so I know what you young marrieds are talking about when you view money events with alarm. I've been there. But I also know you can come through it, as I did, following the money principles my dad laid down for me, never suspecting they were part of God's Master Plan.

In the midst of the shock of the Great Depression, I woke up to the fact that I needed to establish new priorities concerning my life plans and ambitions. So I reminded myself of all my dad had taught me, some of which I had been failing to put into practice in my own life. As I thought about all that, I asked myself some hard questions:

Did I prefer keeping up with the Joneses? Or would I rather begin to pull out of debt and build for the future again? Could I do without certain luxury items to which I had become accustomed? Since there was barely enough money for anyone to keep afloat, the choices almost made themselves.

Having decided in what direction I wanted to head, I sat down and wrote out some thoughts toward a money plan for my little household—my wife and me and our baby daughter, Linda. The set of guidelines went like this:

1. *I would stop living up to the level of my income.* That way, if my income should drop, my peace of mind wouldn't crash with it.

2. *Out of every paycheck, I would always put a certain amount into a savings account, just as I had done when I was trying to scrape together enough for a college education.*

"Oh, but we can't afford to save even a few cents a week in the shape we're in!" I hear the young married couple interrupting.

"Oh yes, you can," I say. "Save a fixed amount every week—this point is crucial—*regardless* of what happens."

You can get money for savings the same way I did in those days. First, I began to steal a little from my cigarette fund, my soda account, my movie money, our dining-out-once-a-week allotment. All these items were things I should have been able to live without.

No, I didn't especially *enjoy* smoking each cigarette down so short it burned my fingers. I didn't like denying myself the indulgence of a refreshment break when everybody else in the office was having one. And not going to the movies whenever I wanted to was a real sacrifice. It hurt to settle for a tube steak at the hot dog joint on the corner to the tune of a raucous jukebox. I'd much rather have dined on a sumptuous T-bone in an elegant restaurant with white linens and sparkling silver and crystal on the table, hovered over by a solicitous maître d' while our ears were caressed by the sweet strains of a violin serenade.

But although I didn't enjoy the sacrifices, the deprivation didn't kill me, and I *did* enjoy the thought that we were building something we could fall back on if we ever needed it. As a result, we survived the depression without being depressed, which was better than you could say for most folks.

It wasn't long after we started this "self-robbery" plan that we began to see such benefits in our diminishing debts and growing savings accounts that we actually became enthusiastic about saving money. Can you imagine? And soon we discovered other "money leaks" we could plug and so have more to put aside for later.

Back in the depths of those depression days, when everyone was still wondering if the world would ever be right-side-up again, we even cancelled our telephone service. That gave us a hefty amount to add to our security fund, as we called it. So that we were not entirely without communication with the outside world, we saved up money to make the essential calls from a pay phone at the local railroad station. Having to keep plunking in those nickels kept calls short almost automatically. For just a few dollars a year, we paid for all our telephoning and eliminated those horrendous monthly bills from the phone company—as well as the piercing ring that could shake you from a snoring good time in the middle of the night.

Don't get me wrong. I believe that in-house telephones are useful instruments, especially when it's raining. And I have one today because it's essential in my business. But in those days, when we were struggling to get out of debt, I programmed myself to think more of their disadvantages than of their good points.

A home garden cut the grocery bill way down. Cutting out my beloved golf games saved another sizable amount, even though I was not "that bad." Other folks were wearing last year's fashions, so my wife didn't feel pressured to succumb to "new clothes" fever. Turning off lights and radios—TV wasn't invented yet—was another plus for our security fund.

By the end of the year, the savings account held several hundred dollars, working *for* us! And it hadn't cost us anything we couldn't live without.

Instead of falling for the "instant everything" syndrome, we were learning to live by a money plan that would enable us to pay cash for whatever we considered indispensable to our life-style. Often, by the time sufficient funds had accumulated in our savings to buy the item that had seemed so desirable, the urgency was gone. It might be no longer an "I can't live without it" item at all, and the money saved could be used for something else. Sometimes we'd just decide to leave it in the bank.

3. *The third part of our plan was to put our savings to work earning interest for us.*

One, two, three—and we were on our way out of debt

and to the top of the heap, as we understood it then. But the best was yet to come.

Meanwhile, now that you see that I know how it feels to be a young married when the financial scene looks like it's headed for falling-down disaster or blowing-up calamity—hold on while I get back to my story.

-4-

THE REAL TURNING POINT FOR ME AND ANY WHOSOEVER

There I was, at the top of the heap. I had pioneered in the field of diesel engines, grown up with that industry, become an authority, had written books and papers, and been recognized for important inventions. In the eyes of the world, I had hit the jackpot. My take was 10 percent of the profit before taxes, and when we hit the multimillion-dollar level, we measured profits in barrels full of the green stuff.

But I had just about used up my boyhood vision.

"Where there is no vision, the people perish," God says in Proverbs 29:18. Man is so constructed that he has to have a vision—or die. Without a goal or purpose, we're programmed to bog down in boredom or frustration—or worse. It doesn't matter what your level of achievement, if you don't have something to look forward to, something to shoot at, life becomes intolerable.

I didn't know that in so many words, but I was feeling the agonizing truth of it down inside. In my gizzard—or where it would be if I had one—*something* was increasingly uncomfortable. As nearly as I could define that something, it was a "positively *nothing*"—but it hurt, like a voracious emptiness clawing at my innards and yammering to be filled. But with what?

Getting desperate one day, I tried to find the answer in my head.

"I know," I said to myself. "I have an airplane and a pilot, but it isn't big enough. *That's* my trouble. I'll get a bigger airplane—maybe a bigger pilot while I'm at it."

I tried that, but it didn't help. My think tank came up with an alternative.

"Maybe it's my boat. I already have a yacht, but my neighbors have a bigger one. I'll get a bigger yacht."

So I did, but there was no improvement inside me. The emptiness was still there, clawing and yammering, yammering and clawing. And growing!

"I have it! If only I had my very own empire. . . ."

That was my final computer program for success and satisfaction in life. So, when I was forty years old, I moved to Maryland from Milwaukee, Wisconsin, where I had gone to run a war production plant.

Baltimore, the land of pleasant living. Chesapeake Bay. A big yacht, a big home, a successful business of my own.

When you move to Maryland from another state, they told me, you remain an enemy alien for at least two hundred years—unless you can outdrink them, and I could. It was a breeze. I belonged from the beginning, and soon my very own company was prospering beyond my fondest dreams.

Knowing how to make a million is one thing. Knowing what to do with the millionaire who has it made is something else. Dad had taught me well how to manage my ambition and my finances, but he hadn't taught me how to manage *me*.

By the time I was forty-five years old, my vision had run out. I had nothing to live for.

What do you do at the top of the ladder when all your dreams have been used up, when anything money can buy is yours for the asking? When you have many wise investments, stock certificates overflowing your safe-deposit box——but nothing to live for? When you wake up in the morning with bad breath, yawn, and say, "So, what else is new?"

Sorry friends, a new mouthwash isn't the answer. What do you do? Maybe you do what I did——you finally take time for a closer look inside, where you really live.

What I saw there called for a sedative, not an encore——that cavernous aching emptiness and a big bunch of the gloppy broken-relationships debris of my skyrocket trip to the top that hadn't bothered to bless other folks along the way, unless it was for my own personal gain.

I didn't like looking at all that ugly gunk. I wished it would go away. But I could feel it growing bigger and bigger.

What to do about it? No one could tell me. The success-unlimited formula and its "implementation procedures" that had worked so fantastically to skyrocket me to the top of my profession had nothing to offer. Neither did any of the "isms" I had tried, and I had tried them all. (Read my first book, *How to Live Like a King's Kid*, for a thorough rundown on this part of my life.)

Somewhere along the way, I had gotten into alcohol—— *not* the rubbing variety for athletic aches and pains. One of my bosses had been a man who couldn't drink——on account of liver problems——and so I had been paid handsomely to drink with his clients. The bootleggers were controlling the social life of the big-time spenders in those days, and I had learned the value of the social drink to break down the barriers of my self-consciousness and put me more at ease in any situation.

I guess it was natural that I began to turn more and more to booze for answers. No, alcohol didn't *have* the answers, but it helped me to forget there were any questions. I mean, the thought of what would happen to me if that inner nothingness took over my life was something I couldn't afford to think about very long at a time without danger of being taken on a one-way trip to the funny farm.

Slowly, sneakily, so gradually that I hardly noticed, alcohol progressively occupied a more and more important role in my life. Day by day, week by week, month by month, and year by year, the life I had once controlled for myself was increasingly taken over by a chemical formula that didn't have my best interests at heart.

Then one day it hit me: I couldn't have stopped drinking even if I wanted to. I was addicted.

On top of everything else, that was simply too much for me to handle.

In 1951, five years after I had started my own company, I downed enough poison to wipe out the neighborhood. I'd always done things to excess and true to form, I took too much, with the result that it bounced, most uncomfortably. I goofed suicide.

A few nights later, I tried again. "This time," I said, "I'll try something that doesn't hurt. Poison hurts, and I don't like to hurt. I'll take a route that leaves no marks; I'll smother myself."

So I set everything up for a suffocation trip and was pretty well into it when the place got so stuffy I had to come up for air.

Nothing was working.

Then, to make a long story short (you can read full details in my first book), came turning point number three in my life, by far the most significant of them all. In utter desperation, one night I cried out, "God help me!"

And He did.

The following week, I was at my first meeting of a fellowship called Alcoholics Anonymous, where I was no bigger a wheel than the ditchdigger from the other side of the tracks with the same problem. The AA message was so simple, even I could do it: "Stay away from the first drink for one day at a time."

To help me along, my fellow alcoholics encouraged me to attend meetings as often as I used to attend the liquor bottle, to help other alcoholics, to pray, and turn my life over to the God of my choice.

"But make sure you get a live One," someone told me.

As far as I had been able to tell, the only people who acted as if they had a live God were the ones who said His name was Jesus, so He's the God I picked. One night I asked Him to come into my heart and clean it out. That was the beginning of a whole new life for me, a life that made the greatest of my former "successes" seem like garbage in comparison.

The live God—Jesus—not only took away all my desire to drink alcohol, He soon removed my addiction to nicotine and my tendency to mow folks down with sharp-tongued criticism; He healed me of all my many physical afflictions; and He moved into that scary emptiness inside me and filled it to overflowing with God Himself. (You can read all the details about this lifesaving transformation in *How to Live Like a King's Kid*.)

I didn't have to worry about emptiness anymore. It was all filled up. Now I had something to live for: the very best that planet earth has to offer and as much of heaven as I can stand on the way to heaven. The most fantastic package deal ever invented!

For the first time in my forty-eight years, I was experiencing the awesome peace I had seen on my mother's face. If she hadn't graduated to heaven while I was still a young boy, I believe she would have told me all about it.

But I wasn't equipped only with the peace that passes all understanding. Dead-slug Hill was gone. I was full of excitement about all this new life had to offer if I lived it according to the instructions in the *Manufacturer's Handbook*. And so I eagerly became what I call a "King's kid in training."

Questions—about anything—no longer bothered me because the One who knows all the answers was living inside me.

I began to study the *Manufacturer's Handbook* with Ed, the man who had introduced me to Jesus. He was a worker in a steel mill, an eighth-grade dropout. Academically, Ed didn't have much to brag about, but oh, how he bragged about Jesus! Ed had a simple, direct faith and an approach to the Bible that was absolutely practical.

"The way I see it," Ed said matter-of-factly, "is that it's so simple, you need help *not* to understand it."

Together, we began to apply the principles we found in the *Manufacturer's Handbook*. And whenever I would be tempted to make a head trip out of it and ask, "What do you think the Bible means there?" Ed would look at me and give the same answer he had given me the last time: "Hal, let's read it and do it and then we'll *know* what it means." It was as if someone had taken an old car— me—and put in it a new engine that not only gave me new aims and purposes to go along with the new outlook but also new vitality to make it work.

Basically, my old human mechanism had been negative, seeing everything in the darkness of the second law of thermodynamics—as falling apart and getting worse. But when the light of the Word of God began to show me things as God sees them, my worn-out mind began to be renewed to know the riches of my inheritance in Christ Jesus, and life began to be a continuous adventure. Instead of wanting to end it all, I wanted to get on with it, to live it up—God's way.

If all that doesn't make sense to you yet, don't worry. It will as soon as you become a King's kid in training.

Now, just in case you didn't pray that rather lengthy prayer in the first chapter of this book, here is a simplified form, the same prayer I prayed back in 1951, which changed my life from death to everlasting life: "Jesus, I don't know if You are the real God or not, I just know I need help. If You are here, and if You can make Yourself real to me right now, will You please do it?"

Doesn't sound like much of a prayer, does it? I mean, you might even call it a prayer of unbelief. But it was the best I could manage, and God took it and used it to get me saved.

One principle the world overlooks in connection with seeking satisfaction and happiness down ten thousand different avenues is that life without Jesus was never intended to work, and it never will. Many of the great business leaders and financial successes of the past either ended in defeat or met God in a personal way.

But now, getting back to money matters:

Soon after I met Jesus, I came across Matthew 6:33, where Jesus says, "Just dare to put My Kingdom methods first in your thinking and considerations, and I'll see to it that what you consider the number-one needs of your life are met as a matter of course" (author's paraphrase).

"Whoa, there!" some cowboy's yelling. "I don't find that Scripture in *my* Bible!"

Well, all right, if you want to be picky, here it is in the lingo of King Jimmy's day, if that will suit you better: "But seek ye first the kingdom of God, and his righteousness; and all these things shall be added unto you" (Matthew 6:33).

There now. Do you like that better? Being an intensely practical King's kid, I have a tendency to take what He says and interpret the thought in language that fits my Educated Idiot Box. It works, either way.

I guess this is as good a place as any to tell you, in case you didn't know it already, that the Bible wasn't written in King James English to start with. It was all done up in Hebrew, Aramaic, and Greek, the languages of the people in the part of the world where it was put down in writing.

All those languages are Greek to me. A *Manufacturer's Handbook* in any one of them would be over my head, good for nothing but to decorate the coffee table. If it hadn't occurred to somebody to translate the Bible into a language I could understand, I'd have to depend on someone else to read the *Manufacturer's Handbook* for me. That sounds second-best, doesn't it?

The first translations wouldn't have helped me much either, since they were from Hebrew into Aramaic and Greek, both equally worse to me. Then there was a translation into Latin—still not much good for most of us. Finally, people began to realize that God could speak in any language, and translations began popping up everywhere—French, Italian, Spanish, German, English, American, Russian, Chinese, Japanese, Portuguese, African, Indian, Polish, Norwegian. . . .

There are already translations of the Bible in all the languages you can name and in many languages you've never heard of. And the languages you *can't* name—well, chances are that someone is working on a translation of the Bible into those languages too. Wycliffe Bible Translators even go to live in remote areas among peoples who have no written language at all! There they learn the language, reduce it to written form, and translate the Bible into that language, so someone can preach the Word to the natives and get them saved.

Fascinating? You bet.

Another side to all this translation business is that language isn't a stable thing. It changes as time goes by. Maybe you remember trying to make heads or tails out of Chaucer's *Canterbury Tales* in high school. Chaucer wrote in the English that all Englishmen understood in his day, but the language has changed so much that twentieth-century folks have a hard time getting a handle on what he was talking about.

The same thing is true of the English of the King James Bible of 1611. People *then* knew what the words were saying, because the translation was into the language the people spoke at that time. But today? I heard about one schoolteacher who read where Jesus says, "Suffer little children, and forbid them not, to come unto me . . ." (Matthew 19:14) and thought Jesus meant that, like her, He couldn't stand the little brats but was willing to suffer putting up with them anyhow.

If that kind of misunderstanding arising out of the changes in the way we use our words doesn't convince you that it's better than okay to have updated American translations now and then—and even paraphrases that help us grab ahold of what the Lord is saying—we're not on the same wavelength.

Almost persuaded, but still a little suspicious of modern translations? Admittedly, some are better than others. You can check them out for yourself by comparing several passages in a modern translation with an oldie that you trust. Does the "modern" translation say the same thing as the oldie—only more plainly? Does the updated version "match" the meaning of a Greek/English interlinear? Lots of people claim the new translations enable them to be better doers of the Word than they could be when the King James language had them stymied about what it was they were supposed to do.

There's a good opportunity for folks to be confused by King Jimmy's language in 1 Peter 3:1, 2:

> Likewise, ye wives, be in subjection to your own husbands; that, if any obey not the word, they also may without the word be won by the conversation of the wives; While they behold your chaste conversation coupled with fear.

Some ladies of my acquaintance have looked at the words *conversation* and *fear* in this passage and taken them as a license to become real blabbermouths, trying to *scare* their husbands into the Kingdom of God by jawing incessantly. Any man could have told them they were taking the wrong approach. All the ladies succeeded in doing was driving their husbands further away from God, of course. What He is saying here through Peter, in language twentieth-century wives can understand, is just the opposite:

> Wives, in the same way be submissive to your husbands so that, if any of them do not believe the word, they may be won over without talk by the behavior of their wives, when they see the purity and reverence of your lives.
>
> *1 Peter 3:1, 2 NIV*

Wives tell me that clamming up and letting the Holy Spirit get their husbands saved really works—when they do it.

If you're *still* not convinced that a translation other than the King James can be God's Word, God might have a solution for you in The New King James Bible-New Testament which, according to its Introduction, sticks as closely as possible to the old King James, but uses "present-day vocabulary, punctuation, and syntax wherever obscurity exists" (NKJB-NT, page iii).

So much for Bible translations. The important thing is not to be hung up and risk missing the best God has for you.

Now where were we? Oh, yes. We were overcoming someone's objections to my paraphrase of Matthew 6:33.

When I first encountered that Scripture, it made no sense to my natural mind. At the time, as a newly appointed corporation president, I had the feeling that successful results all depended on my being at the office by 7:30 every morning at the very latest. Seven days a week had been my workaholic routine as I made my way up the ladder of success as a devout pagan. Now I knew Jesus, but the old habit patterns were still with me.

But the morning I stumbled over the Matthew 6:33 Scripture, Jesus reminded me of what one of my engineering professors had told me years before.

"Where did that formula come from?" I had challenged him one day when he had written a bunch of numbers and letters on the blackboard and told us that was how we were to work a particular problem. His reply was one I had never forgotten:

"At this point, that's none of your concern, Mr. Hill," he had said patiently, peering professorily at me over the tops of his wire-rimmed glasses. "As we go along," he continued, while my ears turned fire-engine red, "you'll learn in another class session all about the derivation of the formula. You couldn't understand it yet if I explained it to you. In the meantime, just take my word for it. I can assure you that the formula is empirical—that is, it has proven to be correct."

He was right, I remembered. His formula *did* work, and by the time I knew enough to understand how the formula came to be, I had sense enough to know that I couldn't have understood the explanation at the time I had asked the question. Sometimes it's necessary to jump into something in the middle, with a blind leap of faith. And after you see how it works, then you're in a better position to understand the how and the why.

You can bet I never asked that professor a presumptuous question again. The Lord was bringing all that back to my consciousness in connection with my attitude toward Matthew 6:33. *It's empirical!* boomed back and forth through my mind as I reread the words.

"All right, Lord," I finally agreed. "It doesn't make sense to me, but I'm going to give it a try, starting right now." And I began spending at least an hour each morning in His Word before going to the office. Arriving at 8:30 instead of an hour earlier, what did I find? The phones were ringing, orders were coming in from all directions, and trucks were rolling *better* than if I'd been there to make it happen. I couldn't get over it! Those crazy-sounding Matthew instructions *were* really empirical. They *worked!*

If I'd let my think tank rule in that situation, the human tendency to put first things last could have robbed me of the beneficial results of doing things God's way.

"But doesn't the Christian life become one of laziness and carelessness when we follow the Matthew instruc-

51

tions? Won't we slouch around looking as bedraggled as last year's cabbage patch?'' people ask me.

"Have you ever seen a lily?'' I ask them. Some of them get the point immediately.

It would be hard to imagine a more exquisitely dressed flower, wouldn't it? And Jesus says that the way He takes care of the apparel of the lilies is the way He's going to take care of everything about us as soon as we put Him and His Word first in our lives.

If you begin to do it His way, I can guarantee you'll begin to look better instead of worse.

"Well, I'll *try* the business of seeking His Kingdom in the pages of the *Manufacturer's Handbook* when I first get up in the morning,'' someone reluctantly agrees. "But I can't yet do *all* things His way—''

"Why not?''

"Well, you don't understand how deeply in debt I am,'' the someone moans. "I simply can't afford to tithe.''

I understand how you feel, because in the beginning I had the same feeling about doing it God's way in the area of the pigskin patch in my hip pocket. For a fellow like me, that was the most sensitive part of my whole anatomy.

Oh how it hurt when I began to tithe! But you know something? After I began to do what the *Manufacturer's Handbook* said about my finances, I *really* began to prosper. Money came in so abundantly that I paid off my mortgage in two years! Ever since I began tithing, I've been able to pay cash for every car and every home I've purchased. Today, I know I can't afford *not* to tithe, because since I began doing things His way, I have no unpaid bills except current ones. Tithing has *increased* my income—and *stretched* it!

"But I don't understand how that works,'' someone's still complaining.

"You will when you do it," my friend Ed told me when I voiced the same objection. And I found out he was right.

I've even discovered *why* it works. You can too, by eavesdropping on a little question-and-answer session that took place between the Manufacturer and His people one day. It's recorded in Malachi, the very last book of the Old Testament:

> THE LORD GOD ALMIGHTY: I the Lord do not change. So you, O descendants of Jacob, are not destroyed. Ever since the time of your forefathers you have turned away from my decrees and have not kept them. Return to me, and I will return to you.
>
> HIS PEOPLE: How are we to return?
>
> THE LORD GOD ALMIGHTY: Will a man rob God? Yet you rob me.
>
> HIS PEOPLE: How do we rob you?
>
> THE LORD GOD ALMIGHTY: In tithes and offerings. You are under a curse—the whole nation of you—because you are robbing me. Bring the whole tithe into the storehouse, that there may be food in my house. Test me in this and see if I will not throw open the floodgates of heaven and pour out so much blessing that you will not have room enough for it. I will prevent pests from devouring your crops, and the vines in your fields will not cast their fruit. Then all the nations will call you blessed, for yours will be a delightful land. You have said harsh things against me.
>
> HIS PEOPLE: What have we said against you?

THE LORD GOD ALMIGHTY: You have said, "It is futile to serve God. What did we gain by carrying out his requirements and going about like mourners before the Lord Almighty? But now we call the arrogant blessed. Certainly the evildoers prosper, and even those who challenge God escape."

Then those who feared the Lord talked with each other, and the Lord listened and heard. A scroll of remembrance was written in his presence concerning those who feared the Lord and honored his name.

THE LORD GOD ALMIGHTY: They will be mine in the day when I make up my treasured possession. I will spare them, just as in compassion a man spares his son who serves him. And you will again see the distinction between the righteous and the wicked, between those who serve God and those who do not.

Malachi 3:6–18 NIV, adapted to dramatic form.

There you have God's answer to *why* tithing works. In my think tank, it all boils down to something like this:

Tithing works because I, the Lord God Almighty, say it works. Do things My way, and I'll always reward you according to all I have promised—whether you understand it or not.

His answer satisfied me completely. How about you? Why does His way work? Because He said so.

-5-
FOR RICHER OR POORER?
What Is God's Will for King's Kids?

For richer or poorer? Poverty or prosperity? Rags or riches? What *is* God's will for King's kids? Do *you* know? I do. Absolutely. How can I be so sure? Because the *Manufacturer's Handbook* makes God's plans for His people perfectly plain so no one will have to be in the dark. Everyone would see it if they'd only approach God's Word with a mind that wasn't laced up tighter than a blimpo's corset with dead denominational doctrines.

Almost everyone will agree that the Great Commission is for everyone: "Go into all the world and preach the good news to all creation" (Mark 16:15 NIV).

Would Jesus have given us such an assignment without providing the resources necessary to accomplish it? Not in my book. He says He'll supply *all* of my needs out of His riches in glory (Philippians 4:19). With the price of plane fare what it is these days, I *need* an abundant supply of shekels to travel the world and tell all the whosoevers about Jesus. Nobody but a prosperous King's kid can afford to make the trip.

55

Let's look at some other things Jesus said on the subject. How about this one: "I am come that you might have life and have it more abundantly" (*see* John 10:10).

"In superabundance" is the way the Wuest translation puts it. Isn't that the best news you ever heard? Doesn't that make you want to find out how to get that superabundance operating in your life, in the lives of your children, in the lives of your parents, and in the lives of your brothers and sisters in Christ? It does me.

Superabundance couldn't *possibly* mean not being able to pay your bills on time or having no money to buy bread and shoes for your children, could it? Not in my dictionary! Besides, I know from James 1:17 that God has only *good* gifts for His children, and poverty is a negative force—the absence of prosperity, just as darkness is the absence of light.

Look into *Webster's New Collegiate Dictionary* with me for a moment. We're right on the verge of discovering something exciting about the Kingdom of God.

abundant = marked by great plenty (as of resources).

plenty = a full or more than adequate amount or supply.

super = surpassing all or most others.

Are you still there, or did you blast out into orbit with that one? I mean, that's good news isn't it? Jesus came so we could have *super*abundant life, which has to mean more than enough of everything good, including material resources. You couldn't want any plainer statement of fact, could you?

And then there's the verse that has been almost my

theme song ever since I became a King's kid: "Beloved, I wish above all things that thou mayest prosper and be in health, even as thy soul prospereth" (3 John 2).

Sure, John wrote that, but he was doing it under the inspiration of the Holy Spirit (2 Timothy 3:16), so it's as if Jesus is saying directly to you, "I wish above all things that *you* would prosper."

Everywhere I look in the *Manufacturer's Handbook,* I find that prosperity *is* His plan for all His people. Don't you find that too? Or haven't you looked lately? As long as you're in doubt about His will, you'll be like a wave of the sea tossed back and forth by the wind, thinking poverty one minute and prosperity the next. That makes you a double-minded King's kid who will never get anything from God—not because He doesn't *want* you to have prosperity but because you have refused to follow His rules for getting it. (*See* some of the rules in James 1:5–8.)

Once you have a solid grip on the fact that God really *wants* you to prosper, and once you come solidly in line with His directions for prospering, you can start watching it happen.

The first thing to do to brighten your financial picture is to blow the dusty cobwebs of dead doctrines of dead men out of your mind with the light of the Word of God. Brainwashing, you could call it, or getting your mind reprogrammed by the Word of God. The *Manufacturer's Handbook* uses slightly different terminology, but it means the same thing: "And be not conformed to this world: but be ye transformed by the renewing of your mind, that ye may prove what is that good, and acceptable, and perfect, will of God" (Romans 12:2).

In other words, don't think as the world thinks; let your mind be reprogrammed by His Word so you will begin to think as God thinks. Then you'll *know* in every cell of your mind and heart that God's will for you is prosperity.

Maybe we should stop and consult Mr. Webster again right here to see what prosperity is, anyhow, and what it means to prosper. *Webster's New Collegiate Dictionary* tells it this way:

> prosperity = the condition of being successful or thriving, especially economic well-being.

> prosper = to succeed in an enterprise or activity; especially to achieve economic success; to become strong and flourishing.

In the background, I can hear the rumbling of dissenters, the folks who all their lives have been conned into believing that for a King's kid, scroungy is spiritual, and success is sin.

You can believe that if you want to, but it's not what God's Word says; those sentiments are like the thieving utterances of a devilish spirit of poverty. So do me a favor, will you? Put all your man-made doctrines on the shelf while we review what God has had to say about His plan for His people from the very beginning. Then, if you have further objections, we'll look at them in later chapters.

''But there's more to life than financial success!'' another religious soul howls, not budging an inch from the poverty line, and not willing to let me present the Word first. Well, let's answer his charges, shall we, just to clear the air before we continue.

Of *course* there's more to life than financial success! I'm living proof of it. My testimony in eight previous books is written proof of it too. Freedom from money worries has enabled me to be a laborer in God's harvest when I might otherwise have had to spend all my time tending the store.

I've found it highly beneficial—for Him and for me—to live the life of prosperity God has in mind for His kids.

Over the years, many have questioned me about what I've been saying here, phrasing their inquiries something like this: "Hill, where did you get the idea that freedom from money worries is God's idea for His people?"

I'm about to show you a whole truckload of answers straight from God's written Word. Let's look at a couple of psalms to start us off, and then head back to the beginning with Great Granddaddy Adam and Great Grandmama Eve.

In the first psalm, God tells us that if we meditate on His Word day and night, whatever we do will prosper:

> Blessed is the man
>   who does not walk in the counsel of the wicked
> or stand in the way of sinners
>   or sit in the seat of mockers.
> But his delight is in the law of the Lord,
>   and on his law he meditates day and night.
> He is like a tree planted by streams of water,
>   which yields its fruit in season
> and whose leaf does not wither.
>   Whatever he does prospers.
>
> *Psalms 1:1–3 NIV*

If God wants you to hang in there with His Word—and nobody could argue with *that*—and if you *do* it, He's going to prosper you, like it or not. He backs that promise up in Psalm 112, where He says:

> Blessed is the man who fears the Lord,
>   who finds great delight in his commands. . . .
> Wealth and riches are in his house. . . .
>
> *Psalms 112:1, 3 NIV*

In other words, if you keep God's commandments, prosperity is going to head your way. It's inevitable, because prosperity has been God's plan for His people from the very beginning.

So that the enemy can't accuse me of picking and choosing Scriptures out of context to prove something conjured up in my own think tank, let's go back to God's first two folks, Adam and Eve. Were they prosperous or poverty-stricken? Look at the record.

In the first chapter of Genesis, God set forth His original plan for the human race, that they would have dominion (they would be the boss) over the entire creation and run it for the owner, who is God. This principle has never changed. Never heard of it? Read it here:

> Then God said, "Let us make man in our image, in our likeness, and let them rule over the fish of the sea and the birds of the air, over the livestock, over all the earth, and over all the creatures that move along the ground."
>
> So God created man in his own image,
>   in the image of God he created him;
>   male and female he created them.
>
> God blessed them and said to them, "Be fruitful and increase in number; fill the earth and subdue it. Rule over the fish of the sea and the birds of the air and over every living creature that moves on the ground."
>
> Then God said, "I give you every seed-bearing plant on the face of the whole earth and every tree that has fruit with seed in it. They will be yours for food. And to all the beasts of the earth and all the birds of the air

and all the creatures that move on the
ground—everything that has the breath of
life in it—I give every green plant for food."
And it was so.

Genesis 1:26–30 NIV

Do you see here that you were made to rule the earth
and that God gave you everything you needed to do it—
including a supermarket full of still-on-the-tree groceries?

God put Adam in the beautiful Garden of Eden "to
work it and take care of it" (Genesis 2:15 NIV). And God
brought to Adam all the beasts of the field and the birds of
the air so Adam could give names to them, and he did.
And Adam began to rule the earth.

When God saw that it would be good for Adam to have
a helper (Genesis 2:18, 20), He put Adam to sleep and
made the original woman for him (Genesis 2:21, 22). (I'm
including verse numbers so you won't have to take my
word for any of this but can check up on me by reading it
in your own Bible.)

Now take a little walk with me through the Garden of
Eden and look around. What's your general impression of
the place? Perfection, eh? No weeds, no litter, no traffic,
no deadlines, no worries, no parking meters, no mothers-
in-law, no commercials, no taxes, no signs telling folks to
keep off the grass, no junk mail, no neighbors' dogs digging dinosaur-bone holes in the middle of your rose garden. *No bills!* Perfectly heavenly place . . . Adam and Eve
wandering around hand-in-hand with gorgeous suntans all
over . . . plenty of delicious food just for picking it off the
tree . . . no work to do except the joyful labor of a man
puttering around in a beautiful garden and taking care of
his luscious wife. . . .

Do you suppose the fanciest estate of the richest bil-
lionaire in the whole world could ever be any finer? No

61

way it could hope to be as good, right? In the beginning, Adam and Eve had absolute prosperity. The Garden of Eden was such a marvelous place that *Almighty God* came there to take His late-afternoon walk! That place was fantastic beyond our imagination. It had everything Adam needed for a perfect life.

God gave Adam only one rule, as far as we know: "Don't eat of the tree of the knowledge of good and evil, because if you do, it will wipe you out" (Genesis 2:17, author's paraphrase).

The same law in the New Testament is called the law of sin and death (Romans 8:2), that is, if you sin, by doing what God told you not to do, it'll kill you every time. That's how these things work.

Anyhow, all went well until old Slue Foot showed up to admire the scenery and talked Eve into a between-meal snack—a piece of fruit from the only no-no tree in the entire world (Genesis 2:17; 3:1–6). Old Slue dangled the bait, and Eve bit—hook, line, and sinker. Then she gave Adam some of the no-no fruit and he ate it, too.

Did they need that fruit? Like they needed another hole in the head. They had plenty to eat already. And they certainly didn't need to know good *and* evil, because up to then, there hadn't been any evil to know. But they ate it anyway.

Things zoomed downhill at a dizzy pace from that time forward. As a partial result of the first act of man's disobedience to God, Adam and Eve

got dressed (3:7)
hid from God (3:8)
told a lie (3:10)
tattled (3:12, 13)
got problems (3:14–19)
and were evicted (3:23).

Can you imagine so much disaster from eating one piece of fruit? In comparison, the old green-apple bellyache I knew as a kid was a picnic. Then get a load of what God did on account of the forbidden-fruit episode:

1. He cursed the serpent
   and said he would always have to crawl on his belly in the dust. (3:14)

2. He told the woman
   she would have increased pain in childbearing and that man would rule over her. (3:16)

3. He cursed the ground
   and said it would produce thorns and thistles. (3:17, 18)

4. He told Adam
   that his labors would be a tough job from now on. (3:17–19)

5. He whipped up some fur-lined snuggies
   to replace their scratchy fig-leaf sinsuits. (3:7, 21)

6. He evicted His first man and first woman from Paradise and made the Tree of Life off limits
   because they'd broken the only rule
   He'd given them. (3:22–24)

Breaks your heart, doesn't it?

Well, the history of mankind is a long story, and I can't get into all of it here. The point I want to hammer home is that God created man to take care of the world He had made and that He gave him everything he needed to carry out his assignment. The only thing man had to provide for himself was obedience to the only commandment. God would have freely given him the grace to do that if Adam had asked Him for it instead of deliberately choosing to do his own thing, to please his wife instead of God.

God wanted Adam to have great abundance, and gave it to him. When Adam ended up in relative poverty, it was his own fault, not God's design.

After Adam ate the no-no fruit, he died, just as God said he would. Yes, I know his body hung around earth for 930 years (Genesis 5:5) before his physical death caught up with him, but it was spiritual death—separation from God—at first bite. Man's continuous, free, intimate fellowship with Almighty God was broken.

By doing his own thing, Adam spoiled everything for everybody everywhere. A person couldn't even go *barefoot* anymore because of the danger of stepping on thorns and thistles (Genesis 3:18)—ouch! Paradise was lost, all right. No one was safe anywhere—one of Adam's sons even murdered his own brother and then lied to God about it (Genesis 4:8, 9)! Oh, it was awful!

About 1650 years later (you can add it up for yourself from the figures given in Genesis 5), things were so bad that God decided He was going to have to wipe out the whole human race and start from scratch (Genesis 6:5–7)—except for Noah, who was a righteous man who walked with God (6:8, 9). Even the earth was corrupt and full of violence (6:11), because the human race was racing so far, so fast, out of God's will.

Wanting to spare righteous Noah and his family, God commanded Noah to build a big house-and-barn boat that could preserve him and his family and at least one couple of every bird, animal, and creeping thing to start a new world population. The ark had to be big enough to hold food for them all. Talk about a seed store! And think how prosperous Noah had to be to *buy* groceries for all those critters! According to Genesis 6:21, it *wasn't* a BYOL (Bring Your Own Lunch) arrangement.

In the midst of dispensing instructions for building the ark, God told Noah, "Everything on earth will perish. But I will establish my convenant with you, and you will enter the ark—you and your sons and your wife and your sons' wives with you" (Genesis 6:17, 18 NIV).

Don't let that word *covenant* throw you. It simply means that God was making a "deal" with Noah. *God's part* of the bargain was to keep Noah and his family safe while everyone else went scuba diving without any oxygen. *Noah's part* was to get busy and build the biggest floating zoo alive.

What did people think of Noah for doing what God said? Everybody was bound to have thought that he had bats in his belfry when he started talking about a flood that would drown the whole world. Up to that time there hadn't been so much as a sprinkle of rain on the earth. The ground had been watered with a mist that came up out of the ground (Genesis 2:5, 6). But no one locked Noah up for his stupidity. Everybody probably just stood by and jeered at him or offered to sell him moldy peanuts to feed the elephants. It's a safe bet that no whosoever pressured him for a reserved seat in the orchestra section.

The building of the boat must have represented quite a challenge for a man with no Sears Roebuck power tools to speed things up. Awesome responsibility!

Well, it took a long time, but Noah "did all that the Lord commanded him" (Genesis 7:5 NIV). When the ark was finally finished, and all of Noah's family and the necessary numbers of birds, animals, and creeping things were safely inside the ark, it started to rain.

That must have been some downpour! Just listen to it:

In the six hundredth year of Noah's life, on
the seventeenth day of the second month

... all the springs of the great deep burst forth, and the floodgates of the heavens were opened. And rain fell on the earth forty days and forty nights . . . and as the waters increased they lifted the ark high above the earth . . . and all the high mountains under the entire heavens were covered . . . to a depth of more than twenty feet. . . . Every living thing on the face of the earth was wiped out. . . . Only Noah was left, and those with him in the ark.

Genesis 7:11–23 NIV

Man, what a bath! That should have been enough to clean up everything in sight. But God let the world soak in the tub for days before He pulled the plug and let the water gurgle down the drain. Afterward, there was a mud-pack to beat all mudpacks. But at last, after a year and ten days, the earth was completely dry, and God told Noah to come out of the ark.

The very first thing Noah did was to build an altar to the Lord and sacrifice burnt offerings to Him. When the Lord "smelled the pleasing aroma" of the burnt offering, He was so blessed, He "said in his heart" (Genesis 8:21 NIV) that He would never again curse the ground because of man, and He would never again destroy all living creatures. Furthermore, He made a promise to Noah:

As long as the earth endures,
seedtime and harvest,
cold and heat,
summer and winter,
day and night
will never cease.

Genesis 8:22 NIV

66

Then God set His rainbow in the clouds as a reminder to Noah and to Himself that He would keep His promise. The rainbow was at least as good a memory jogger as a string around a pinkie, I guess, in addition to being a whole lot prettier to look at. For *his* part this time, Noah was to "Be fruitful and increase in number and fill the earth" (Genesis 9:1 NIV).

Were there any no-nos for Noah? Only one: he was not to eat meat that still had its lifeblood in it (Genesis 9:4). And God said that if anyone killed another person, He would personally demand an accounting (Genesis 9:5, 6).

After the flood, Noah lived in prosperity for 350 years, and things more or less rocked along until God made another deal—with Abram, this time. And what a deal! Just listen:

The Lord had said to Abram [that was his name before God changed it], "Leave your country, your people and your father's household and go to the land I will show you.

"I will make you into a great nation
and I will bless you;
I will make your name great,
and you will be a blessing. . . ."

"All the land that you see I will give to you and your offspring forever. . . . Go, walk through the length and breadth of the land, for I am giving it to you."
Genesis 12:1, 2; 13:15, 17 NIV

A man couldn't want more prosperity than that, could he? Imagine owning all the land that you could see—forever! If that's poverty, my head's past due for a tune-up.

Later God changed Abram's name to Abraham (Genesis 17:5) and told him that if he would walk before Him blameless, God would make him "very fruitful" (Genesis 17:6 NIV) and would give him "the whole land of Canaan . . . as an everlasting possession to you and your descendants after you; and I will be their God" (Genesis 17:8 NIV).

The whole land of Canaan? That's quite a bundle of free real estate.

A further requirement on Abraham's part was that he and all the males in his outfit were to be circumcised. Abraham didn't argue with God, he just did what God said, and God blessed him so abundantly that even today we talk about "the blessings of Abraham."

After Abraham's death at 175 years of age, the Lord appeared to Abe's son Isaac and told him how many ways He would bless him—because Abraham had followed the rules God gave him. And Isaac, too, became very wealthy (Genesis 26:13).

Coming on down the years toward today, we see that Jacob, Joseph, Moses, David, Solomon, and many others—all King's kids, on assignment for the King, doing what God told them to do—were blessed with plenty to do *with*. None of them ever had any trouble paying his bills.

And now latch onto the loaded promise God made to all the Israelites in the wilderness:

> And it shall come to pass, if thou shalt hearken diligently unto the voice of the Lord thy God, to observe and to do all his commandments which I command thee this day, that the Lord thy God will set thee on high above all nations of the earth.
>
> *Deuteronomy 28:1*

That's how King Jimmy's version of the *Manufacturer's Handbook* begins the promise-packed chapter. Before we go further, let's come up for air for a minute to make sure we're on the same wavelength, all right?

How do you "hearken diligently" to God's Word? Every day you read the Bible out loud so you can hear it. Or maybe you listen to Bible tapes as you're driving along, washing dishes, or jogging to the bus stop. Listening to Bible tapes is a good way to soak yourself in God's Word. A friend of mine turns on his tape player when he goes to bed so the Word of God can be feeding him even while he sleeps.

In Deuteronomy 28:1 God is telling us, "Look, kids, if you will listen to My voice and do everything I tell you, then I will set you high above all the nations of the earth."

I don't hear a hint of poverty in that, do you?

Let's look at that verse in a modern translation and see if it still says the same thing. Here it is in the NIV: "If you fully obey the Lord your God and carefully follow all his commands I give you today, the Lord your God will set you high above all the nations on earth."

That translation reminds us that to hearken to the Word of God means more than just to take it in with our ears; it means that we are to *hear and obey* what He says. In this case, reading two translations doubled my understanding of the verse.

And now look at what follows! "And all these blessings shall come on thee, and overtake thee, if thou shalt hearken unto [*obey* NIV] the voice of the Lord thy God" (Deuteronomy 28:2).

Fantastic! In other words, "Get out of the way! These blessings are going to *overtake* you! If you don't watch out, the blessings will run right over you!"

Notice that He doesn't say, "*If* the prime rate behaves,

69

if the recession lifts, *if* the economy improves." He says, "Just listen to Me, obey Me, and I'll dump these blessings all over you."

When I first heard that verse, I said, "Whoopee! That's the greatest thing I've ever heard in all my life!" I never took a college or graduate course where the professor said, "Now, I'm *guaranteeing* that you'll prosper because you took this course."

What he said was more like, "Pay as you go out. That's it. You got it. Good luck. Maybe it will work for you." There were never any guarantees.

But just look at the blessings God guarantees for those who do His will:

> You will be blessed in the city and blessed in the country. The fruit of your womb will be blessed, and the crops of your land and the young of your livestock—the calves of your herds and the lambs of your flocks. Your basket and your kneading trough will be blessed. You will be blessed when you come in and blessed when you go out. . . . The Lord will send a blessing on your barns and on everything you put your hand to. The Lord your God will bless you in the land he is giving you. The Lord will establish you as his holy people, as he promised you on oath, if you keep the commands of the Lord your God and walk in his ways. Then all the peoples on earth will see that you are called by the name of the Lord, and they will fear you. The Lord will grant you abundant prosperity—in the fruit of your womb, the young of your livestock and the crops of your ground—in the land he swore to your forefathers to give you. The Lord will open the heavens, the storehouse of his bounty, to

send rain on your land in season and to
bless all the work of your hands. You will
lend to many nations but will borrow from
none. The Lord will make you the head not
the tail. If you pay attention to the commands of the Lord your God that I give you
this day and carefully follow them, you will
always be at the top, never at the bottom.

Deuteronomy 28:3–13 NIV

Still listening? Or did you lift off into the Rapture at all
this good news that belongs to you if you belong to God
and act like it? Can you think of anything better than what
He has promised here? I can't.

These blessings of Abraham are ours, too, when we
are walking by faith. Same blessings, same promises.

"Now wait just a minute!" someone's squawking.
"Where do you get that? Exactly what do the blessings of
Abraham have to do with *me?*"

Believe it or not, God answered that in Paul's letter to
the Galatians:

Those who believe are children of Abraham.
The Scripture foresaw that God would justify
the Gentiles by faith, and announced the
gospel in advance to Abraham: "All nations
will be blessed through you." So those who
have faith are blessed along with Abraham,
the man of faith.

Galatians 3:7–9 NIV

"Those who have faith are blessed along with Abraham." Do you have faith? Of course you do! In Romans
12:3, God says that He has given to every man "the
measure of faith." How's that for God's Word for it that
the blessings of Abraham are yours? Couldn't be plainer.

Before we get too far away from the Book of Deuteron-

71

omy, take a look at one more mind-boggling verse about prosperity: "But thou shalt remember the Lord thy God: for it is he that giveth thee power to get wealth . . ." (Deuteronomy 8:18).

Wow! Did that make your eyes light up? Read it again, in another translation, to make sure you've got it: "But remember the Lord your God, for it is he who gives you the ability to produce wealth . . ." (NIV).

The other translations I consulted render it ". . . strength to become prosperous" (New English Bible); ". . . the power of gaining wealth" (Moffatt); ". . . power to make wealth" (New American Standard). They all say about the same thing, don't they?

Now fasten your seat belt and listen to what the last half of the same verse has to say about *why* God gives us the power to get wealth: ". . . that he may establish his covenant which he sware unto thy fathers, as it is this day" (Deuteronomy 8:18).

Do you hear it? He gives us power to produce wealth *so He can establish His covenant*—in other words, *so He can keep His promises!*

If you've never danced before the Lord, now would be a good time to try it. I mean, did you *hear* what He said? Percolate that with your prosperity pros and cons for a minute. Does it say to you what it says to me? That it isn't just merely *all right* if we prosper but that we're *called* to prosper for *His* sake, *so He can keep His promises!*

SO
      HE
           CAN
                KEEP
                    HIS
                        PROMISES!

If that doesn't blow your mind, nothing ever will. And now let's carry our understanding one step further:

Want to make a liar out of God? Want to prove that He *doesn't* bless His people? Here's how:

> *Refuse* to prosper.
> > *Go* to the poorhouse.
> > > *Be* head over heels in debt
> > > with no way out.
> > > > *Owe* everybody and his brother.
> > > > *Let* your children beg for bread.

Looking at it backwards and upside down that way *might* jolt some of you out of your second-best theology long enough for a blessing to get through.

After God had told the Israelites—and us—of the prosperity that would happen if they obeyed Him, He told them the bad things that would happen if they chose their own way. If you have a strong stomach and want to risk it, put on your heaviest suit of armor and turn to Deuteronomy 28:15–68. There you can read about how people who choose *not* to obey God have chosen disastrous things, including

> to turn into cannibals,
> > to eat their own babies (28:53),
> > > and become so worthless in the end,
> > > their enemies wouldn't have them
> > > > on a Christmas tree—
> > > > > not even as *slaves!* (28:68).

That's probably about as low as you can get.

"But all that's Old Testament stuff!" someone's growling at me.

73

Wait a minute! Do you think we have things *less* good because Jesus has come? According to my copy of the *Manufacturer's Handbook*, we have them *better* now that Light has come into the world.

Don't think of Old Testament and New Testament as if they belonged to different ages. The entire written Word of God belongs to King's kids *now*. When God was speaking His perfect will of prosperity for His people in Deuteronomy 28, it was for them back there and for us right now too, because God's promises never change, His gifts are never taken away (Romans 11:29). He always says, "I am God; I change not" (*see* James 1:17; Hebrews 13:8).

Did you realize that Jesus Himself said He came to preach the *good* news to the poor (Luke 4:18), and that He talked "more about money and possessions than about any other subject except the kingdom of God"? (From *Life Abundant*, by Dr. Edward Bauman in "Your Money or Your Life," in the November 1978 issue of *Ministry of Money*, published by Wellspring, Germantown, Maryland 20767.)

Could *good* news to the poor *ever* mean that they were destined to remain poor? That wouldn't be good news to me. Listen carefully to what He said:

> *The Spirit of the Lord is on me,*
> *because he has anointed me*
> *to preach good news to the poor.*
> *He has sent me to proclaim freedom for the prisoners*
> *and recovery of sight for the blind,*
> *to release the oppressed,*
> *to proclaim the year of the Lord's favor.*
>
> *Luke 4:18, 19 NIV*

Did you *hear* it? The *good* news to the poor was that their condition of poverty was about to be *reversed,* just as the other things Jesus mentions in this passage were to be changed. He was proclaiming freedom for prisoners, sight for the blind, release for the oppressed, the year of the Lord's *favor* for everyone!

When? Pie in the sky by and by? Or right now? Read Jesus' answer in the same chapter: "Today this Scripture is fulfilled in your hearing" (Luke 4:21 NIV).

Now, while you're still sputtering your surprise, "But—but—but—I always thought—" and your old dead doctrines are clattering to the floor, read another New Testament passage often quoted by proponents of the poverty/piety hogwash, and have the eyes of your understanding opened even wider:

> Blessed are you who are poor,
> for yours is the kingdom of God.
> Blessed are you who hunger now,
> for you will be satisfied.
> Blessed are you who weep now,
> for you will laugh.
>
> *Luke 6:20, 21 NIV*

Have you always thought this passage meant that the *good* news was that the poor would remain poor, the hungry would remain hungry, and that those who were weeping would keep on weeping forever? What kind of *good* news would that be? Read the passage again, setting aside all the old *bad news* doctrines you have learned from men, and let the light shine through.

Did you see the *good* news this time? It's as plain as the surprise in your eyes that Jesus is proclaiming

that those who were hungry
were going to be fed so much
that their hunger would be completely satisfied;
that those who were weeping and mourning
were going to be so comforted
they would actually laugh.

75

What about the poor? Because Jesus had come into the world,
the
    poor
        were
            going
                to
                    be
                        poor
                            no
                                more!

They were going to be set free from poverty!

You had never realized that before? That's what the dead doctrines of men can do to you—they can completely blind you to the good-news truth of God's Word.

What's the next thing that happened? Jesus went about doing the things He said He had come to do, and when John's disciples came to ask Him if He was really the Messiah, He told them:

> "Go back and report to John what you have seen and heard: The blind receive sight, the lame walk, those who have leprosy are cured, the deaf hear, the dead are raised, and the good news is preached to the poor."
>
> *Luke 7:22* NIV

Could there be any more *now* good news than that?

What *kind* of good news did Jesus preach to the poor? The kind that would show them how to get out of their poverty! Details of that later, but meanwhile, hold on for more good news if you think you can stand it.

God's promise of prosperity to His people as recorded in Deuteronomy 28 sounded suspiciously like abundant life, didn't it? I mean, if a man had all that, it would be more than enough. And yet centuries later, Jesus said *He* had come to give us abundant life (John 10:10).

Why wasn't the first promise of prosperity enough for God's people? Because they were human, that's why. And being human, they goofed it every time. Adam, Eve, Cain. . . .

Oh, once in a while, there was someone who was *almost* able to keep the requirements of the law, but mostly they struck out before they ever got to first base. Don't blame them—you're just like them, because "All have sinned and fall short of the glory of God" (Romans 3:23 NIV).

But it was different when Jesus came and said He would give us abundant life we could keep forever—for eternal life. Why could He make such a promise? Because for the first time, the law wouldn't be external, written on tablets of stone. It would be internal, written on our hearts (Ezekiel 36:26, 27; Romans 8:1–14). He would take all our failure and disobedience upon Himself, and give us His righteousness and obedience in exchange, His very own right standing with God!

When He went to heaven, He would actually ask the Father to send His own perfectly sinless Holy Spirit to live inside us to see to the keeping of the law *for* us (John 14:15–21). When the Lawgiver inside us is the one doing the keeping of the law for us, we can't possibly fail to measure up. How come?

> I am crucified with Christ: nevertheless I live; yet not I, but Christ liveth in me: and the life which I now live in the flesh I live by the faith of the Son of God, who loved me, and gave himself for me.
>
> *Galatians 2:20*

And Jesus *is* the perfect fulfillment of the law (Matthew 5:17). Do I hear any hallelujah choruses breaking forth out there? You can understand why Paul cried out, "Thanks be to God! He gives us the victory through our Lord Jesus Christ."

What a way to go! What a perfect guarantee that we will keep headed for heaven, on the way there enjoying the heavenly prosperity that comes from the obedience of Christ. I could never have dreamed up such a plan for myself, could you?

All I have to say is, if you don't like the prosperity message, you'd better not get mixed up with this Jesus.

Did you ever stop to think how much trouble Jesus went to in order to *provide* prosperity for His people? You can get a whiff of it in this verse:

> For you know the grace of our Lord Jesus Christ, that though he was so very rich, yet for your sakes he became so very poor, so that you through his poverty might become rich, abundantly supplied.
> *2 Corinthians 8:9* NIV *and* AMPLIFIED

Hallelujah, hallelujah!

If you can read *that* and *still* think Jesus wants you poor, you should have your head examined by the best shrink in the business. Jesus left enormous riches in glory so He could meet all your needs, making you rich so you could glorify God by the way in which you used those riches to meet the needs of others for Him. A delicious circle, I call it. And I like being involved in it.

The Wuest translation of the familiar "Abide in me . . ." Scripture (John 15:7, 8) is a real eye-opener about all this. Hold onto your hats, here it comes:

If you maintain a living communion with me and my words are at home in you, I command you to ask, at once, something for yourself, whatever your heart desires, and it will become yours. In this my Father is glorified, namely, that you are bearing much fruit.

John 15:7, 8 WUEST

How's that for making it plain that all the prosperity promises are for King's kids who recognize that nothing is their own to "spend on their own pleasures" (*see* James 4:3 NKJB-NT) but that everything belongs to their heavenly Father who puts it in their hands so they can enjoy using it to bear fruit for His glory?

Summing it all up, then, we *know* King's kids are *supposed* to prosper because:

1. God's original plan for the human race was that they would run the entire creation under God's ownership. He would supply everything they needed to do the job right. This principle has never changed (Genesis 1:27–30).

2. Prosperity is God's idea for carrying out His Kingdom work on earth (Deuteronomy 8:18). How could we expect to carry out the Great Commission of preaching the Gospel to every creature and represent God as His ambassadors worldwide unless funds were available? (Matthew 28:18–20).

3. We are God's holy people. Will He withhold any good thing from those who love Him and serve Him? (Deuteronomy 28; Psalms 84:11; John 10:10).

79

4. As Abraham's descendants, we are to prosper exactly as God decided that Abraham would prosper. *See* Deuteronomy 28 for the delicious details and Galatians 3:7 for the key that makes the blessings of Abraham ours.

5. We are God's handpicked ambassadors (1 Peter 2:9). What sort of influence does a grubby ambassador have on the pagan world, or even among the brethren? First class is God's idea for those who will simply take Him at His Word and do it.

6. Third John 2 says that prosperity and health, as our souls prosper, are God's intention for us.

If you don't like the prosperity message, you'll have to take it up with God, not me. I didn't invent it, He did. But I'm glad to have been let in on it.

Well, this chapter has been long enough to be almost a book in itself, but it accomplished something for me. All that sloshing around in the goodness of God's Word has made me confident I'll never again, for even a fleeting second, fall for the lie of Satan that says God wants me poor.

And now, prosperity, watch out! Here we come!

-6-
WHERE DOES POVERTY COME FROM?

"But if God wants me to prosper, how come I'm so poor?" someone's wailing from the back row. Don't apologize for asking. That's an important question, one that needs to be answered in a book of this kind.

In the light of God's very real promises of prosperity to His children, why *do* so many really sold-out-to-Jesus King's kids find themselves wallowing in poverty and want?

The answer to the question *has* to be, "The poor, the sick, the lost sinners, and all others who are not experiencing God's salvation——which includes eternal life, prosperity, and health——must be doing something wrong." There's no other conclusion we can reach after studying the *Manufacturer's Handbook* about these things.

Be careful! This *isn't* an excuse for you to point an accusing finger and jeer, "Nyah, nyah, nyah," as Brother Job's friends did at him. That King's kids are doing something wrong is no excuse for faultfinding and blaming. It's a reason for finding out what is wrong so it can be made right.

What Are You Doing Wrong?

So, what *are* unprosperous King's kids doing wrong? As I have asked the Lord this question, He's given me answers. Right in the pages of the *Manufacturer's Handbook*, naturally. We'll check them out in a minute, but first, let's reaffirm some basic meat-and-potatoes truths.

It isn't enough to *hear* the Word and *know* that God wants us to be prosperous. We have to *act* on His prosperity promises before they can be ours in experience. We have to *become* prosperous by following His instructions, being obedient to *do* the Word.

That's how it is with a lot of God's promises, even salvation. Every day people are dying and going to hell. Is that God's will? No way. Jesus paid the price for eternal life in heaven for every human being who would receive Him. But we have to respond to that provision before we can enjoy the results.

Here's how He says it in one place: "As many as received him, to them gave he power to become the sons of God . . ." (John 1:12).

Have *all* been given power to become sons of God? No, only those who are *obedient* to receive Him. Are they automatically sons of God? No, they have power to *become* sons of God, but the process of *becoming* requires *obedience*, and the choice to obey or not to obey is in their hands.

In Deuteronomy 28:1, the blessings God promises His people aren't automatic. They are *contingent upon our doing what He says*—hearing and obeying His Word. Even in the often-quoted-out-of-context Scripture that God

is no respecter of persons (Acts 10:34), there are conditions and qualifications to be met by persons before they
can receive God's blessing: "I now realize how true it is
that God does not show favoritism but accepts men from
every nation who fear him and do what is right" (Acts
10:34 NIV).

See? God doesn't show favoritism between nations,
but does that mean He accepts all individuals without
qualification? No, He accepts all *who meet His conditions
of fearing Him and doing what is right!* Keep that in mind
as we go along.

The Answer

A big part of the reason some King's kids prosper and
some don't is wrapped up in Jesus' parable of the sower.
Let's read it together to refresh our memory of how these
things work. Where will you find it? Matthew 13, Mark 4,
or Luke 8—take your pick. The parable is told in all three
places, from the distinctive viewpoint of each of the writers
of the first three Gospels. Each account has something
the others lack, as eyewitness accounts invariably do.

Maybe, for study purposes or to give an orderly overview to a brand-new King's kid, you have sometimes
wished for a four-in-one composite Gospel combining all
of Matthew, Mark, Luke, and John in a single chronologi-
cal narrative. If you've ever wanted something like that for
whatever reason, rejoice. It's on the way.

For several years—between books, she tells me—my
collaborator has been working on a composite Gospel,
and it's about ready for the printer. The title? *The Manufacturer's Handbook for King's Kids,* of course. The first
volume contains the interwoven Gospels; the next will
have the Book of Acts interwoven with the Epistles. If

King's kids find these helpful, she may tackle a chronologically arranged Old Testament next, who knows?

The Manufacturer's Handbook for King's Kids isn't some flaky paraphrase that could make you wonder whether or not it is faithful to the original. The content is very carefully woven, word for word, from the highly respected and readily understandable New International Version of the Bible.

I like the idea. TMHFKK will never take the place of the original Matthew, Mark, Luke, and John, of course—it's not intended to—but it should be mighty helpful as a study book. Interested? For ordering information, send a stamped, self-addressed envelope to:

Star Books
408 Pearson Street
Wilson, NC 27893

and let me know how you like it.

Now, let's take a look at the composite parable of the sower from the forthcoming *Manufacturer's Handbook for King's Kids*, with all three NIV accounts woven together.

The Parable of the Sower
(Matthew 13:1–9; Mark 4:1–9; Luke 8:4–9)

That same day, Jesus went out of the house and sat and began to teach by the lake. While a large crowd was gathering around him and people were coming to Jesus from town after town, he got into a boat and sat in it out on the lake. All the people stood along the shore at the water's edge. Then he taught them many things by parables, and in his teaching told this parable:

"Listen! A farmer went out to sow his

seed. As he was scattering the seed, some fell along the path; it was trampled on, and the birds of the air came and ate it up. Some fell on rocky places, where it did not have much soil. It sprang up quickly, because the soil was shallow. But when the sun came up, the plants were scorched, and they withered because they had no root [and] moisture. Other seed fell among thorns, which grew up with it and choked the plants, so that they did not bear grain. Still other seed fell on good soil. It came up, grew and produced a crop, multiplying thirty, sixty, or even a hundred times more than what was sown.''

When Jesus said this, he called out, ''He who has ears to hear, let him hear.''

His disciples asked him what this parable meant.

Jesus Explains the Parable of the Sower
(Matthew 13:18–23; Mark 4:13–20; Luke 8:11–15)

Then Jesus said to them, ''Don't you understand this parable? How then will you understand any parable? Listen then to what the parable of the sower means:

''The seed is the word of God. The farmer sows the word. Some people are like seed along the path where the word is sown. As soon as they hear the message about the kingdom and do not understand it, then the evil one—Satan, the devil—comes and snatches away from their hearts the word that was sown in them, so that they cannot believe and be saved.

85

"Others, like seed sown on rocky places, are the ones who hear the word and at once receive it with joy. But since they have no root, they last only a short time. They believe for a while, but in the time of testing, when trouble or persecution comes because of the word, they quickly fall away.

"The seed that fell [sown] among thorns stands for still others who hear the word, but as they go on their way, the worries of this life, the deceitfulness of wealth [riches], pleasures, and the desires for other things come in and choke the word, making it unfruitful. They do not mature.

"But the seed sown on good soil stands for those with a noble and good heart,
   who hear the word,
     accept it,
      understand it,
       retain it,
   and by persevering produce a crop—
     yielding thirty,
       sixty,
        or even a hundred times
         what was sown."

Isn't that delicious? Three in one. Makes you want to have a noble and good heart, doesn't it? And persevere until you produce a real crop for the Kingdom.

Now let's look at a Scripture found only in John's Gospel, and then we'll see what a combination of these two passages tells us about where poverty comes from. This verse from John is probably familiar to most King's kids:

"The thief does not come except to steal and to kill and to destroy; I alone came in order that they might be possessing life, and that they might be possessing it in super-abundance.''

John 10:10 WUEST

Now, stir these ingredients together in your think tank and mix well:

1. God's Word, promising His people prosperity;

2. Jesus' parable of the sower;

3. John 10:10

What do they tell you about where poverty comes from?

Poverty—a negative quality, the absence of our God-promised prosperity—comes when the thief, the master deceiver, Satan, robs us of our most priceless earthly possession, the Word of God.

Had you ever noticed that Slue Foot's role is described in the very same verse in which we read that Jesus gives us superabundance? Notice it now, and underline it ten times in every Bible you own. And never blame God again for anyone's poverty.

Why would Satan steal God's Word from God's children? Because God's Word is the source of His blessings for His children, that's why. Just look at some of them!

FAITH comes by hearing of the Word. (*Romans 10:17*)

NEW BIRTH—without which we cannot enter God's Kingdom—comes by the Word of God. (*1 Peter 1:23*)

SPIRITUAL GROWTH comes by hearing the Word. (*1 Peter 2:2*)

FREEDOM comes by the Word. (*John 8:31, 32*)

PERFECTED LOVE comes by obedience to the Word. (*1 John 2:5*)

HEALING comes by the Word. (*Proverbs 4:20-22; Psalms 107:20*)

PROSPERITY comes by the Word. (*Deuteronomy 8:18; 28:1; Joshua 1:8; Psalm 1*)

OUR INHERITANCE AND STRENGTH come by the Word. (*Acts 20:32*)

The list could go on and on, but this is more than enough to make the point. No wonder Satan comes to steal the Word! The Word is of infinite value for King's kids. Without the Word, we don't have enough left to go on.

How does Satan steal the Word and with it our prosperity? A zillion different ways—often with our unwitting but full cooperation, just as he used Eve's cooperation to steal God's best from the residents of Eden.

Reduced to its simplest terms, with a special focus on the subject of our study, the parable of the sower says that God has sent His Word to earth. That Word includes His promise of prosperity. The promise is the same for all His people but the fulfillment of the promise varies from person to person, according to their different levels of receptivity, determined by their attitudes toward Him and His Word.

1. *Sometimes the Word falls on people who in their IGNORANCE fail to understand it.* Satan quickly grabs the Word away from them so they can't believe and be saved (rescued) from their poverty.

2. *Sometimes the Word falls on people who* do *under-*

stand and receive it, but fail to put their whole depen-
dence on it and nurture it faithfully so it can produce fruit in
them. They soon succumb to UNBELIEF and have little
benefit from the Word.

3. Sometimes the Word falls on folks who are so
caught up with doing their own thing, DISOBEDIENCE to
the commands of God, that they never give the Word a
chance to show what God can do.

4. And then sometimes, hallelujah, the prosperity
promises of God's Word fall on sold-out King's kids who
are so glad to hear the good news that they cooperate
with it in every way they can and produce a bumper crop
for the glory of God.

The *Manufacturer's Handbook* said it would be like
that:

> Every Scripture is God-breathed, and is
> profitable for teaching, for conviction, for
> improvement, for training with respect to
> righteousness, in order that the man of God
> may be complete, fitted out for every good
> work.
>
> 2 Timothy 3:16, 17 WUEST

Who is going to be complete, thoroughly fitted out for
every good work? Everybody? No, only the man of God.
Are all King's kids living as men of God, out doing God's
work, seeking His way of doing business (Matthew 6:33),
leading lost sinners to Jesus (John 15:16), and thus *entitled* to all the equipment necessary for carrying out His instructions?

You know the answer to that as well as I do.

God, in His love and mercy for all mankind, has something to offer everyone, but what each one *receives* is dependent on his attitude toward God and His Word.

Attitudes determine the level of a person's receptivity to God's promises.

Think about it like this. Imagine a great apple orchard full of fruit—God's promise to supply all our need for apples. The orchard is free for all whosoevers—but each whosoever must bring his own container to receive the apples. Who takes home the most apples? The one who comes with a two-quart plastic bucket—or the one who arrives with ten bushel baskets in the back of his pickup truck so he will have plenty to share with his neighbors—who aren't yet whosoevers—when he gets home?

I heard your answer. You get the picture. The ones who are convinced of the generosity of God's promises and who are being OBEDIENT to do the things He said to do, are the ones who benefit most from His prosperity promises.

The promises don't show partiality, because God is no respecter of persons. But some people show more partiality to God's Word than others. Those who respect it the most receive the greatest benefits.

And so it is that real King's kids, on the go to brag about the King, find it impossible even to leave home for the sake of Jesus and the Gospel without receiving a huge return for their efforts. In this, King's kids in high gear are different from all other types of people. Out on God's assignments, putting His Word first in their lives, meditating on His Word day and night (Psalms 1:1), they stay on the wavelength of prosperity and abundant living far beyond what hydramatic King's kids—that's my word for "shiftless" Christians—or unsaved people can ever expect.

King's kids in high gear for Him are able to reap the full benefits of all He has to offer because they first give Him all of themselves, with an attitude that says, "Here am I, send me to do Your work in the world" (*see* Isaiah 6:8). Sounds suspiciously like the sowing (GIVING) and reaping (GETTING) principle at work, doesn't it?

God's Master Plan offers all His goodies of prosperity and health to whosoever *will* meet His qualifications, but some whosoevers simply *won't,* and that's what makes all the difference.

Let's say it again another way. Because of varying levels of receptivity to His Word, all do not benefit equally from God's promises, but it's not because *He* shows favoritism. It's because people make wrong choices. Some choose never to advance much beyond calling upon the name of the Lord and being saved. Others go just a little further and serve God sparingly, in their spare time, when the boob tube is on the blink, or it's too rainy to play golf, and they have nothing else to do. Still others go whole hog and serve Him all the time.

Now which of these do you suppose is able to receive the greatest blessings from God? Those who give Him the most of themselves, right?

The parable of the sower also gives us some clues about *how* the evil one is able to rob us. We can look around us—or into our own lives—and see how that works out. Satan has plenty of tricks to get our cooperation so he can rob us of the Word of God that's the source of our prosperity. Here are just a few of them:

causing us to fall for the deceitfulness of riches
  where we spend all our time watching the ticker tape
    or perusing the latest financial report
      instead of feeding on God's Word;
choking the Word out of us
  by the troubles and cares of the world;
making us too lazy to read the Word;

91

catching our attention with TV—or any other idol—
   so we neglect the Word;
causing us to listen to dead doctrines
   of dead men and get so saddled with UNBELIEF
     that we refuse to DO the Word,
       fearing it will make us look foolish;
exalting the human intellect
   to make us think we have to understand
     why the Word works
       before we can apply it;
causing us to do our own thing
   in DISOBEDIENCE to the Word. . . .

In these and a carload of other insidious ways, Satan robs us of the Word, so that instead of living the abundant life, filled to overflowing with the promises of His Word, and producing a rich harvest for the Kingdom, we are limited to dragging around as barren, unfruitful, down-at-the-mouth, defeated King's kids.

Satan's methods for stealing the Word from us, and so making it ineffective in our lives, can be classified under three headings: IGNORANCE, UNBELIEF, and DISOBEDIENCE.

Wow! Just look at those three big bad guys standing there. Do you see what I see?

I gnorance. U nbelief. D isobedience.

I'd never noticed it until this minute, but the Lord of glory has just opened my eyes to see the initial letters of those words: I U D.

In today's medical parlance, IUD stands for *intrauterine device,* a widely used contraption that prevents conception when it is planted in the uterus of a woman. For some reason no one has ever explained to me, the IUD prevents the seed of the man from uniting with the seed of the woman to make a baby. The IUD makes her barren and unfruitful.

And that's exactly what I, U, and D do in the life of a whosoever! Just think of it!

> *IGNORANCE*
> *UNBELIEF*
> *DISOBEDIENCE*
> *in a whosoever*
> *prevent the seed that is God's Word*
> *from coming together*
> *with the seed of faith*
> *to bring forth fruit!*

IGNORANCE, UNBELIEF, and *DISOBEDIENCE* make the Bride of Christ barren and unfruitful—unable to receive the implanted Word for His glory. I, U, and D literally make the promises of God "inconceivable"! *Something that is not even conceived can never come forth as fruit.*

What's all that white space doing there? A printer's error? No, it's there on purpose to give you time to catch your breath, sing hallelujahs, thank Jesus for this far-reaching new insight, and praise God with me. As I meditated on this brand-new, fresh-off-the-press revelation word of knowledge, He brought a flood of Amens! to my mind:

"The seed is the word of God." (*Luke 8:11*)

I would not have you ignorant. . . . (*Romans 1:13; 1 Corinthians 10:1, 12:1; 2 Corinthians 1:8; 1 Thessalonians 4:13*)

The word preached did not profit them, not being mixed with faith . . . they to whom it was first preached entered not in because of unbelief. . . . Let us, therefore, make every effort to enter that rest, so that no one will fall by following their example of disobedience. (*Hebrews 4:2, 6; Hebrews 4:11 NIV*) [Their unbelief kept the Israelites from bringing forth the fruit of the Word—entering the land that God had promised. Their unbelief made them disobedient.]

"Be not faithless, but believing." (*John 20:27*)

"If ye have faith as a grain of mustard seed, ye shall say unto this mountain, Remove hence to yonder place; and it shall remove; and nothing shall be impossible unto you." (*Matthew 17:20*) [The tiniest seed of faith united with receptivity and obedience to God's Word can produce great wonders. Nothing will be impossible for us when we provide the conditions under which the seed of our faith can come together in union with the seed of God's Word.]

Even as Abraham believed God, and it was accounted to him for righteousness. Know ye therefore that they which are of faith, the same are the children of Abraham. (*Gala-*

tians 3:6, 7) [Abraham's faith made him obedient to God's Word.]

For as the rain cometh down, and the snow from heaven, and returneth not thither, but watereth the earth, and maketh it bring forth and bud, that it may give seed to the sower, and bread to the eater: So shall my word be that goeth forth out of my mouth: it shall not return unto me void, but it shall accomplish that which I please, and it shall prosper in the thing whereto I sent it. (*Isaiah 55:10, 11*) [Think of all the things His Word was sent to accomplish—in us and for us.]

His divine power has given us everything we need for life and godliness through our knowledge of him who called us by his own glory and goodness. Through these he has given us his very great and precious promises, so that through them you may participate in the divine nature and escape the corruption in the world caused by evil desires.

For this very reason, make every effort to add to your faith goodness; and to goodness, knowledge; and to knowledge, self-control; and to self-control, perseverance; and to perseverance, godliness; and to godliness, brotherly kindness; and to brotherly kindness, love. For if you possess these qualities in increasing measure, they will keep you from being ineffective and unproductive in your knowledge of our Lord Jesus Christ. . . . For if you do these things, you will never fall, and you will receive a rich welcome into the eternal kingdom of our

Lord and Savior Jesus Christ. (*2 Peter 1:3–11 NIV*)

If you ever come across anything better than that last Scripture, let me know, will you? It's enough, all by itself, to change the whole universe!

These Scriptures reaffirm to me that IGNORANCE, UN-BELIEF, and DISOBEDIENCE—*knowing not* the Word, *believing not* the Word, and *doing not* the Word—rob us of the manifestation of the prosperity promises of God.

But when there are no IUDs around to prevent it, the seed of the Word of God will penetrate to the heart of the tiniest mustard seed of faith to fertilize it and cause it to grow. Then, after the prescribed fullness-of-time gestation/incubation period in the womb/hearts of His people, the promises of God will come forth in manifested reality as fruit that will glorify God and bless His people.

His kingdom will come on earth as it is in heaven. *Nothing will be impossible for us King's kids!*

"Quick!" I hear someone hollering. "How can I get rid of IUD so all these things can come to pass in *my* life?"

That's the best question I've heard all day. And the answer is so simple:

Let your IGNORANCE be overcome
by KNOWLEDGE of the Word of truth;
Let your UNBELIEF be overcome
by FAITH in the Word of truth;
Let your DISOBEDIENCE be overcome
by OBEDIENCE to hear and do the Word of truth.

And then what will happen? Something too wonderful for words, according to that mind-blowing promise in Isaiah, repeated in the New Testament:

> But as it is written, Eye hath not seen, nor ear heard, neither have entered into the heart of man, the things which God hath prepared for them that love him. But God hath revealed them unto us by his Spirit. . . .
>
> *1 Corinthians 2:9, 10*

Can you take all that in, or has it blown all the fuses in your finite think tank?

But now, if you are able, float down from the mountain-top with me to look at a picture of what happens when IUD is permitted to take over:

Ol' Zeke

Ol' Zeke is a flesh-and-blood caricature of how the three big uglies can cause poverty to happen and keep on happening among God's children:

"I guess it's jes' God's will for me to be pore," Ol' Zeke whines. He pauses to squirt a stream of terbaccy juice at the three-legged cat in the debris-strewn yard, shifts his cud into his other toothless cheek, then continues to deliver his learned theological pronouncements:

"Our family's always bin pore, and we jes' don't go along with all this hyar prosperity-teachin' stuff. The way I figger it, poverty must be our cross to bear till we git up yonder."

Having delivered himself of this profundity, Ol' Zeke hitches up his baggy britches, hunches his frayed suspenders back onto his sloping shoulders, and plops back down in the cane-bottom rocker on the dilapidated front porch to whittle himself a new whistle—"jes' to pass the time o' day afore Mandy gits the vittles on the table fer supper," he explains.

97

Notice the holes in his shoes? The three-day growth of beard on his spittle-stained chin? Purty, it ain't. God's will for him? No way. But by his IGNORANCE, his UNBELIEF, the DISOBEDIENCE of the negative confession of his mouth, and other things he's doing wrong, Ol' Zeke's stuck forever in a life-style of poverty.

"But I'm not that bad!" I hear you bellowing.

Of course you're not that bad. I didn't say you were. You're reading this book, aren't you? That's bound to put you light-years ahead of Ol' Zeke, chawin' his 'baccy and whittlin' away. Chances are, Ol' Zeke cain't even read nuthin'.

But some of the same poverty principles that are operating in Ol' Zeke's life could be operating also in yours:

If you remain in IGNORANCE of God's highest will for you, you'll miss it every time.

If you cement yourself in UNBELIEF by continually bad-mouthing your prospects, poverty will remain your lot in life.

If you indulge yourself in the DISOBEDIENCE of sloth-fulness, prosperity will never risk plowing its way through the junk in your yard to knock on your door.

Looking at this dreary derelict in Hillbilly Holler, we could invent a new beatitude: "Blessed be the bad examples—who show us what *not* to do."

The universal Bible principle of sowing and reaping (Galatians 6:7) was really at work in Ol' Zeke's life—against him. The old codger was sowing seeds of poverty while he sat and spat and whittled. His harvest was already upon him; he was reaping a bountiful supply of what he was still sowing. Of course, he didn't *know* that. But ignorance of a principle doesn't make it inoperative. It might even make it more deadly dangerous!

You could tell by looking at Ol' Zeke and his tumble-down shanty that he had been sowing the same kind of 100-proof poverty seed last year and the year before that. There's no way Ol' Zeke could ever hope to reap something good—like prosperity—with all his conception-preventing IGNORANCE, UNBELIEF, and DISOBEDIENCE cemented so securely in place.

Did I hear an "Ugh!" in the audience? Or did it come from me?

Maybe we should revive ourselves with the refreshment of a word or two from the Lord to renew our faith in God's promises of prosperity. Here are a few verses we didn't include in the last chapter, just in case someone might need a booster shot along about now:

> There will be no poor among you, for in the land the Lord your God is giving you to possess as your inheritance, he will surely richly bless you, if only you carefully listen to the voice of [and] fully obey the Lord your God and are careful to follow [and] do watchfully all these commands I am giving you today. For the Lord your God will bless you as he has promised, and you will lend to many nations but will borrow from none; And you shall rule over many nations, but they shall not rule over you. (*Deuteronomy 15:4–6 KJV and AMP*)

> This book of the law shall not depart out of thy mouth; but thou shalt meditate therein day and night, that thou mayest observe to do according to all that is written therein: for then thou shalt make thy way prosperous, and then thou shalt deal wisely and have good success. (*Joshua 1:8 KJV and AMP*)

Did those clear your mind of all of Ol' Zeke's negativity? Did they set you back on the right track of faith in God's promise of prosperity for you? I hope so. And now that you're fortified to go on, let's look a little more closely at the ugly big three.

Ignorance

"My people are destroyed for lack of knowledge," God says (Hosea 4:6). Too many King's kids are robbed of God's best simply because they are IGNORANT of what God's Word has to say about their rightful inheritance of abundant life. Others realize they are supposed to be living some better way, but are IGNORANT of how to get prosperity *operating* in their lives.

Folks IGNORANT of God's Word are suckers for all kinds of flaky teachings of dead denominational theologians—teachings that attempt to dispense with God's miracle-working power for today, and teachings that try to push off on us a big, gloppy mess called "unworthiness" to make us think that we're not fit to receive what God wants us to have. I almost fell for that one myself, once upon a time.

"Brother Hill," one unworthy fellow croaked at me in my early days as a King's kid, when I was so bubbling full of freedom and joy that others perceived it as a threat to their misery, "Jesus surely did die for our sins and carried our sorrows as the Bible clearly teaches, but at the present time, He expects us to live by the sweat of our brows because we are unworthy of His blessings and favors."

That kind of sick, self-sanctified, counterfeit "humility" came at me from all directions in the beginning. And, since I was still largely IGNORANT of God's Word, it wasn't long before I began to pick up on that "unworthiness" theme and identify with it. I was told that I was simply a hell-deserving sinner, saved by God's grace—but saved for later, not for now.

Another thing they pushed off on me was that my salvation was very fragile, and that I might lose it at any moment. I didn't know any better than to fall for that too.

"Certainly God has forgiven you your *past* sins," they said, standing a barn's length away from me to prove that *they* hadn't forgiven me yet for *anything*. Then they issued the grim warning: "But you had better watch your step in case you goof all over again and suddenly die outside of repentance."

According to them, the shed blood of Jesus on the cross of Calvary paid for all of my *past* sins, right up to the moment I received Jesus as my Savior. But, watch out! Nothing beyond that was covered.

To me, that was about like having an auto-insurance policy that covered only past accidents and was absolutely worthless for the future. Who needs insurance like that? This King's kid wouldn't give you a plugged nickel for it.

As I considered all that, even my sick head branded it as deception. How *could* the blood of Jesus cover my *past* sins when I hadn't even been born yet at the time He said, "It is finished"? I hadn't committed *any* sins until I showed up in my birthday suit many centuries later.

Hearing all their false doctrine didn't leave me very comfortable inside, even though I knew they had to be wrong. But it did get me worried enough to really dig into the Word. That's where I found deliverance forever from their dead theology.

In 1 John 1:9, I discovered that as long as my confession of sins remains up to date, they're *all* covered—through all eternity—by His blood shed on the cross for me. Whew!

Think that's too good to be true and that I'm just making it up? Check it out in the *Manufacturer's Handbook:*

> But if we really are living and walking in the Light, ordering our behavior in the Light as He Himself is in the Light, we have true, unbroken fellowship with one another, and the blood of Jesus Christ His Son keeps continually cleaning us from all sin and guilt in all its forms and manifestations. '. . . If we continue to confess our sins, faithful is He and just to forgive us our sins, and continuously to cleanse us from every unrighteousness—everything that is not in conformity to His will in purpose, thought and action.
>
> *1 John 1:7, 9* AMPLIFIED *and* WUEST

Plain enough for you? It made me feel squeaky clean.

Then when I found Romans 11:29 said that God's gifts and calling were "without repentance" (*irrevocable* NIV), that is, that He had given them and wasn't planning to take them back, I quit worrying that I might accidentally lose my ticket to life everlasting. It was a gift, all paid for, and God isn't in the give-and-take-back business. I had God's Word for all that:

> For God's gifts and His call are irrevocable—He never withdraws them when once they are given, and He does not change His mind about those to whom He gives His grace or to whom He sends His call.
>
> *Romans 11:29* AMPLIFIED

And when I read in Matthew 5:45 that He makes the same rain to fall on the just and the unjust, I saw no reason not to get what I had coming in every area. The only catch was that I had to become a "doer of the Word." And that was so much fun, once I tried it, that I kept on doing it.

It should be plain to everybody that guilt-trip Christianity and edge-of-poverty "salvation" can never be a witness to the pagan world. Fear of losing my salvation because God was "out to get me" was no better than some of the pagan religions in which I was involved before I met the real God.

When I found these great truths in the *Manufacturer's Handbook*, I was completely set free from feeling unworthy and released to literally enter into the promised land in the here and now. No longer would I let the enemy rob me of my inheritance by keeping me IGNORANT so he could deceive me with the dead doctrines of dead men.

One day when I opened my mouth, rejoicing about God's prosperity promises for King's kids, some holes-are-holiness theologians let me have it with both barrels:

"Look at all God's people who are poor and struggling to make ends meet," they said, wagging their heads at me. "Why, some of the sweetest Christians we know have lived on the ragged edge of poverty all their lives—and they really love God. Aren't they as worthy as you of all these financial blessings? Why do you suppose you're worthier than they are to be financially blessed?"

If I had been still IGNORANT of God's Word, I would have had no answer, and Satan would have had a good chance to rob me. But I had caught on to the fact that I could judge circumstances by God's Word if I wanted to, but I could never judge His Word by circumstances. Besides, I was flying high by that time with my growing knowledge of God's Word. So I was able to say to them,

"Of *course* they're worthy of God's best, because it's not our worthiness, it's the worthiness of Jesus that counts."

In my search of the Scriptures, I had discovered that His worthiness is the only worthiness there is, that the best worthiness of the most impeccable saint is no better than stinking, filthy rags in God's sight (Isaiah 64:6). But since He gives us *His* worthiness to go with, we're fully entitled to anything God has to offer in His current catalog.

As a little piece of doggerel puts it:

> *"I'll never be*
> *good enough for heaven."*
> *"No, child,*
> *thou wilt never be;*
> *But GOD is good enough*
> *for thee* and *me."*

The *Manufacturer's Handbook* says it like this:

> It is because of him that you are in Christ Jesus, who has become for us wisdom from God—that is, our righteousness, thus making us upright and putting us in right standing with God; and our Consecration—making us pure and holy; and our Redemption, providing our ransom from eternal penalty for sin. Therefore, as it is written: "Let him who boasts boast in the Lord."
> *1 Corinthians 1:30, 31* NIV and AMPLIFIED

"Boast in the Lord"—that's where I get my license to go into all the world and brag on Jesus. And the more I learn of His Word, the more I find to brag about.

And now let's look at the second "ugly" in the IUD— UNBELIEF.

Unbelief

The *Manufacturer's Handbook* is full of case histories demonstrating that our attitude toward God's promises is what makes them either overtake us to bless us or blast off out of our reach. To benefit from God's promises about prosperity or anything else, our attitude must be right:

> Without faith it is impossible to please him: for he that cometh to God must believe that he is, and that he is a rewarder of them that diligently seek him. (*Hebrews 11:6*)

> For we are God's own handiwork, re-created in Christ Jesus, born anew that we may do those good works which God planned beforehand for us (taking paths which He prepared ahead of time) that we should walk in them—living the good life which He prearranged and made ready for us to live. (*Ephesians 2:10 AMPLIFIED*)

Why did He prepare those good works for us to do? Matthew tells us: "Let your light so shine before men, that they may see your good works, and glorify your Father which is in heaven" (Matthew 5:16).

What God has promised—a good life—and why—so men would see our good works and glorify Him—is glorious all the way, right? So, what is UNBELIEF and why have men been so stupid as to fall for it? UNBELIEF is not an innocuous lack of faith; UNBELIEF is a deliberate saying, in effect, "Please do not confuse me with the facts. My mind is made up."

From an engineering standpoint, UNBELIEF is a powerful negative force generated in the human mind, having the power to block the blessings prepared by God for us so that men would see them and glorify Him. UNBELIEF

105

slams the door in the face of God's blessings, when we listen to the thieving, devious doctrines of men who have exalted their own intellects against God's Word. The *Manufacturer's Handbook* warns us against them:

As you have therefore received the Christ, [even] Jesus the Lord, [so] walk——regulate your lives and conduct yourselves——in union with and conformity to Him. Have the roots [of your being] firmly and deeply planted [in Him]——fixed and founded in Him——being continually built up in Him, becoming increasingly more confirmed and established in the faith, just as you were taught, and abounding and overflowing in it with thanksgiving. See to it that no one carries you off as spoil or makes you yourselves captive by his so-called philosophy and intellectualism, and vain deceit (idle fancies and plain nonsense), following human tradition——men's ideas of the material [rather than the spiritual] world——just crude notions following the rudimentary and elemental teachings of the universe, and disregarding [the teachings of] Christ, the Messiah. For in Him the whole fullness of Deity (the Godhead), continues to dwell in bodily form——giving complete expression of the divine nature. And you are in Him, made full and have come to fullness in life——in Christ you too are filled with the Godhead: Father, Son and Holy Spirit, and reach full spiritual stature. And He is the Head of all rule and authority——of every angelic principality and power.

Colossians 2:6–10 AMPLIFIED

Doesn't all that make you want to go into a pure glory fit? It does me. I mean, if every person was aware of and believed in God promises like that, none of us would ever have fallen for UNBELIEF or settled for anything second best.

The classic example of what happens when folks have an attitude of UNBELIEF is the experience of the Israelites. Their UNBELIEF forced them to wander in the wilderness for forty years instead of living it up in the promised land flowing with moo juice and bee sugar. They doggedly refused to enter the promised land, in spite of all God did to convince them that He had made the way safe and had prepared the victory for them.

What was God's reaction to the Israelites' theology of UNBELIEF? In our modern vernacular, it would be translated, "Drop dead." And they did, thousands of them. The *Manufacturer's Handbook* account says they all died in the wilderness because of their attitude of UNBELIEF— except for Joshua and Caleb. Only those two BELIEVED that God had told the truth and was able to do what He had promised. No wonder God says that we should be on guard and see to it that we don't fall "after the same example of unbelief" (Hebrews 4:11).

Unfortunately, some King's kids have failed to heed the warning, and acted like Israelites, mixing the promises of God with a hefty dose of "I'll believe it when I see it." And *then* they have the nerve to wonder why the things for which they have prayed haven't come to pass! But God had already told them that would happen:

The word preached did not profit them, not being mixed with faith [*the leaning of the entire personality on God in absolute trust and confidence in His power, wisdom and*

107

goodness AMPLIFIED] in them that heard it.
Hebrews 4:2

UNBELIEF sounds like a pretty fatal thing, when you get right down to it. A sure way *not* to get anything from God. A wrong attitude toward the Word of God will cheat you every time. A right attitude is absolutely essential if we're to get any of the blessings God has promised. With faith, all things are possible. Without faith, forget it.

To get yourselves out of the doldrums where all that weight might have dragged you, let's look at three New Testament cases demonstrating that the right attitude makes all the promises *work.*

Do you remember the time when Jesus was on His way to raise a young woman from the dead? (Refresh your memory by reading Matthew 9:18–26.)

As Jesus walked along, a woman came up behind him, touched the edge of His cloak, and was healed of an ailment she'd had for twelve whole years.

What was her attitude? Total faith in Jesus. "If I only touch his cloak, I will be healed," was how she put it (Matthew 9:21 NIV). When Jesus turned and saw her, He said, "Take heart, daughter, your faith has healed you" (verse 22 NIV).

Pretty persuasive, isn't it, that faith (attitude) matters when we need something from God?

Look at what happened next.

Jesus went on His way to the home of the certain ruler whose daughter was dead. What was her father's attitude? Complete faith in Jesus. Listen to what he said: "My daughter is even now dead: but come and lay thy hand upon her, and she shall live" (Matthew 9:18).

What did Jesus do in the face of faith like that? He went in and took her hand, and she arose (Matthew 9:25). Then what?

After raising the ruler's daughter from the dead, Jesus went on His way again, and two blind men came crying after Him. The first thing Jesus did was to check on their attitude toward Him and His healing power.

"Do you believe that I am able to do this?" (Matthew 9:28 NIV) He asked. When they told him they *did* believe, He touched their eyes and said, "According to your faith [attitude] will it be done to you," and suddenly the formerly blind men could see! (Matthew 9:29 NIV).

The *Manufacturer's Handbook* is loaded with other instances where the right attitude—faith in Jesus—always brought blessing to the believer. The wrong attitude always spelled less than good news. In Jesus' hometown, people had an attitude of disapproval and UNBELIEF. What did it get them? A big fat nothing: "And He did not do many works of power [*miracles* NIV] there, because of their unbelief—their lack of faith" (Matthew 13:58 AMPLIFIED).

Their wrong attitude toward God's Word was the means by which Satan was able to rob them of what Jesus wanted to do for them.

"Just go ahead and take Me at My Word!" God seems to be shouting at us from every page of the Bible. "Don't let unbelief block you from My best. Try Me and see that I am good. Bring your tithes into My storehouse and let Me prove to you that I can shower down blessings" (*see* Malachi 3:10).

I'm ready to go for it, whole hog, aren't you? But doubters caught in UNBELIEF would rather wallow in their misery than take a leap of faith.

"We must be very careful, Brother Hill, that we do not frustrate the grace of God," a deacon shot at me one day. Just offhand, I couldn't think of anything more frustrating to God's grace than for His people not to believe it and take advantage of it.

We frustrate the Word of God when we prevent it from uniting with faith in us so it can accomplish His purpose. If Jesus had not found faith in anyone when He came, no one would have been saved. He would have left His riches in glory for nothing.

Once I nearly missed out on a worldly blessing because of the same kind of stupid attitude of UNBELIEF.

A while back my Uncle Bob died, practically penniless as far as we knew. His estate consisted of one elderly coonhound, one beat-up shotgun, a few odds and ends of personal effects, and a tumbledown cabin back in the wilds of western Massachusetts. Uncle Bob's last years were spent puttering around the few acres surrounding his ramshackle dwelling, growing just enough garden vegetables and fruits to live on, shooting an occasional squirrel or rabbit for stew, and living as close to the earth as he could.

When notice came from a law firm that I was named in Uncle Bob's will, I wasn't too impressed. In fact, I didn't even bother to sign the papers entitling me to claim my share of the estate.

One day I received a "third and final" notice which I finally signed and returned to the sender, expecting nothing in return. Who needed a fractional portion of an old coonhound, beat-up shotgun, and dilapidated hunting cabin? Not me.

What I didn't know was that the ramshackle old cabin was in reality a museum piece for which the New England Historical Society was eager to pay a large sum. Through my stupid attitude of UNBELIEF toward the whole situation, I nearly cheated myself out of a sizable sum of cash, which arrived a few weeks later.

So often we cut ourselves off from what God has in mind for us by being full of IGNORANCE and UNBELIEF that allows Satan to rob us blind.

At this point it might be good to summarize some of the causes of an attitude of UNBELIEF in the financial area of our lives as a further guard against the danger of coming down with it. Here are a few sources of contamination:

1. Listening to the losers who have stubbornly held onto the traditions of men and invented new doctrines without first checking it out with Him.

2. Relying totally on the common sense of the five senses for guidance through this life, refusing God's supernatural guidance, just as the Israelites did.

3. Hanging onto that feeling of unworthiness, mumbling coyly, "Oh, but I don't deserve all that." You think that makes you look humble? Wrong! The Bible calls it pride.

4. Being not too sure that salvation means total completeness—including prosperity—in everything that concerns us. It does, you know. If you still can't take my word for it, hear this definition from *The Master Study Bible:*

> Both in the Hebrew and the Greek terms for salvation the underlying thought is deliverance from evil, *oppression of any kind,* and safety from danger, and ultimately, welfare, peace and happiness.

Now, if that doesn't include prosperity, someone has tampered with my dictionary.

Once we have disposed of IGNORANCE by giving top priority to reading the Word to find out what it says, and once we have dispatched UNBELIEF and mixed the Word with faith in our think tanks, we're ready to scuttle the third "ugly" and get God's Master Plan in gear, working for us.

Disobedience

What does DISOBEDIENCE have to do with poverty? Plenty. Do you remember the Malachi Scripture toward the end of chapter 4, where the Lord God Almighty was giving His people down-the-country for their DISOBEDI-ENCE? He said they had turned away from His decrees and not kept them, that they had actually robbed God by their DISOBEDIENCE.

What an indictment! Have *you* ever willfully robbed God by refusing to do the will of God? Think about your answer while we recheck the prosperity verse we found in Brother John's letter: "I wish above all things that thou mayest prosper and be in health, even as thy soul prospereth" (3 John 2).

What makes a soul prosper? Being obedient to hear and do the Word of God (Psalm 1 and Joshua 1:8).

If your obedience—your doing of the Word—isn't up to par, don't look for prosperity to be dropping in for a prolonged visit, because that's *not* how these things work. If you are shortchanging God in any way, DISOBEDIENCE can cheat you of prosperity and health. Let's look at a few things that are bad news for the prosperity of your soul:

being on the outs with your neighbor;
fudging "just a little bit" on your income tax;
harboring resentment against your mother-in-law;
soaking up hours of boob tube every week
    while letting a quick verse
        from the promise box on the breakfast table
            serve as your total daily Bible reading;

*praying only during the commercial break
on your favorite soap opera. . . .*

If you're doing any of these things that are DISOBEDI-ENT to His commandment to seek first the Kingdom, don't be surprised when poverty moves in to stay. By your actions and priorities, you've given it an engraved invitation.

If, on the other hand, you are being OBEDIENT to love and serve the Lord your God with all your heart, soul, strength, and mind; to love your neighbor as yourself (Matthew 22:37–39); to repent and believe the good news (Mark 1:15), your soul will be prospering, and you can expect your health and prosperity to follow suit.

DISOBEDIENCE takes many forms. Laziness is another one of them. Nowhere does God tell anyone to be lazy, but to be "not slothful in business" (Romans 12:11), "working with his hands the thing which is good" (Ephesians 4:28), doing everything "with all your might" (Ecclesiastes 9:10 NIV).

> Whatever you are doing, from your soul do it diligently as to the Lord and not to men, knowing that from the Lord you will receive back the just recompense which consists of the inheritance.
> *Colossians 3:23* WUESTE

Warnings about laziness and its effect on prosperity and poverty are scattered throughout the Word. Here's one from the Old Testament and one from the New:

> The sluggard will not plow by reason of the cold; therefore shall he beg in harvest, and have nothing. *(Proverbs 20:4)*

113

If any would not work, neither should he eat. (*2 Thessalonians 3:10*)

Have you ever known any King's kids who claimed they were "living by faith," when the truth was that they were too shiftless to do anything to produce income, and were just looking for an excuse not to work for a living? I have. That's one form of soul sickness in action.

Other causes of soul sickness? Look at the catalog mentioned in Galatians 5:19 NIV:

> The acts of the sinful nature are obvious: sexual immorality, impurity and debauchery; idolatry and witchcraft; hatred, discord, jealousy, fits of rage, selfish ambition, dissensions, factions and envy; drunkenness, orgies, and the like. I warn you, as I did before, that those who live like this will not inherit the kingdom of God.

For best results in the soul department, leave all that junk out of your diet and tank up on soul nutrition from the "legal" fruit department: "But the fruit of the Spirit is love, joy, peace, patience, kindness, goodness, faithfulness, gentleness and self-control. Against such things there is no law" (Galatians 5:22, 23 NIV).

Have you seen yourself anywhere in our comments on the big three uglies? If you have, don't think that this discovery is bad news, and don't feel condemned about it. Actually, it's good news——because if your eyes have been opened to see how you have brought less-than-best circumstances upon yourself, you can ask God for wisdom to correct the situation, and He will give it.

Doesn't all this make you wonder how people——especially King's kids——ever got in the habit of blaming God for their poverty and giving Him a bad reputation in a lot of places?

It must really grieve the heart of God, who has planned so many good things for us, to be blamed for our failure when we listen to the wrong voices, do the wrong things, and suffer second-best results. It would bother me if I were God.

Because the human mind is so flaky about all these things, God keeps trying His best to get our minds reprogrammed, our attitudes entirely changed, "by the renewing of our minds, that we may prove the good, acceptable, and perfect will of God" (*see* Romans 12:2) through simply KNOWING, BELIEVING, AND DOING the will of God as it is written in His Word. The scoffers and ridiculers will continue to shoot barbs at us as they did at Jesus, but we'll be too delighted with the results we're getting to even notice.

Finally, then, in the sense in which we usually use the word *sin*, it's not a sin to be broke—but it sure is a shame. And since sin really means "missing the mark" of the high calling God has for us, poverty *is* sin, because it means we have failed to receive the promises He died to give us.

Now, is that settled for you? Poverty can't come from God, because the One who is so rich He owns all the cattle on a thousand hills (Psalms 50:10) and paves His streets with gold (Revelation 21:21) simply doesn't carry any poverty in His inventory. He doesn't have any poverty to give.

If it was up to me, I'd let the devil keep all the poverty for himself. I've thought it over and decided I don't need any of it. How about you?

-7-
BUT
WHAT ABOUT JOB?

"But what about Job?" someone always asks whenever I begin to talk about how God wants us to prosper
and be in health. The asker usually puts on a holier-than-
thou expression so sanctified that I almost need sun-
glasses to look him in the eye.

Don't misunderstand. This is another good question,
one that should be looked at and not discouraged. It's just
that usually the folks who ask it think they are so brilliant—

"The Book of Job is simply an allegory, and a mytho-
logical something-or-other . . ." droned the ecclesiastical
voice over my car radio one day as I rode along, tuned to
a local religious station.

So reasonable and persuasive were the statements of
the renowned theologian that I found myself in agreement
with what he was saying. But suddenly the Holy Spirit
made a strong suggestion somewhere down in the middle
of my gizzard: "Hill, why take this man's opinion about My
Word? Why not check it out with Me?"

"Right on, Lord," I replied. And being in no hurry to reach my destination, I pulled into a roadside rest area, opened my Bible, turned to the Book of Job, and read the following statement of fact from God Himself: "There was a man in the land of Uz, whose name was Job . . ." (Job 1:1).

"Thank You, Lord!" I shouted. "I don't care what anyone else says, theologians included. Your Word is dependable, and if You say that black is white, I'll praise You for a brand-new kind of white. The fact that it might appear black to me is beside the point. You don't say that Job is an allegory, You say he was a man. So I'm not going to take the Book of Job as anything less than a true story about a man who really lived, too long ago for me to shake his hand before we meet on the other side, but recently enough for me to learn a lot from what You taught him—so I won't have to tribulate through the same raunchy set of circumstances that hit him. Hallelujah!"

Besides, I said to myself, if Job was only an allegory, why would Moses have included his story as a part of God's Word to His people? And why would God have referred to Job as an example of righteousness in Ezekiel 14:14, 20, and as an example of patience in James 5:11 if he wasn't a real man with real tragedies happening to him? I decided I'd stick to what I said in the beginning—that since God said there was a man whose name was Job, I'd believe it.

That settled, I turned on the ignition and continued down the highway, listening to my Bible tapes this time, and not to some educated idiot's misguided opinion of what the Bible is all about. And from that time until this, I've never paid any attention to those who quibble about the Word of God as it is written.

Later, when I sat down to study the Book of Job for

117

myself, I wasn't surprised that Satan is so eager for God's people to ignore what it says about the role he plays in human sufferings and disasters. The Book of Job puts the blame where it belongs, clearly exposing Satan as the author of all sickness and destruction, and God as the deliverer of all who call upon Him.

In Job's life, there is a special test case, arranged between God and Satan, in response to Satan's lying accusation that God's people serve Him only for what they can get out of it. God gave Satan permission to prove his point, and Satan, true to his slimy nature, proceeded to steal, kill, and destroy (John 10:10) everything of value in Job's life and affairs, including his physical well-being. But Satan didn't succeed in proving what he set out to prove. He didn't win the argument. He never does. The only thing Satan can prove is that he is a defeated liar. He's good at that wherever God's people know God's Word and are faithful to do it.

"But," you sputter, "how could such a good man as Job get himself into such a mess?" Again, the answer is right there for you to read. God had built a hedge around Job, as He had around all His people back in Old Testament times. They needed a hedge before the Holy Spirit was poured out as He has been in these last days. That hedge was fully protecting Job, enabling him to prosper in every way. As long as he walked uprightly, trusting God, Satan could not touch Job in any way—except by God's special permission.

"The just shall live by faith" (Habakkuk 2:4; Romans 1:17) was true then, just the same as in our time. King's kids like Job were living by faith in God's promise that a Savior would come in the future, just as we can live by faith in the promise of God, who has already come in the form of Jesus.

But somehow, maybe because God had blessed him

so abundantly, Job had developed a feeling of self-righteousness in his own eyes (32:1), which hatched out a spirit of fear—as it always does—that somehow the righteousness would leak away and leave him subject to judgment. That fear, which is literally "faith in failure," made an opening in the hedge of God's protective covering around Job. In came Satan, killing people, destroying property, and stealing the truth of God's Word from Job's life.

Instead of continuing to enjoy his God-given prosperity and health, Job came down with an almost terminal case of sickness and poverty. If he'd hung onto the Word, and stuck to confessing it in spite of his pitiful circumstances, he'd have had a quicker victory.

"How can *you* know all that about Job?" one of my critics asks sarcastically.

Because Job tells us himself, right there in Job 1:5, where it is written that he feared his children might be doing something wrong, and in 3:25, where he says, "I incubated the spirit of fear, and it came upon me just as I thought it would" (author's paraphrase). Did you know that things work this way—that we can brood on a situation and hatch it out, just like a mother hen on a nest of eggs turning into chicks? If the concept is new to you, read *How to Live the Bible Like a King's Kid* to learn how these things work.

Not being aware of why all the disasters were coming upon him, Job and his friends tried to diagnose his case through human wisdom and intellectual reasoning—all of which resulted in a horrendous rhubarb. That's the inevitable result of relying on the human think tank instead of consulting God about our problems. Human answers can never be any better than second best. I want first best, myself, don't you?

Not once did Job or any of his friends take all the

119

calamities and disasters to God in prayer and ask Him to give them the wisdom to discern what they were all about. Instead, they revved their sick heads into high gear and wound up blaming one another—and God!—for the awesome tragedies for which Satan alone was responsible. Can you believe it? If they'd consulted God and learned that old Slue Foot was behind all the tragedies, Job could have submitted himself to God, resisted the devil, and old Slue would have been long gone (James 4:7). But ignorance prevailed, as is usual when the Educated Idiot Box is in control.

In literally dozens of statements of perverted truth and downright lies throughout the first thirty chapters of the book, Job bad-mouthed God. Just listen to some of them:

He destroys the perfect with the wicked. (*Job 9:22*)

He is cruel.   (*30:21*)

You [God] oppress and despise me.   (*10:3*)

You [God] destroy the hope of men.   (*14:19*)

There is no justice from Him [God].   (*19:7*)

On and on Job raved, accusing God of all sorts of ugly things that came directly from Satan, until finally God had heard all the complaints He could stomach. Then He said, in effect, "That's enough out of you. Now you listen to Me for a few chapters. Who are you to bad-mouth Me?" (Job 38:2; 40:2, author's paraphrase).

Then God proceeded to remind Job of some of the great and mighty and good things He had done. God is a loving God, and it is impossible for Him to do bad things.

Wising up at last, Job finally repented (40:1–5; 41:1–6) and received God's forgiveness, something he had previously denied himself as he chose to engage in self-righteous accusations of everyone and everything in life that didn't suit him exactly. But once Job's thinking got turned around, back in line with God's thinking, his mind being renewed by the Word of God, his soul began to prosper.

Did you ever notice that Job's full deliverance and double restoration of everything he had lost came when he prayed for his friends? (see 42:10). With friends like that, I've thought, who needs enemies? Anyway, it took all those chapters of misery for Job to admit he was wrong, to accept the fact that God is a good God, and that human reasoning is the pits when dealing with spiritual matters. Amen and amen.

God teaches so many lessons in the Book of Job when our ears are open to receive the truth, and when our heads aren't clogged by the theological doctrines of man. It is unfortunate that so many Christians use Job's miseries—which they think came from God—to justify their belief that poverty is God's will for their lives. Instead, they should read the book for themselves with their eyes wide open and discover for themselves that Satan is the master deceiver behind all the calamities.

Instead of utilizing what Jesus has done for them, and taking authority over the enemy, such persons often get together for pity parties where they sing such "happy pilgrim" refrains as, "Oh, it's not an easy road," "Suffer on, you faithful ones," and "Cheer up, my brother, we'll understand it better by and by." Such songs have crept into Christian thinking courtesy of the prince of this world and of the powers of the air, the great destroyer and deceiver, Satan himself.

"Well, then, why doesn't God step in and boot Satan

out?'' someone wants to know. Because He has delegated that authority to us, that's why.

In the beginning, God gave Adam complete dominion over planet earth. Since Adam chose to sell out to Satan, God has no legal right to operate here except through doors opened by a member of Adam's fallen race, a human being who will literally invite God into a particular situation. When we pray as directed by the Spirit of God (Romans 8:26), Jesus, our Great Intercessor (Hebrews 7:25), comes through the doorway into what was formerly Satan's domain to tear it up and break down his strongholds (2 Corinthians 10:4) and thus glorify God and bless His people.

Don't take my word for it. Look up the Scriptures and check it out for yourselves.

One of the lessons I learned from the Book of Job is that wrong use of the tongue can make matters go from heavenly perfect to completely hellish in short order.

Another lesson I learned from my study of the Book of Job was not to rely on human reasoning for answers to the ''why'' questions of human experience. In his first letter to the Corinthians, Paul is talking about this principle when he reminds us, ''[Spiritual things] are spiritually discerned'' (1 Corinthians 2:14), that is, they cannot be intellectually understood. The natural man—relying on his human think tank—will produce nothing but confusion and deception for answers to questions only the Holy Spirit can answer.

Still another lesson I learned from Job was the lesson of patience, taught in a number of places in the *Manufacturer's Handbook*. Here's how it reads in the Book of James:

We consider those who patiently remain under their trials spiritually prosperous and fortunate. You heard of the patience of Job, how he patiently remained under the trials to which he was subjected, and you saw the consummation [of those trials] brought about by the Lord, that the Lord is compassionate and merciful.

James 5:11 WUEST

The patience lesson was further reinforced by Hebrews 12:1, 2, where we are told to "run with patience the race that is set before us, Looking unto Jesus, the author and finisher of our faith. . . ."

"Speaking of authors, who wrote the Book of Job?" someone wants to know. Can't tell you, since I wasn't there looking over his shoulder at the time. But many folks think it must have been Moses.

The most important lesson in the Book of Job for us King's kids is that if things begin to go wrong in our lives, we're not to blame God, ever. We're to keep our antennae up to see what He has to say to us in it all. And if our conscience condemns us, saying we've not been spending the time we should in Bible study and prayer for best results, we should remedy that—fast.

And now look what happened once Job got back into right relationship with God: Once his soul started to prosper again, prosperity and health were on the way. In the end, Job was more prosperous than he had ever been before. And he lived happily ever after. Glory!

Get a vision for that happening in *your* life now that your thinking about prosperity has been reprogrammed by the Word of God that cannot lie. And get ready to be more prosperous than you've ever dreamed.

-8-

AND WHAT ABOUT THE CRITICS?

"But didn't Jesus say we were to sell all our possessions and give them to the poor?" some diehard always asks me.

Well, He said that, all right—to the rich young ruler—in each of the first three Gospels (Matthew 19:21; Mark 10:21; Luke 18:22). But let's look at the rest of the story. The first thing I notice is that Jesus' invitation to him, "Come, follow Me," was reserved exclusively for disciples and not for everyone Jesus met on His journeys. Sometimes He actually told people *not* to follow Him, remember, but to go back to their hometowns and tell what God had done for them (*see* Luke 8:39, for example).

As I've read about the rich young ruler, it has come to me that Jesus had a very special plan in mind for that particular successful businessman—treasurer of His ministry here on earth. Knowing ahead of time that His money man, Judas, was going to sell out to the authorities, Jesus had handpicked the highly qualified rich young ruler as his successor for the job.

What an opportunity the rich young ruler missed, being so in bondage to his wealth that he had to turn down such a position. There's no telling how great an increase the Lord would have put in his hands had he been able to sow (GIVE) all that he had into the Kingdom.

This "sell all you have" Scripture is often taken out of context, resulting in great confusion. Soon after I became a King's kid and began to travel for Jesus, a man came up to me after a meeting with this piece of news: "The Lord told me to tell you to sell all you have, give it to the poor, and follow Jesus."

Not being aware at the time that Satan can speak Scripture through human beings if it suits his slimy purposes, I started to panic at the thought of uprooting my entire life-style. I envisioned myself ending my days in total poverty, in the heart of darkest Africa. The picture in my mind was of an emaciated me, clad in a dusty black burlap robe with Tarzan-vine chains around my waist, my toes sticking out of palm-leaf sandals, smelling like the "before" picture in a deodorant commercial.

Praise God, the Holy Spirit came to my rescue with a word of wisdom before I could make an utter fool of myself. He suggested that I check the whole thing out with Jesus—before I sold my Sunday suit—and ask Him to give me a confirmation through the mouth of two or three witnesses. I knew that was scriptural, because I had run across it one day in Matthew 18:16. While I was waiting for the confirmation that never came, I asked Him directly, "Lord, is this what You mean for me to do?"

His answer came back in the form of a question that helped me learn how to test many things for myself.

Hill, are you a rich young ruler? He asked.

"Not me, Lord," I replied. "I'm a middle-aged businessman eager to do Your perfect will."

125

Then behave like one and don't listen to folks who take My Word out of context, He said.

So I thanked Him for my narrow escape and continued in the better way, bypassing the disaster trips that await the man who listens to the advice of others who speak from an emotional or think-tank level instead of under the anointing of the Holy Spirit.

"But didn't Jesus say, 'The poor you have with you always'?" some sad sister asks from way back in the corner of almost every meeting.

"He surely did," I reply. "But that doesn't mean that poverty comes from God any more than that it's His will for any to perish, to be sick, or to go to hell. These things happen all the time, because people don't *do* what He said to do to keep their souls in a state of prosperity."

The next question someone is sure to ask when I begin talking on the subject of prosperity goes something like this: "Well, maybe God doesn't *send* poverty, but doesn't God sometimes *use* poverty as part of His Master Plan for our lives?"

Sure He does. God uses everything that happens to us in His Master Plan, no matter where it comes from. Garbage and all, like an organic gardener with a big pile of compost. We know He works all kinds of things together for good for us because He says so in Romans 8:28. And one of the ways in which He uses bad things for good is that He shows us in His Word where the bad things come from—and how to get rid of them so we don't have to be stuck with any junk.

Can anyone crank up a hallelujah about that? I keep my hallelujahs going full tilt all the time when I think about how our God has given us *richly* all things to enjoy (1 Timothy 6:17), and no bad stuff at all!

"But money isn't everything," some sanctimonious soul on poverty row always lets me know.

True, money isn't everything, but it's mighty handy for some things—like sending missionaries wherever they're needed around the world, buying Bibles to give to folks who don't have them, feeding widows and orphans who get hungry, supporting the TV ministries that beam God's Word into dark areas to bring light.

Meanwhile, here comes another question from the peanut gallery. Does it ever sound holy!

"But doesn't God sometimes take away prosperity and health from His people to teach us humility?"

No, He never does that, so far as I have been able to discover in His Word. (Search the Scriptures for yourself, and if you find God saying He does, let me know, will you?)

Then there comes another, more sophisticated question from someone trying to justify his own inability to pay his bills. "But isn't it true that some of us are called to 'walk to the beat of a different drummer' and that there are 'different strokes for different folks'?"

You are so right! But not the way you're thinking. You've put your finger on a real clue as to why some prosper and some don't: the poverty of soul that comes from paying attention to the wrong voices and acting on the wrong advice. Paul describes the causes of that dis-ease among King's kids in 2 Timothy. They had "wandered away from the truth" (2:18 NIV), he said, and needed to shape up and "avoid godless chatter, profane and vain babblings" (2:16 NIV and KJV) so they could be cleansed from ignoble purposes and used as "an instrument for noble purposes, made holy, useful to the Master and prepared to do any good work" (2:21 NIV). God didn't mince any words in telling them to depart from their iniquity (verse 19) and to purge themselves from youthful lusts (verse 22), did He?

If you have been listening to the folks who've been following the wrong drummer and saying, "That's not for today," or "Poor is piety," or "Riches are sin," it's past time to stop doing that and get your soul in an attitude of faith where you can begin to benefit from God's promises instead of looking for excuses as to why they won't work for you.

The critics and I have had a sparring acquaintance for the last thirty years, so none of their jibes are new to me. When I was a new Christian back in 1954, I became excited about all God had to say about success, health, abundant living, and top-level affluence for His people right here on planet earth. Naturally, I was tagged as a fanatic, dreamer, greedy-grabber, someone who needed someone else to straighten out my thinking so I would realize that, for some of God's children, poverty *is* God's will.

Checking that out with my *Manufacturer's Handbook,* I did find God saying, "You always have the poor among you" (Matthew 26:11 AMPLIFIED, with echoes in Mark 14:7; John 12:18; Deuteronomy 15:11), but I didn't find Him saying anywhere that He *wanted* it to be that way. It's just that He recognized there would always be some folks who were IGNORANT of God's will, who were full of UNBELIEF, or who were DISOBEDIENT, simply refusing to follow His instructions about prosperity—the old IUD crowd we met in chapter 6.

Everywhere I go teaching these success principles, some folks are sure to argue with me, comparing the teaching of Brother So-and-So, who doesn't see these things quite the same way I do. It doesn't bother me that everyone doesn't agree with everything I believe. But sometimes it seems to bother them that I don't think exactly the way they do and so they think they have to put me down.

One barb that came to my attention recently will serve

as an example. A member of a huge, affluent church suggested to his pastor that I be invited to share my testimony with his congregation.

"Humph!" the pastor snorted. "We would not want Brother Hill to speak at *any* of *our* services. He preaches only success and wealth."

The last time his congregation voted to give him a raise in pay and increase his fringe benefits, he was glad to accept them. How inconsistent can you get? Maybe everyone should check his own motives in all this.

If you really believe God wants you poor, why do you stretch out your hand for your paycheck when the end of the month rolls around? Why do you read the sale ads and head for the best bargains? Why do you enter the sweepstakes that promise to make you a millionaire overnight?

Have you ever thought about getting your actions and your words lined up with each other? You could probably get poorer faster if you bent all your efforts in a single direction instead of heading pell-mell for prosperity and poverty both at the same time.

Meanwhile, I'll continue to teach these things the way the Holy Spirit reveals them to me. How could I teach them any other way? I notice that Peter and Paul didn't see eye-to-eye on everything, and look how powerfully God used them anyhow!

So far, in the years since I've been a King's kid, I've met a lot of folks—churchpeople especially—who didn't find quite the joy in the promises of God's Word that I found. You'll just have to excuse me, because since I decided to take God's Word for everything, in spite of how circumstances looked or what men might say, I've stayed excited about what He promises His people. But taking the Word of God literally can keep you in hot water with a lot of people. I've had plenty of practice in being the outcast of the traditional bunch. Even before I became a King's kid, I was in rejection training camp. Maybe that's why it doesn't bother me anymore. Just look at a few examples, details of which can be found in my other books and in other chapters of this one:

1. As I grew up, a poor boy wearing hand-me-downs, the more fortunate kids never allowed me to forget that I was the "kid least likely to succeed" in my high-school class.

2. A college classmate, a real brain, gave it to me point-blank one day: "Why don't you wise up and give up? You'll never amount to anything. You just haven't got it upstairs." He knew I was working my way through, while he had his dad's millions at his disposal.

3. This kind of pecking order—with everyone else always pecking on me—showed up again when I began to put into practice the unlimited-success formula described in chapter 2 of this book.

4. Then, after I quit drinking alcohol through the help of Alcoholics Anonymous, my boozy former friends began to cut me off with scornful epithets like "Holy Joe"—and worse.

5. Three years later, when I met Jesus Christ as my personal Lord and Savior, my personal "higher power" in AA, my rummy pals called me a Christer, water-walker, and much worse.

6. As a baby Christian in the Baptist church, when I asked for divine healing for my disinte-grated spinal disk, I was told, very condescend-

ingly, "Don't be a fanatic, Hill. That's not for today. All that petered out when Peter petered out. God relies exclusively on doctors in these last days."

7. When I went and got healed in Oral Roberts' tent in 1954 anyway, the only reason they didn't throw me out was that I was by then a tither, and they couldn't afford to lose me!

8. A few months later, when I met Jesus as Baptizer in the Holy Spirit and began using that power to lead other sinners to Him for salvation, I was tagged with "Holy Roller" and other choice handles.

9. As I began to apply God's methods for sickness and poverty removal and to encourage others to do the same thing, the dissenters were always standing by, ready with a put-down or a well-chosen word of criticism whether they were Christians or pagans. Actually, I find it hard to tell the difference between King's kids and the devil's urchins when all that negative garbage starts dribbling down their chins about the faults and weaknesses of one another's religious beliefs and doctrines.

10. And I really blew it in their eyes when, after turning my life and affairs totally over to Jesus, I began teaching the "faith walk" over twenty-five years ago. The criticism and ridicule that began then continues through the present moment with such terms as "Cadillac conscious," "money mad," and "health freak"—and worse—being pasted on me.

Can you imagine where I'd be today if I had let the opinions of the critics sway me? If I had tried to be a men-pleaser instead of a God-pleaser? Why, I'd be the yo-yo-est, see-saw-iest King's kid in creation. It would make you dizzy just to look at me. People who try to please other people instead of God are always headed straight for the goofy barn, their heads split into a thousand pea brains, each with a different conflicting opinion.

Remember the old Aesop's fable about the man and his son who bought a donkey and tried to bring it home? Some people thought the old man should ride the donkey while the boy walked, some people thought the boy should ride while the old man walked, some people thought they should both ride, some thought they should both walk. They tried some of everything, and in the end, what was it? Didn't the old man and the boy wind up so confused that they tied the donkey's legs to a stick and carried him upside down between them, to the tune of a horselaugh from all directions all the way home?

Is that kind of foolishness for you? It's not for me!

Doesn't all this nit-picking contain a message for us all about our individual doctrines, biased beliefs, pet schemes, and favorite formulas? When we jealously nurture them, wanting everyone else to think exactly as we think, it's at the expense of our spiritual growth, because we cut ourselves off from any possibility of learning from one another, lest our pet doctrines be stepped on.

But isn't that exactly what we can expect of babies—be they Christian infants or flesh-and-blood offspring—a complete mess? But we don't throw the baby away just because he's a mess. We wash him and feed him and trust he'll grow up someday. But unfortunately, he doesn't always. His Royal Highness, King Brat, may still be sitting on his royal potty-throne when the undertaker arrives to take him under, a hundred years old but still straining at gnats and swallowing camels when anyone in sight or earshot disagrees with his outlooks and beliefs.

I learned a long time ago to respect the other fellow's right to be wrong. You stay healthier that way. If God wants to change the other fellow's mind—or yours—about something, He's big enough to do it without your "help" if you'll just keep out of the way.

Just for the exercise, a while ago I searched the Scriptures to locate the one "perfect church" which the Holy Spirit might have addressed in at least one of the Epistles. Do you know how many I found? Not a single one. All had sinned and fallen short of the glory of God.

The Galatians were addressed as "foolish ones."

The Corinthians were top-level tongue-talkers—-but they had things going on in the church that pagans wouldn't have considered!

The Colossians were told to quit lying to one another and to get rid of a lot of other non-Christian activities.

The only perfect church I found in the Scriptures is the one Jesus wants to find when He comes back—a church without spot or wrinkle or blemish, a church full of love and unity instead of division. From my observation, I'd say it hasn't yet come into being. But God's still working on us all, still-carping critics included.

The words of Jesus about His own lack of ownership of anything, even a place to lay His head, is used by some as a big stick to try to intimidate those of us who own mortgage-free homes, through putting into practice the Master Plan that God has given us to use.

What some of the critics never suspect as they sit on their lofty thrones of judgment is that many of us have sold out, long ago, and become complete stewards of God's resources so that we actually own nothing for ourselves. In my own case, some years ago I gave it all to Jesus, with a prayer that went something like this:

> Lord Jesus, from now on I refuse to be an owner of anything. From now on I choose to be a steward of Your bountiful supplies and blessings. It's Your job, Lord, to see that I'm a faithful steward, knowing as You do all my weaknesses and selfish tendencies inherited from my granddad Adam. But Lord, I now have Your own nature within me. Please make me aware of my own foolish desires when they threaten to take over, and show me how to override them. Please reprogram my appetites and desires to conform them to Your own. And please plant in my heart Your own desires so that Your promise to give me the desires of my heart will simply refer to Your own desires planted there by You personally. I receive all this by faith, with the request that in case I'm not entirely sincere in this prayer, You go ahead and do it anyhow. Thank You, Lord. Amen.

Since I have prayed that prayer and turned my life and will completely over to the management of Jesus Christ, how can anyone legally criticize me? They can't—because my motives, tendencies, biases, attitudes, and selfish interests are now God's property. If you don't like my life-style in any respect, you'll just have to take it up with Jesus.

Actually, the expert nitpicker can take just about any Bible verse and use it as a Bible bullet to shoot down another brother whose doctrine varies the least bit from his own.

"Lay not up for yourselves treasures upon earth" (Matthew 6:19) is one often laid on those of us who teach the health and prosperity message. Just what is treasure? The definition would vary with each one of us. Whatever I idolize, whatever occupies the major part of my attention, is my treasure.

In my own case, my treasure has changed over the years. Where once it was a big bank account, a large yacht, fine clothes, and a palatial home, my present ambition, my treasure today, is to be in the center of God's will at all times. For me to judge someone else's motive toward money or worldly goods is to shove God off the judgment seat and attempt through my limited, finite outlook—like a little kid trying to see a game through a knothole in the fence—to tell where they're coming from when God's the only One who knows their hearts.

Each of us has arrived at his own perspective through painful experiences and glorious insights which have biased us one way or another. Therefore our attempts to judge one another are warped by our own inner hurts and pet peeves. "Judge not, that ye be not judged" (Matthew 7:1) is the safest way to bypass criticism from others. What we don't sow in that department, we won't have to reap. I'm probably still collecting the harvest from all my pagan years of planting the wrong seed. It serves me right.

What about the critics then? As they keep persecuting me, I'll keep praying for them, and according to Matthew 5:11, 12, I can rejoice and be glad, knowing that I've got a great reward waiting for me in heaven. What will that reward be? The *Manufacturer's Handbook* doesn't spell it out, but I know it will be a good one. Somewhere down in my gizzard is the feeling that the reward will be directly in line with the sowing and reaping principle He seems to like so much. The best reward I can think of is that the nastiest of the critics will be in heaven when I get there, covered with glory grins themselves. Standing in line to hug my neck, they'll say something like, "Hey, Hill! I've found out that you were right after all!"

Then we can praise the Lord together.

Who could want a greater reward than that?

-9-
HOW NOT TO DO IT

I discovered a long time ago that people are so consti-
tuted that when you want to help them, it's often a good
idea to tell them in the beginning what they ought *not* to
do. Giving them a detailed list of everything guaranteed
not to work helps ensure that they get on the right path
and stay there without any costly side trips that set them
back further than they were in the beginning.

One reason this is so is that the "good" is often the
worst enemy of the "best" in the area of God's blessings.
Had you ever noticed? Worldly wisdom has us well trained
to always consult our common sense as the final authority.
Whenever God says something contrary to men's ideas of
what's appropriate, we're likely to go running backward
into the second best our human think tanks have conjured
up. Later, we blame God for our failure to succeed, but
we brought it all on ourselves by using our Educated
Idiot Boxes for purposes for which they were never designed.

These things being almost invariably true, let's take a

look at how folks are enabled to miss God's best every time. Here's how the plan generally evolves:

1. *Whatever your problem, face it with fear, trembling, and panic, consulting everyone you know as to what you should do about it.* Listen to all opinions indiscriminately, mixing those of successful people with those of the derelicts—to make sure you get a broad sampling. It's usually a lot easier to get advice from failures, because they're so flattered to be asked. Besides, they have nothing better to do with their time. The successful fellows often have crowded calendars.

Since most of these opinions will be based on total ignorance of the problem, ignore whatever slivers of good advice they might come up with and stick to your own opinion no matter what. When you finally find someone who agrees with you, even if he's the worst failure in town, congratulate him for his high wisdom and turn your back on all those other dummies who seemed to think that your predicament was in some way connected with your own less-than-wise actions in the past.

2. *Next, apply human wisdom and reasoning, based on our "best thinkers" and assorted philosophers of the ages.* Delve deeply into the mysterious "psychic causes" behind the whole mess. If your problem happens to include "drinking too much" now and then, maybe psychoanalysis would reveal that your mother dropped you on your head in front of a brewery horse when you were an infant. Apply TA, ETS, ESP, TM, TC, ABC, XYZ, IUD, and every other acronym and anachronism you can come up with. After all, something's *bound* to work. That's known as the alphabet cure, otherwise titled the Tag-It-and-Gag-It syndrome, or the EIB (Educated Idiot Box) system, all of which are guaranteed to snatch failure from certain victory.

3. *When all else fails, read the instructions in the* Manufacturer's Handbook *to see what God thinks about it.* List all the Scripture promises which hint at solutions. Study the results they have produced in the lives of others—but don't put the principles into operation for yourself. Just talk about them. Consult "highly spiritual Christians" on the subject and ask them to pray for you. But be sure not to take their advice. Tell them how unworthy you are and how you don't really expect God to do much for you, considering how undeserving you are and all. Continue this line of phony piety as long as your stomach can stand it, or until you have convinced yourself that a) it might work for others, but you're just too much for God to handle; b) it's probably your "cross to bear," and God is undoubtedly trying to teach you something through whatever adversity has you in its grip; c) the particular Scriptures that seem to promise something for your situation were true in Bible times but they no longer work, a conclusion based on your careful perusal of the highly erudite treatises by the renowned theologians Dr. Sounding Brass and Dr. Tinkling Cymbal of Unbelief Cemetery—er, ah, I mean, Seminary.

4. *Now begin to blame everyone and everything— people, places, things, and circumstances beyond your control—for your continued failure.*

5. *Be sure to cut back on your tithes and giving to God's work so that disaster will* really *hit.* Or maybe you had already gotten into that devil's trap of robbing God and that's where all the trouble started? It'll do it every time.

6. *Last of all, for the very best guaranteed way to fail financially, begin—or continue—to rob God at every opportunity.* Malachi 3:10 seems to promise that if you *don't* bring your tithes into the storehouse, He *won't* shower down blessings upon you, an idea that is further con-

firmed in 2 Corinthians 9:6, 10, which says it this way: "Whoever sows sparingly will also reap sparingly, and whoever sows generously will also reap generously" (2 Corinthians 9:6 NIV).

That's plain enough, isn't it? Guaranteed failure if you don't do it God's way.

Oh! I almost forgot. There's another way guaranteed to fail, too. Want to hear about it? This is just one of several "get rich quick" schemes guaranteed to have you flopping on your face in failure in nothing flat.

One of the most currently rampant ways to lose ground financially is to fall into the trap carefully laid by the get-rich-quick operators of so-called pyramid schemes. To enable you to spot one if it comes your way, let's look at an example of how they work:

You're out mowing the lawn, minding your own business, when the swift-talking promoter approaches, flatters your fescue, and bends your ear long enough to tell you he has a foolproof way to have you rolling in dough before the next year rolls around. Your eyes light up, your ears twitch, and he launches into the incredibly easy-as-pie details. For an investment of only one hundred dollars, you can become a sergeant in the army of the affluent by buying a bunch of nylon spark plugs "guaranteed to double the gas mileage of anyone's car."

Hmm. You think about it a few minutes. Sounds great! You've been wanting to get out of the nine-to-five rat race anyhow. Here's your big chance. Be sure not to crack the Bible at this point, especially in the vicinity of Proverbs 28:20, because you might read it and wise up to what happens to people who fall for get-rich-quick schemes.

Instead of giving the fast-talking promoter only one hundred dollars of your hard-earned bucks, you twist his arm and talk him into letting you invest one thousand dollars. I mean, he's convinced you this is a sure thing, so why wait until tomorrow?

Visions of indoor/outdoor swimming pools, air-conditioned stables, a mink for the missus, finishing school in Europe for your teenagers, to get them out of *your* hair, and a private golf course all for yourself begin to dance in your head. He made it sound so *good!* So easy! So foolproof! In the bag!

The shipment of plugs arrives and you sign for them. They don't look all that great, but after all, machinery is only machinery. Looks don't matter. Beauty won't sell them—efficient performance will. You move your car and lawn mower out to the street, park the plugs in your half of the garage, and read the instruction manual about how to sell them to all your friends.

"Shucks, these here plugs'll practically sell theirselves, once you tell folks what they kin do," the not-too-literate salesman had assured you.

But something goes wrong. You've read the manual, followed the instructions, but your friends aren't buying. They seem perfectly content with the antiquated, inefficient plugs they've been using for years.

"I guess I'm just not a salesman," you wail to the promoter when he checks back to see how you're getting along.

"That's a cinch to fix," he booms, giving you a too-hearty pat on your sunburned shoulder. "Lots of folks can't sell nuthin'—but hundreds of others has sold the Brooklyn Bridge. What you need is some sergeants working under you to unload the merchandise. They'll make a tidy profit, and you'll get a hefty cut of their sales just for lettin' 'em in on it. Actually, you can make more that way than by selling yourself," he confides, after first casting a sharp-eyed glance around to make sure none of your potential sales crew is within earshot. Sounds appealing, and since the bottom line for this upper level of operation is that you'll need an inventory worth five thousand dollars to make it work, you up the ante—never admitting even to yourself that you're borrowing it on 18 percent credit cards. When the merchandise arrives, you strain your back storing it in garage, attic, basement, and broom closet. But you figure it's the course of prudence to keep your mouth shut about your back.

"It's only for the time being," you attempt to console the missus, who's been panting for her fur coat two months already and seems a mite miffed that now *her* car has to sit in the street with yours. "Once these things start to move—"

You'd like to dance a little jig to demonstrate your enthusiasm, but you're back is killing you, and besides, you're almost late for your next appointment with the chiropractor.

The missus is beginning to raise her eyebrows at the whole business, but your confidence is still running high—until it turns out that the hot sales crew of sergeants you expected to recruit is just as uninterested in your job offer as they were in your spark plugs. No one wants to break his neck working so you can effortlessly mop up your percentage. But who can blame them? Then in Saturday's paper, you see that the most popular discount store in town is advertising what looks like spark plugs identical to yours for half of what you paid for them wholesale with your special general's discount.

It's the end of the world.

You're flat broke, in debt, stuck—maybe forever— with tripping over spark plugs at every turn the rest of your life or renting a miniwarehouse until you can figure out what to do with them. And worse, how to pay off those credit-card charges your wife hasn't seen yet. You start looking at the classified ads to see if the Foreign Legion or someone's Antarctic expedition has any vacancies.

Sound farfetched? You wouldn't believe how many King's kids fall for this sort of swindle, how many basements and attics are crowded with car-bars, do-it-yourself oil filters, household products of questionable quality and negligible usefulness, and other assorted oddments never designed to be sold but only to be used as bait for the old pyramid swindle.

How to avoid them? Make sure your motives are pure. Never get into anything as a greedy get-rich-quick money-making scheme. Be confident that the product or service you're going to provide is worth what you're asking. Try it out. If everything passes your scrutiny, double-check the outfit's success record with the Better Business Bureau. If they've never heard of 'em, find someone who has, someone whose word you can trust.

If suddenly the whole outfit turns up vanished into the woodwork, you'd be better off to get ahead by picking aluminum cans out of the gutter for recycling or collecting candy wrappers for mail-in refund offers. I read about a woman in her seventies who picked up cans and netted about twelve bucks a week, with no overhead. Doesn't sound like riches to you? It beats a five-thousand-dollar 18 percent debt, a sprained back, an overflowing garage, and a mad wife by a country mile.

Any questions? Folks are too busy blushing to ask anything about *that,* but here comes a question on another subject: "What about all the sweepstakes and contests making the rounds these days?"

Enter 'em all—as long as you have time to spare—and the entry requires no postage out of your pocket. Sure, people win 'em all the time, but the odds are astronomically slimmer than slim. And some folks fall into the trap of being so cocksure they're going to win whatever it is that they waste half their lives watching for the mailman and the other half dreaming of how they're going to spend their great reward. The great reward might become so real in their minds that they forget it isn't *in* their pockets, and they go in hock for unaffordable luxuries before they learn the loot will never be theirs.

And did you ever stop to figure how much you'd have in the bank if you'd saved all those postage pennies and invested them at compound interest?

Talk about superabundance! That's how many irresistible tricks the enemy has to lure King's kids from Wednesday-night prayer meetings where *real* miracles happen. Watch out for his seductions that come in many guises.

All this reminds me of a ''pome'' a friend of mine wrote years ago after being sorely disappointed on the win-this-contest scene. The friend didn't know the Lord in those days, so the ''pome'' doesn't have a spiritual bone in it, but it does make a point:

The Prize*

Our prospects were dismal, no hope was in store.
Our debts seemed abysmal, we kept piling up more.
I picked up the paper to read the day's news
And what I saw there, I couldn't refuse:
ENTER THIS CONTEST! WIN FIVE THOUSAND
SMACKERS!
JUST TELL WHY YOU LIKE
MCGUSTEY'S GRAHAM CRACKERS!
ENCLOSE WITH EACH ENTRY—WE ASK THIS OF
YOU—
THE TOP OF A CRACKER BOX—
FACSIMILES WON'T DO.
I read the ad and thought, ''Why not?
We surely can't lose more than we've got.''

I hied to the store for crackers a la McGustey.
The boxes were large ones, and smelled rather musty.
They tasted just terrible, but we ate 'em and faced it.
The money was spent, we couldn't just waste it.
We had graham cracker salad, smorgasbord, and steak
graham cracker omelette, McGustey quiche, and cake.
We had no more dinner guests,
our friends had diminished.
My good-cook reputation
was decidedly finished.
But I kept a stiff upper lip—
winners would soon be announced.
The mailman brought me a letter, and on it I pounced.
"It's finally come kids! Now we'll be rich!
Take McGustey's old crackers
and dump 'em in the ditch!"
I tore open the envelope—
A CHECK!
Not *for five thousand smackers—*
but second prize!
Ten years' supply
of
McGustey's
graham
crackers.

Name withheld by request, and I don't blame her, do you?

But now, on with what you've been waiting for—a positive program for real success. Meanwhile, as a quick-to-the-rescue bicarb antidote for all the miseries in this chapter and whatever miseries you may be enjoying, try this ten-point intake (from my *How to Live in High Victory*) to keep you alive until you can read through the next few chapters and get started on the real program:

1. Wrap everything in praise and turn it over to Jesus as a joint heir with Him of the results.

2. Refuse to be impressed by appearances.

3. Do the next thing, and trust Jesus for guiding your paths (Proverbs 3:5, 6).

4. Form the habit of praise in the midst of, in spite of, or on account of whatever is going on (1 Thessalonians 5:16–18; Ephesians 5:20; Hebrews 13:15).

5. Learn to listen to God. Frequently say, "Speak, Lord. I'm listening for further instructions." But first be sure you've carried out the last instructions He gave you.

6. Don't ask anyone else's opinion about the guidance God gives you. Wait for confirmation from another source if you are in doubt.

7. Stop doubting God really did speak to you.

8. When guidance comes, act immediately, praising Him for results.

9. When doubt enters, tell Him, "I'm going into action, Lord. If I'm on a second-best course of action, it's up to You to block me. But if I'm on the right road, open all the doors and benefit everyone concerned."

10. I find this to be a good prayer: "Lord, make me as holy as You can make a sinner saved by grace" (origin unknown).

Doing all this will result in high victory, because it is written, ". . . and this is the victory that overcometh the world, even our faith" (1 John 5:4). And what is our faith? The faith of Jesus Himself (Galatians 2:20), on loan to us!

-10-
WHAT IS MONEY ANYHOW? WHOSE IS IT?

And Why Does Your Gizzard Quiver When Anyone Talks About It?

To get you on the right track with God's Master Plan for your prosperity, let's explore some basic facts about the relationship between money and you and God. For instance:

What is money?
  Who invented it—and why?
    Where does it come from?
      Why is it so hard to control?
        Is money really the root of all evil?
  What does God think about money?
    Are credit cards no-nos for Christians?

All the questions are good ones; it makes sense for us to look into a few answers. I'm indebted to Liz Rogers, who runs the King's Kids' Korner, for researching these things for me.

What Is Money?

Most King's kids are accustomed to thinking of money in terms of our modern coins and currency, but many different kinds of mediums of exchange have been used in various places throughout the course of history. In the beginning, there was no such thing as money. Who needed it? There was plenty of everything for both members of the earth's human population, and it was all free. Adam and Eve could pick their breakfast off a tree—not even a cover charge.

Adam didn't have any pockets in which to jingle any loose change if he'd had any. Later, when there were more folks, and when one person wanted something of which another person had more than enough, they just traded their surplus with each other. Everything that changed hands was used for money—animals, salt, corn, other grains, shells, tools. . . . You name it, somewhere, sometime, someone has used it for money.

In China, tea was once the major medium of exchange. You could buy a horse or camel if you had enough tea. Can you imagine the size of the pocketbooks the ladies had to carry when they went to the supermarket? Or the size of the warehouses landlords had to maintain just to keep the day's receipts?

In Mexico, the Aztec Indians used sacks of cocoa beans to buy the things they wanted. Coconuts served for cash on some islands near India. Fishhooks were the medium of exchange for the Aleut Indians of Alaska; blankets were money to certain Indian tribes in Canada; strings of shells to American Indians and Pacific islanders, whale's teeth for Fiji islanders, hair from an elephant's tail to some African tribes. The biggest and heaviest money the world has known are the yap stones used for money in the

Caroline Islands in the Pacific. Some of them are twelve feet high—as big as two tall men standing on top of each other. Think of the trouser-pocket mortality rate from carrying clunking change like that!

As civilizations grew more sophisticated, people began to use chunks of metal of all sizes and shapes as a medium of exchange. How much could you buy with a chunk of copper? It depended on the weight of it; a heavier chunk could buy more than a lighter chunk.

Every time a piece of metal was used in a transaction, it had to be weighed by the buyer of merchandise and the seller. Sometimes the buyer's weight and the seller's weight didn't agree with each other. The dis-agreement could lead to heated argument—and even to war between two tribes.

Dishonest merchants kept two scales—one that would make their chunks appear heavier, another that would make their customers' chunks appear lighter. The person who cheated in that way was in bad trouble with the Lord. In Proverbs 11:1, God went to the trouble of saying that He abhors dishonest scales but delights in accurate weights (NIV).

As you would imagine, it was a lot of hassle for folks to have to weigh their chunks of metal every time they wanted to buy or sell something—to say nothing of the endless risks of getting cheated out of your shirt. Then one day someone came up with a brilliant idea: a piece of metal should be weighed one time, and a mark put on it to show the "official" weight. After that, the piece of metal would never have to be weighed again. The metal with the official weight marked on it was called a "coin."

But there was still no guarantee that the metal was correctly labeled. It wasn't just a case of "Let the buyer beware." Sellers had to beware, too!

Then, almost three thousand years ago, the king of Lydia, in Asia Minor, made a new law, forbidding people to weigh their own metal and mark it. From then on, the king and his men were the only ones allowed to make metal into coins. These gold and silver coins were the first *official money,* made by the government as our money is made today.

Standard, government-made coins proved very convenient, but as soon as they became widely circulated, men began to try to figure out how they could cheat with the new money. Financially hard-pressed rulers reduced the amount of metal in their coins, or substituted brass for some of the gold, and hoped no one would notice. This debasement of coinage was said to be one of the causes of the fall of Rome.

It wasn't long before others discovered they could clip or shave a few micromilligrams of precious metal from each coin that went through their hands. Our expression, "He got clipped," didn't come from the barbershop; it came from this practice of actually "clipping" coins of some of their metal content with a sharp instrument.

Counterfeiting also sprang up, and as early as 540 B.C., Polycrates of Samos is said to have cheated the Spartans with coins of simulated gold. In great trading cities, where coins of several jurisdictions might appear in the marketplace, people were inclined to use the "bad" coins for trade and to hoard the "good" ones. "Gresham's law," this tendency is called today.

And Why Does Your Gizzard Quiver When Anyone Talks About It?

Why are you cringing? What is it inside you that covers its face, looks away, changes the subject, or pretends to

151

be out to lunch whenever the subject of money is mentioned?

Have you ever wondered about that? I have. And one day when I asked the Lord about it, He gave me some answers.

If you don't enjoy feeling uncomfortable, you may want to skip the rest of this chapter. But if you want to be healed of your hang-ups, hang in there while we get to the root of them.

The reason money is such a no-no subject for most folks is that we are emotionally involved with it in the very depths of our personalities. That's why the mere mention of money among "religious folks" brings on the sniffles—"Oh, my deah, it's such poo-ah taste to mention that dreadful subject." Can't you just see the plump old biddy, dripping with diamonds, her precious little pinkie crooked just so at the side of the fragile china teacup?

"Baloney, honey!" I say to her. "You *know* the subject of money stays uppermost in your mind." While she sits there registering her shock with her mouth wide open so you can admire her gold inlays, let's get to the heart of *your* uncomfortable aversion to the very mention of money. The truth will set you free, and here it is:

You feel threatened by the subject because money represents *you*—the portion of your own life you sell to your employer for slaving away at his sweatshop when you'd rather be staying at the golf course on a perpetual vacation, or the part you've invested in someone else's enterprise with expectation of a substantial return. Whenever that hard-earned cash is threatened by anyone—even another King's kid in distress—the tendency is to shelter your money behind whatever cover-up you can find.

"I gave at the office," is one we've all heard—and used. "I'm sorry, I just don't have my checkbook with me," is another. (Did you leave it at home on purpose?) "I'll have to pray about it," is sometimes just a pious, impolite excuse from the same barrel of rotten apples so you can forget about the request as quickly as possible.

If my ego or self dominates me, I will always be overly nervous when my money is threatened. Even though I may make myself toss big bills into the plate at church—openly and in full view of the congregation—inside I may be in pain and distress at the thought of someone "clipping" me out of a few dollars.

Our clinging attitude toward money is often indicative that we're in bondage to ourselves, to fear of poverty, or to loss of our misplaced security. The Bible calls all this clinging, for whatever reason, the love of money.

The Love of Money

"Yes, money is the root of all evil," I hear some sanctimonious soul clucking to her neighbor while she pretends not to need to know how she can get out from under the mountain of debt she should never have incurred in the first place. But the aforementioned, oft-quoted phrase isn't found in my Bible.

What the *Manufacturer's Handbook does* say is that the *love* of money is the root of all evil (1 Timothy 6:10). And that's a different story.

If the love of money, just for the sake of having money, grips your heart and dominates your thinking—if you think more about making money than you think about loving God—money has become a false god, an idol in your life. Behind this kind of love of money lies a really destructive principle—self-love, selfish motives. The evidence of self-love is what God labels the root of all evil, not the greenery in your pocket.

Rich and poor alike can come down with the no-no love of money. No one is immune. The person without a penny in his pocket can be just as worshipful of money as the richest three-piece-suited banker in town. You can be literally wallowing in the evil coming from the love of money even if you are penniless, flat broke, and deeply in debt. The love of money can itself lead to poverty, because for a King's kid, prosperity is indissolubly linked to loving God and your neighbor above all else.

When I first learned these things as a new Christian, I said, "Lord, how can I know if I am the victim of this cancerous thing called self-love? How can I get free of the love of money?"

Why did I feel guilty of that sin? Because I'm no different from anyone else. We all have a built-in selfishness problem and only Jesus can do anything good about it.

I've learned that one effective way to test your motives in the money department is to ask yourself *why* you would like to have a million dollars. Here are some answers I have heard from listening to other folks——or when I was eavesdropping on what was going on in my own gizzard:

1. To be independent of all financial woes forever.

2. To have a bigger house than my stupid relatives.

3. To prove to Grandma Pruneface that I don't need her money when she dies.

4. So I can travel in style and dog it over my neighbors.

5. To go into all the world and preach the Gospel to every creature (Mark 16:15), winning the lost for Jesus as I go.

154

Did any of those motivations strike a responsive chord? That little evaluation test was an eye-opener, wasn't it? If you identified with number five, you're on God's team, and He will bless you with so much prosperity you'll hardly know what to do with it. But if you're wanting the big bucks to "consume on your own lusts—to use on your own pleasures" (*see* James 4:3) as indicated in items one through four above, prepare for perpetual poverty, because it's all you're going to get.

God has shown me that the way to get rid of all uncomfortable hang-ups about money is to recognize the true answer to the big question: Whose money is it?

Whose Money Is It?

I used to think that *some* money was mine, and I was always worried about losing it. Yet there was a gut-level uneasiness about the lasting security that money promised but never quite seemed to deliver. If money really delivered security, why did I read about wealthy men and women leaping from skyscraper windowsills and high bridges?

To *that* uneasiness was added the fear that my money would vanish, that my investments would "erode," or that someone would make off with my hard-earned cash. When anyone mentioned anything about the dying dollar in my presence, I would sense myself moaning deep down inside, and my collar would be suddenly too loose, like my neck was shriveling up. Fear will do that to you.

Did you ever stop to think about who owns all the money in the world? I did one day, while I was reading the *Manufacturer's Handbook*. The truth I saw there got me so fully liberated from the strangling strings that had been tying my gizzard to my pocketbook, that I could use those strings for shoelaces. And I no longer needed to swallow hard and screw up my courage to unglue my billfold from my hip pocket when folks came around taking up a collection for a good cause.

Want to know the liberating Scripture? Here it is: "For we brought nothing into the world, and we can take nothing out of it" (1 Timothy 6:7 NIV).

The way I understand that verse, since we bring nothing into the world and can take nothing out of it, wealth can't possibly be ours except on a very temporary basis, loaned to us by God during our sojourn here on planet earth so we can be equipped for doing His work. That must mean that all wealth belongs to God—not merely all the cattle on a thousand hills.

When the truth of all that hit my think tank, I knew I could look to God, who thought it all up in the first place, not only to furnish the financial supply out of His riches in glory (Philippians 4:19) for every need I had, but to take good care of all His own riches—even the part temporarily in my hands.

Since I didn't own any wealth to start with, there was no way I could lose it. Since it was God's money, and all I was doing was managing it for Him, I could relax and enjoy my assignment. No need to pile up treasures for myself. I couldn't take them with me to heaven, and they'd only be an unnecessary nuisance if I could. Certainly the God who made the whole universe was well able to watch over His own money. That settled, my worry over losing "my" money came to a screeching halt and slithered away.

Whew! What a relief!

Let Jesus Clean Up Your Money Motives!

Until you understand that all money, like all wealth of any kind, belongs to God, you're bound to have trouble in the money department. This basic truth about money shows up in the *Manufacturer's Handbook:* "Whoever loves money never has money enough; whoever loves wealth is never satisfied with his income" (Ecclesiastes 5:10 NIV).

Once I asked a multimillionaire how much money it would take to make him happy.

"Just one more million," he said. And I suspected that once he had that million, I could ask him the same question again—and get the same answer.

I've heard large landowners say they would be happy if they could add to their holdings just a little bit more—only the land that adjoined theirs. That "modest desire" could take up the whole continent, gobbling up land until it hit the big water.

We'll never be able to be completely pure in the financial realm or any other as long as we're this side of heaven. We're too good at fooling ourselves for that. But, as usual, God has a perfect antidote for our ailment, beginning with a most uncomfortable procedure called "self-honesty." Instead of denying our shortcomings, pointing at the other fellow and saying, "I'm not *that* bad," we have to admit we've fallen short, and ask God to search our hearts and root out everything not pleasing to Him (Psalms 139:23, 24).

In order to make any real progress in the upward direction in this area of financial success, we have to start with being honest with God. Care to try it with me?

Lord, I'm no doubt as phony as a three-dollar bill deep down in my motive department. You say that the heart is more deceitful than anything else, desperately wicked and who can know it (Jeremiah 17:9). You say that every imagination and all the thoughts of a man's heart are only evil continually (Genesis 6:5). You say that greed, gluttony, and the grabbies are built into my human mechanism. All my inner motives are probably contrary to Your perfect will for me.

All this I readily acknowledge.

But Lord Jesus, I know You have come to do something about this horrendous Hill mess [feel free, reader, to substitute your own name in place of mine]. I hereby turn it all over to You for Your full treatment. Just help Yourself to me and change things to suit Yourself. From now on, I consider myself——including my attitudes in money matters——to be Your problem. I'm going to continue in Your Word, which You say is the heavenly detergent for doing this cleanup job (Ephesians 5:26). And I'm going to keep on bragging on You and acting like a King's kid. Amen.

If you have joined me in the prayer and substituted your name for mine, you know how relieved I was the day I first prayed a prayer like this so many years ago. It was truly liberating to acknowledge that I'm simply not my own, I'm His. I've been bought with a price (1 Corinthians 6:20; 7:23), as the *Manufacturer's Handbook* puts it. And He's in charge of *me!* That means no condemnation ever again! (Romans 8:1).

Does all my victory make you feel uncomfortable? If you want the best for yourself, do what I did. Be simply grateful that God has done for us what we could never have done for ourselves. Admit to your phoniness and unfitness for the Kingdom of God, and look to Jesus for the changes He can make in your flawed human nature to qualify you for God's Master Plan in your life and affairs.

The "blessed are the poor in spirit" principle (Matthew 5:3) taught by Jesus in the Sermon on the Mount relates to those who are totally honest with themselves, with God, and with one another. They're the ones who can say, "Yes, Lord, I'm truly a spiritual pauper. I have nothing of my own to recommend me to Your love and mercy. I have no righteousness of my own, but Jesus is my righteousness" (1 Corinthians 1:30). To that group Jesus said—and is still saying, "Yours *is* the Kingdom of heaven"—really top-level King's kid living in the here and now.

When Jesus preached the good news to the poor, He was addressing folks who were honest about their needs. They were there to learn, and were childlike enough to accept the words of Jesus without quibbling. We are blessed when we acknowledge, "I can't do it, Jesus, and if You can't, that makes two of us. But just go ahead anyway and see what You can do with a mess like me."

In dealing with the area of financial success, remember that unless Jesus has full charge of our motives and deep-down heart drives, complete success from God's standpoint will never be reached in this lifetime. He warns us about this in many places. Look again at 1 Timothy 6:9, 10 NIV:

> People who want to get rich fall into temptation and a trap and into many foolish and harmful desires that plunge men into ruin and destruction. For the love of money is a root of all kinds of evil. Some people, eager for money, have wandered from the faith and pierced themselves with many griefs.

What are some of the bad guys He's advising us to steer clear of in these verses? Check them out for yourself so you'll know what to watch out for:

> The acts of the sinful nature are obvious: sexual immorality, impurity and debauchery, idolatry and witchcraft; hatred, discord, jealousy, fits of rage, selfish ambition, dissensions, factions and envy; drunkenness, orgies, and the like. I warn you, as I did before, that those who live like this will not inherit the kingdom of God. (*Galatians 5:19–21 NIV*)

> Put to death, therefore, whatever belongs to your earthly nature: sexual immorality, impurity, lust, evil desires and greed, which is idolatry . . . you must rid yourselves of all such things as these: anger, rage, malice, slander, and filthy language from your lips. Do not lie to each other. . . . (*Colossians 3:5–9 NIV*)

Apparently the early Christians as well as modern-day ones had tendencies toward such satanic activities as horoscopes, games of chance, lotteries, zodiac signs, Ouija boards, reincarnation, seances, and so on. Have you kicked these roadblocks to God's best out of your life so you can receive His very best for you? In my pagan days, I carried the moon-sign book with me at all times and consulted it for every decision I made. It worked! Satan does have some very impressive tricks, and without the Holy Spirit to guide me, I was drawn into the spook scene. The results, as you can read in *How to Live Like a King's Kid*, were very nearly fatal forever.

Because of what I've experienced, when people call to my attention the Scriptures reminding me that some of us King's kids have a tendency to backslide in the money department, and sanctimoniously inquire, "How do you handle that, Hill?'' I give a hearty *Amen* to the Scripture and ask them how *they* handle it.

I know that everything the verses say is true. I've been there, but Jesus has rescued me out of them all.

Meanwhile, if you have so much gold that it makes you uncomfortable, try giving it away to a needy person. But don't do away with all riches this side of heaven just because some of us goof it occasionally.

Does money sometimes cause backsliding? Can it cause Christians to get into such bad trouble that they would have been better off to stay poor? No argument. That's why it's so important for us to invite Him to keep our motives pure in all this.

Doesn't the wrong use of food result in gluttony? But if you quit eating altogether, dead-itis sets in, and someone will have to call the undertaker.

Doesn't the wrong use of motor vehicles result in death on our highways? But are you hoofing it everywhere? Or saddling yourself with the inconvenience of straddling a hayburner?

Don't some people who enjoy the healthful exercise of swimming find themselves on the mortician's table from drowning when things go wrong? But has that made you give up all your beach trips for the duration of your sojourn here on planet earth?

Does fire, so necessary to cook our food and keep us warm, sometimes get out of hand and cause great death and devastation? But did that turn you into a raw vegetarian and force you to throw away your furnace and take your chances on freezing to death?

You get the picture. Instead of giving up the things that could be dangerous, we need to learn to use them responsibly so that good and not evil may come from them.

I have come to see all that green stuff for what it is:
a tool for doing God's work in the world,
an instrument for good in the hands of King's kids
whose motives are under God's control,
a means of fulfilling the Great Commission
taking the good news of the Gospel
to the uttermost parts of the earth.

All things considered, the more riches He wants to send my way to manage for Him for these purposes earthside, the better I'll like it, and He'll get all the glory.

And now, finally, with all that settled at last, hurrah and hallelujah, we're ready to get you out of poverty and poverty out of you so you can get God's Master Plan for prosperity working in your life.

-11-
HOW YOU CAN GET OUT OF POVERTY

And Live Like a Millionaire

Me—get out of poverty? Me—live like a millionaire?
Of course! Didn't you know you could? And you can start today.

Does Satan have the right to keep us IGNORANT of God's Word, full of UNBELIEF, and DISOBEDIENT to God's Word so as to rob us of the prosperity God has promised? Only if we let him.

You may never have realized before that if any human being on planet earth can make a million dollars, so can you. If anyone else has ever succeeded and become free from debts, mortgages, loans, and unpaid bills, it can happen to you.

"I never heard such crazy talk in all my life," someone's muttering under his breath. You might just as well say it out loud, because I hear you anyhow.

Well, it may *sound* crazy, but it's the best kind of crazy you'll ever know. If I can do it, you can do it, and I have done it. Once you have learned the principles that govern these things, prosperity is waiting for you just around the corner.

"Around *what* corner?"

Around any corner where you will begin to put into operation the laws that govern money and prosperity.

Everything in life works according to precise laws or principles that God, the Designer of it all, cranked into the system in the very beginning of things. Those laws and principles have never changed, and they still bring results for anyone who puts them into practice.

The first thing to do is to get rid of the influence of the robber in our lives. How can we do that? The *Manufacturer's Handbook* says that if we will submit ourselves to God and resist the devil, he will have to flee from us (James 4:7).

What does it mean to submit yourself to God? Simply read His Word, do His Word, and report on results. The reporting on results is called our testimony, and God says that our testimony, together with the blood of the Lamb who has already been slain, will clobber old Slue Foot right in his tracks:

> And I heard a loud voice saying in heaven, Now is come salvation, and strength, and the kingdom of our God, and the power of his Christ: for the accuser of our brethren is cast down, which accused them before our God day and night. And they overcame him by the blood of the Lamb, and by the word of their testimony. . . .
>
> *Revelation 12:10, 11*

And what will become of the overcomers? Wait'll you hear!

To him that overcometh

> will I give to eat of the tree of life,
>> which is in the midst of the paradise of
>> God. (Revelation 2:7)
>
> will I grant to eat of the hidden manna,
>> will I give a white stone
>>> with a new name. (*See* 2:17)
>
> will I give power over the nations:
>> And he shall rule them with a rod of
>> iron. . . .
>>> And I will give him the morning star.
>>> (2:26–28)
>
> [he] shall be clothed in white raiment;
>> and I will . . . confess his name before
>> my Father. (3:5)
>
> I will make him a pillar in the temple of my
> God . . .
>> and I will write upon him the name of
>> my God. (*See* 3:12)
>
> will I grant to sit with me in my throne.
> (3:21)
>
> [he] shall inherit all things;
>> and I will be his God,
>> and he shall be my son. (*21:7*)

There's a lot more of it, so full of glory you should get out your concordance and make a list of all the benefits to overcomers you find there.

Once we have overcome the enemy and recovered our inheritance of abundant life that Satan had stolen from us by taking away the Word of God, we can follow God's instructions and be on the road to prosperity again. Satan knows he's licked once we have the Word back in our grasp and are equipped to use the spiritual weapons of warfare against him (2 Corinthians 10:4).

Remember that we are never fighting against flesh and blood, but against "principalities, against powers, against the rulers of the darkness of this world, against spiritual wickedness in high places" (Ephesians 6:12).

To have the victory in our hands, we must
   1. clothe ourselves in the full armor of God,
      including truth,
           righteousness,
           the gospel of peace,
           faith, and
           salvation (Ephesians 6:11–17)
   2. battle all the bad guys with
      the sword of the Spirit,
        which is the Word of God (Ephesians 6:17),
      the blood of the Lamb
      who has already been slain, and
      the word of our testimony
      declaring the truth of His Word.

In all that, we are more than conquerors, and all the uglies will have to flee, every member of the whole devilish army of ungodliness, and keep their slimy hands off God's property.

"Is it that simple?" someone asks.

It's that simple.

"Why wasn't I taught all about this in my college training?"

Because the eggheads don't know anything about it, that's why. They've missed it themselves, and they've gone to a lot of trouble to see that others miss it too. The Gospel is so simple, so literal, so easy, folks with big heads who are always trying to complicate things just naturally miss it, as my friend Ed explained to me long ago.

You might be surprised to learn that God actually planned it that way so men wouldn't think *they* had dreamed up the good news and hog all the glory for themselves. Here's what Jesus said about it one day when He was praying:

> "I thank You, Father, Lord of heaven and earth, and acknowledge openly and joyfully to Your honor that You have hidden these things from the wise and clever and learned, and revealed them to babies—to the childish, untaught and unskilled. Yes, Father, [I praise You that] such was Your gracious will and good pleasure."
>
> (*Matthew 11:25, 26* AMPLIFIED)

If you think that's a misprint, turn to Brother Luke's Gospel, 10:21, and read essentially the same thing. It's no misprint, it's God's choice; it's how He wanted to do these things. We have to become like little children to enter into the Kingdom, He says (Mark 10:15), and this is one of the reasons.

The first step in the new life of financial success instead of failure is to get your mind reprogrammed by the Word of God. Its light and truth will flush out all the old religious laws about money, wealth, and prosperity that are hanging around in your sick head. It will fully persuade you that poverty is *not* your "cross to bear."

Only God's Word can reprogram your mind and make it think God thoughts. That's why I've jammed these pages with prosperity Scriptures from the *Manufacturer's Handbook.*

As you have been soaking in the Word of God concerning financial matters in these pages, your inner vision should have literally changed from poverty to wealth, from fear to faith, and from failure to success. Has it happened? If not, you should go back to the beginning and read it all over again, because FAITH IS THE ONLY ATTITUDE THAT CAN RECEIVE THE PROMISES OF GOD. The change has to come first in your inner vision, and then your circumstances, which you thought were stuck forever in failure, will begin to lift off and move over into success—if your motives are right.

It's so important for you to get a firm hold on this principle that we're going to look at another Scripture on the subject:

> For, though we are ordering our behavior in the sphere of human experience, not in accordance with mere human considerations are we waging warfare [against evil], for the weapons of our warfare are not human but mighty in God's sight, resulting in the demolition of fortresses, demolishing reasonings and every haughty mental elevation which lifts itself up against the experiential knowledge [which we believers have] of God, and leading captive every thought into the obedience of the Christ, and being in readiness to discipline every careless, apathetic hearing of and disobedience to the Word. . . .
> *2 Corinthians 10:3–6* WUEST

That's a mouthful, isn't it? And a headful too. In those words, Jesus is telling us that we must let all our thoughts be conformed to His thoughts before we can experience the life God wants us to have. When our thoughts are conformed to His thoughts, we'll have a powerful weapon at our disposal to wipe out the enemy who has robbed us of our prosperity. Again, what is our weapon? If you didn't understand it in this passage, Ephesians 6:17 will make it plain to you: "And take the helmet of salvation, and the sword of the Spirit, which is the word of God."

How do we *use* the sword of the Spirit in warfare? We *believe* it and we *speak* it out with our mouths.

The last part of that 2 Corinthians 10:3–6 Scripture makes it sound as if any neglect of the Word of God by anyone is something he'll be sorry for later on. Is that how you read it?

The best antidote for trouble, financial or otherwise, is to HEAR, BELIEVE, AND DO THE WORD OF GOD—with no quibbling. As God thoughts fill our hearts and think tanks, God's Word will become so real in our lives that it will be continually issuing from our lips to clobber the enemy.

And now, back to how these things relate to the state of health of your pocketbook.

How would you like to have your first million in your hand this very moment? Your answer to that question may hold a clue to your present scroungy condition. Most folks to whom I put that question reply something like this:

"A million? You've got to be kidding. I'd be happy if I had just enough money to pay all my bills. I believe it's God's will for me to be broke and humble—but I don't believe He wants me to be quite *this* broke."

Recognize your trouble now? You've programmed your mind to poverty instead of the abundance God wants for you. Remember that in the *Manufacturer's Handbook* Jesus says, "According to your faith [attitude or inner vision] it shall be done unto you in your life" (Mark 5:34, author's paraphrase). In other words, whatever your inner vision, reflected in the confession of your tongue, *that* is what you are likely to achieve—failure or success, poverty or wealth.

It's not enough for God to open the windows of heaven

and pour out blessings for you. Unless you're programmed by an attitude of faith to receive them, you'll be like a leaky sieve. The rain of blessings will drain away onto the territory of a man who is equipped to receive it.

Now, there is a big difference between a heavenly promise and an earthly contract that is specific as to the time when it will be fulfilled. Sometimes the long delay between God's giving of a promise and the time of its fulfillment causes a problem for people. But the delay is never God's fault. It's for our good. Sometimes He has to wait for us to be *ready to receive* what He has for us. Not understanding that, sometimes folks lack the patience God says we're supposed to exercise to the full. They have a tendency to be discouraged and say, "Well, things just don't work that way anymore. God blesses others, but He sure leaves me out."

That's a wrong confession that will never get us anywhere except further in the pits. The truth is that in spite of feelings, symptoms, and appearances, we still have a promise from God on which we can rely because He has committed Himself to carry it out and has bound Himself by His own Word to do it. "I will hasten my word to perform it," He says (Jeremiah 1:12).

The contract is there, it is valid, and repeated promises are given to build up our faith, so it will be strong enough to RECEIVE what God has promised. Looking over and over again at God's contract, or "deal," helps us develop the faith muscles we need in order to overcome the hangups of our five senses and enter that victory ground where, having done all, we can stand and see the salvation of the Lord (Ephesians 6:13).

God's Master Plan provides for us to live in the best of two worlds, right here, right now, in this lifetime:

1. The very best this natural world has to offer—as much of it as we can handle without being ruined by it and without letting it become a false god in our lives. (God in His mercy will see to it that the Christian who is chained to his money is set free by being stripped of his captor, the big buck.)

2. The best that heaven has to offer—as much as we can stand without being "so heavenly minded we are of no earthly use" as fruit-bearers and laborers in His harvest in this world of darkness.

The *Manufacturer's Handbook* traces the ups and downs of God's people under conditions of poverty and conditions of plenty. In the beginning, Adam and Eve had it made. Then they blew it.

Later, the children of Israel were forever experiencing yo-yo conditions of extremes in their lives, up and down, down and up, prosperity and poverty, poverty and prosperity. Why the fluctuation? Not because God chose to torment them and make them humble through poverty and lack but because they, like God's people today, had a tendency to look away from God when things were going well. When they had it made, they tended to leave God out of their lives and affairs.

The natural result of looking away from God was poverty. When things really hit bottom, they remembered where they came from and who the God of their salvation really was, and went caterwauling back to Him. He always forgave them and restored them again to a life of prosperity.

Again and again poverty made them cry out to Him for

help—and then they'd be on their way up again. If they'd been smart enough to *keep* their attention on Him all the time, they could have continued in perfect peace without the roller-coaster ride. How do I know that? God says so, right there in Isaiah: "Thou wilt keep him in perfect peace, whose mind is stayed on thee: because he trusteth in thee" (Isaiah 26:3).

How about you? When things become *too* prosperous, what happens to your prayer life? Do you tend to forget all about God and chase after false idols? Let's think that through with a hypothetical illustration.

Suppose, for instance, that the morning mail brings you an unexpected check for a million dollars—maybe from some sweepstakes you entered months ago, spending your last two dimes on a stamp. Or maybe some unknown, long-lost second cousin died and left all of his vast holdings to you.

As a brand-new millionaire, will you show up tonight for that witnessing session in the Down-and-Outers Mission in the slums of Hometown City, USA? How about prayer meeting in your little church next Wednesday night? Will you keep on with your early-morning devotions? Will you continue to teach that small Bible class in that tiny church in Booneytown?

Have you just come forth with a whole string of unanimous, apologetic, negative answers? That's what I thought. At least you're being honest.

God is fully aware of our tendency to forget Him during times of great plenty and financial blessings. He knows we are prone to let our eyes wander away from Him and to look to *things* He has given us. He knows how easily we are attracted to the gifts instead of to the Giver. And so He has cranked into His Master Plan a natural law for our good, a safeguard called "leanness."

Whenever we show a tendency to head for left field, wherein He knows lies total disaster for us, the wall of His protection against the enemy is automatically lowered, and the financial—or other—miseries creep through, settle in, and get our attention.

What's the first thing we do when our worldly "goodies," our health and prosperity, or that of our loved ones, start to fade away out of sight? We get our prayer life back into high gear, right? As false idols are removed through the natural circumstances of life, we return to the One who is the Rock of our salvation, the One who is always ready to forgive us, to give us a new beginning, and to restore the years the locust has eaten. The way is made for the true and living God to get us back in gear for His Master Plan of prosperity to operate in our lives.

Yes, you might say that the same prosperity and good health that are His perfect will for us can be the greatest hindrances to our spiritual growth and maturity. But when we are no longer ignorant of those dangers but understand how these things work, we can have the best of two worlds by doing what God recommends in Matthew 6:33—seeking first His Kingdom and His righteousness—and watching all these things being added unto us.

A word to the wise: When you see your worldly riches disappearing, focus intently on God, ask Him to show you how to grow spiritually so you can handle prosperity, obey what He says you are to do, and then watch His Master Plan unfold in your life with accelerated speed.

In line with the good news of Romans 8:28 that He's always working all things together for the good of those who love Him, we know that poverty—if it turns us back to Him—can actually become the pathway to plenty, because it is the Father's good pleasure to give us the Kingdom! (Luke 12:32).

173

If your mind has been renewed by the Word of God to expect the best, according to His promises, and if you're walking in righteousness before Him but your fortunes are *still* largely on the red ink side of the ledger, your second-best position just *may be* the result of satanic influences that can be gotten rid of by the right kind of spiritual warfare. *Then* the blessings can flow. How does that work?

Think in a new way for a minute about some very familiar words from the *Manufacturer's Handbook*. Try to think about the Scriptures in the very literal way a child would think about them. Don't spiritualize anything away. If you can do that, you're in for a real treat:

1. *Jesus taught His disciples to pray, "Thy kingdom come. Thy will be done in earth, as it is in heaven"* (*Matthew 6:10*). In other words, He told us to ask the Father to let God's Kingdom come in our here and now. Since heaven's streets are paved with gold, giant pearls are the gates of the city, and there's no crying there, I'm pretty certain poverty isn't free to roam around heaven all day and gobble up God's children, aren't you?

It's okay with God—is it okay with you for *that* kind of heavenly Kingdom of righteousness, peace and joy (Romans 14:17) to prevail here?

Sure it is. Read on.

2. *Next, look at what Jesus said to Peter immediately after Peter made the good confession:*

> "Blessed art thou, Simon Bar-jona: for flesh and blood hath not revealed it unto thee, but my Father which is in heaven. And I say also unto thee, That thou art Peter, and upon this rock I will build my church; and the gates of hell shall not prevail against it. And I will give unto thee the keys of the kingdom of

174

heaven: and whatever you bind on earth [forbid to be done], shall have been already bound [forbidden to be done] in heaven; and what you loose on earth [permit to be done], shall have already been loosed [permitted to be done] in heaven."

Matthew 16:17–19 KJV and WUEST

Now for the big surprise. Why did Jesus give to Peter and to us that big King's kid key ring that day? A little child wouldn't miss it. A little child would say that Jesus gave us the keys to the Kingdom of heaven so we could open the door and see inside.

Then, a little child would understand that in the light of God's Word in Matthew 16:17–19, whatever we saw happening *there,* we could cause to happen *here,* just as Jesus did. Remember, He said He *did* nothing except what He saw His Father doing (John 5:19) and He *said* nothing except what He heard His Father saying (John 8:28). That last verse is a real mind-jogger in another sense. Look at it in any translation you happen to have on hand and see if you see what I see: ". . . I do nothing of myself; but as my Father hath taught me, I speak these things" (John 8:28).

Does it sound to you as if Jesus is saying that what He *does,* He does by *speaking* what the Father has taught Him? Sounds that way to me, too. And as I look through the *Manufacturer's Handbook,* from beginning to end, I find that's true. Could it be that that's how we're to operate in the spiritual realm? We've already seen Scripture after Scripture confirming that thought, right?

Now look at one more question. *Where* was Jesus' heavenly Father doing and saying the things that Jesus duplicated on earth? In heaven, of course. Where is heaven? In the midst of you, Jesus said (Luke 17:21), and

He confirmed that when He explained, "the Father that dwelleth in me, he doeth the works" (John 14:10).

Had you ever realized the implications of *all* that before? I hadn't.

The keys of the Kingdom give us *access to heaven— the right and the power to see what He has done in heaven and the right and the power to do the same things here by speaking God's Word. And we will see—and do—greater things because Jesus has gone to the Father.* Where will we see them? In the Kingdom that dwells down inside *us* when we are right with God.

Wow, Lord! Are you sure? I mean, that's almost more than we can take in. But Jesus said it would be like that, didn't He? Here is another confirmation from the *Manufacturer's Handbook:* "Verily, verily, I say unto you, He that believeth on me, the works that I do shall he do also; and greater works than these shall he do; because I go unto my Father" (John 14:12).

More? How about this one:

> "I tell you the truth, the Son can do nothing by himself; he can do only what he sees his Father doing, because whatever the Father does the Son also does. For the Father loves the Son and shows him all he does. Yes, to your amazement he will show him even greater things than these."
>
> *John 5:19, 20* NIV

What does that do for you? Do you suppose there's any connection between the greater things we will do and the greater things the Father will show the Son? I do.

Well, we could stay in John's Gospel all our lives and not begin to see all He's saying to us there, but let's go back to the practical application to your money matters.

Since poverty isn't on the loose in heaven, that must mean that we can bind it—forbid it to operate—in our lives here on earth. How can we bind poverty? Do we have to traipse to the hardware store and shuffle home with a hundred yards of rope dragging our shoulders down, catch poverty in a trap, and bind it by tying it to a tree with a boy scout knot? Not the way I read it. The way I read it, King's kids can bind poverty, disease, and all the other bad guys in life the same way God created the world—by the words of their mouths: speaking the things that are not on earth as though they are, because they are already in heaven, and praying that His Kingdom will come here as it is there.

The only way you'll ever know how it works is to try it for yourself. For openers, if you've become really convinced that God could use you better rich than He can use you poor, that He wants His Kingdom-of-heaven will to be done on earth for you exactly as it is done in heaven, you might begin by praying something like this:

Father, I come in the name of Jesus, and I thank You that every word of Your Word is true. I thank You that You love me and want the best for me in the here and now as well as in the hereafter and thereafter. You want Your Kingdom to be established on earth as it is already established in heaven. Father, I freely confess to You that I've made an unheavenly, hellish botch of my finances and it looks impossible for me ever to get them straightened out. But I thank You, Lord, that nothing is impossible with You.

In this matter of binding and loosing, Lord, I thank You for the authority You have given me in Your written Word to bind on earth the things You have bound in heaven. I'm persuaded by Your Word that, according to Your perfect will, poverty is bound and forbidden to operate in heaven. Therefore, I choose to exercise that binding authority here and now so that heaven's best will be accomplished on earth as it is already accomplished in heaven.

Spirit of poverty, in the name of Jesus, by the authority given me in the Word of God, I command you to take your filthy hands off my life and affairs forever. I bind you and forbid you to operate any further in my financial affairs or the financial affairs of my family.

Finances, I loose you completely from all the destructive influence of poverty and set you free to work, in the here and now, for the prosperity which *is* God's will for my life, and which is already present in superabundance in heaven as more riches in glory than I could ever ask or imagine.

And now, Lord, I thank You that because I have done what Your Word gives me authority to do, I am delivered from all bondage to poverty, now and forevermore. I believe that because Your Word is true, prosperity will have to begin to flow in my life as I become OBEDIENT to DO according to the principles You have established. For *Your* glory. Hallelujah! Amen!

Prayers are not formulas; they're living communication with a loving, living God. But if you've prayed, and honestly believed the Word of God behind the words that have come from your mouth, you can expect things to start happening.

In this matter of attitude control concerning your financial affairs, it isn't enough to stop talking yourself into poverty and to bind the forces that have been operating against you. You must replace your former poor-mouth complaining with power-packed Bible statements of truth, agreeing with what God says in His written Word. Here are a few to get you going:

> I am beginning to prosper, because it is written I shall prosper, because I am meditating on God's Word day and night.   (See *Psalm 1*)

> I am beginning to get wealth because I am agreeing with God's Word, and it is written that my God has given me power to get wealth.   (Read *Deuteronomy 8:18*)

> I thank my God that I *have* all my needs, because He is continually supplying all my needs out of His riches in glory.   (Read *Philippians 4:19*)

> The Lord is my shepherd, I shall lack for nothing.   (*Psalms 23:1 NIV*)

> I am the lender and not the borrower.   (See *Deuteronomy 28:12*)

> I am the head and not the tail.   (See *Deuteronomy 28:13*)

> It is written that Jesus came to set the captives free (*Isaiah 61:1; Luke 4:18*). I shall therefore no longer be a slave to banks

and other lending institutions, or to bill collectors.

Success is mine according to the Word of God (*Joshua 1:8*). I refuse to be defeated and beat down by circumstances and mere outward appearances any longer; I have total victory through faith in Jesus Christ my Lord. (*1 John 5:4*)

Hearing yourself say the positive words in line with God's truth will help renew your mind by the Word of God by programming it to think God's thoughts. Your poor-pitiful-me attitude will begin to change into one that boldly affirms, "I am more than conqueror through Jesus Christ who loved me and gave Himself for me" (*see* Romans 8:37).

"I am rich and not poor, because my Father owns all the cattle on a thousand hills" (*see* Psalms 50:10) has power to change your bad-mouthing into a glory grin— and your dismal circumstances into situations full of hope. Meditating on and speaking forth God's Word will speed you on your way to high victory in Jesus.

"But isn't that some kind of hocus-pocus, positive-thinking, deception?" somebody wants to know.

No indeed. Meditating on God's Word day and night and speaking it forth is God's own recommendation for changing our circumstances. Don't try a few statements a few times, as some have done, and then quit, grumbling, "Well, I tried it, but it didn't work for me." Keep at it! They *have* to work, and they *will* work, because they're God's promises, not mine. "Let patience have her perfect work, that ye may be perfect and entire, wanting nothing" (James 1:4).

If we fly off the handle and quit too soon, nothing good will happen.

"Yes, but——" someone's Educated Idiot Box is sure to be clamoring along about now. "You don't understand! I'm out of work, thousands of dollars in debt, and there *is* no way out."

According to the *Manufacturer's Handbook,* if you're *that* bad off, that deep in trouble, you're actually in *good* shape——because God says: "Call upon me in the day of trouble: I will deliver thee, and thou shalt glorify me" (Psalms 50:15).

Be OBEDIENT. *Do* the Word. Call upon Him. A simple "Help, Lord!" has activated that promise of God for many people who didn't even *know* it would work. He *will* deliver you. But be certain you do verse 14 first. It's the other half of the equation, necessary to make the next half work: "Offer unto God thanksgiving; and pay thy vows unto the most High" (Psalms 50:14).

You can start right now to stop the negative talking that can only keep sinking you deeper and deeper into the horrendous pits of despair. And you can begin right now to confess the Scriptures that will make a difference in the right direction, speaking the things that are not as though they were, and watching them come to pass.

Now let me sum it all up, and then give you a case history to show you how these things work in actual practice.

The summary: Repeatedly rehearsing the symptoms of poverty and failure makes these baddies feel at home. They're guaranteed to stay with you as long as you keep making them feel so welcome. Putting into words God's antidote by agreeing with His Word and repeating positive Scriptures reverses the direction of things. When your confession changes, the circumstances have to fall in line. When you begin speaking the things that are not as though they are, they have to become yours in manifested reality. Hear the confirmation from the *Manufacturer's Handbook:*

181

"Out of the fullness—the overflow, the superabundance—of the heart the mouth speaks. The good man from his inner treasure brings forth good things, and the evil man out of his inner treasure brings forth evil things. Moreover I am saying to you, Every word which men shall speak which has no legitimate work, which is inoperative (idle, non-working) and thus morally useless and unprofitable, they shall give account of at the day of judgment, for by your words you shall be justified and acquitted, and by your words shall you be condemned and sentenced."

Matthew 12:34–37 WUEST and AMPLIFIED

What kind of words "work"? Only the words that are in perfect agreement with God's Word, because His Words alone are Spirit and life (John 6:63).

Now faith is the title deed of things hoped for, the proof of things which are not being seen. . . . By means of faith we perceive that the material universe and the God-appointed ages of time were equipped and fitted by God's word for the purpose for which they were intended, and it follows therefore that that which we see did not come into being out of that which is visible.

Hebrews 11:1–3 WUEST

Fascinating, isn't it—that everything you see was made by God's Word from something that was invisible? And if that's how God operated once, that's how He still operates, because He doesn't change (Hebrews 13:8). Stretch your powers of credulity a bit and believe it. Don't forget that Jesus said we would do the things He did—

and even greater things, because He was going to the Father (John 14:12).

Now for the case history, a demonstration of how these things work, the proof of the pudding, you might say.

George, a newborn Christian brother, telephoned me one day, asking if we could have lunch together to discuss his impossible situation—out of work and no jobs available.

Right away, I was encouraged. I mean, the no-job situation clearly offered the raw material of invisibility for God to make a job out of, right? It offered the trouble from which God had promised to deliver His people.

"Too highly qualified," "Overeducated for our needs," "Don't call us—we'll call you," and other similar brushoffs were getting stale fast. The bottom line was that his newly earned doctorate in biophysics was excess baggage that had no value in the marketplace. In his locality, no one was hiring that kind of talent, and there was no hope for any immediate improvement in the job situation. George's scores of applications had borne no fruit. Since he had a sizable family to support, and since all his savings had been exhausted in paying for his education, he was in desperate trouble.

Did you notice the plentiful supply of invisibles, the raw material for glory? Just look at it:

no sale value,
    no one hiring,
        no hope,
            no fruit,
                no savings—
                    in other words, plenty of nuthin'.

"I may never be able to get a job calling for my particular qualifications," George wailed. "I'm even thinking about lying about my training in order to *be* qualified for a lower-paid position. Do you think I should do that?''

Before I could open my mouth to give him the right positively negative answer, he was wailing some more.

''Oh, why did I ever spend all that money for an education that turns out to be a liability instead of an asset? Why did I ever sacrifice all those years—for nothing? They're a stinking albatross around my neck. Oh, woe is me!''

His pity party was in such high gear, it would have been a shame to interrupt it. I quit trying to answer his questions and just let him rave while I finished my soup and sandwich. On and on he went until I could tell his spiritual temperature was well into the subzero range. Negative vision will do that to you. It will drain all your spiritual energy and literally continue the ''curse'' on yourself that you put in down gear with the first discouraged word.

If you think I haven't experienced that for myself—in unbelievable abundance—you haven't read *How to Live the Bible Like a King's Kid*. If you think *you're* good at pity parties, try that book and find yourself a raw amateur compared to me. My wrong confession on that overseas bragging-on-Jesus trip brought me so low, it's the eighth wonder of the world that I lived to tell about it.

Anyhow, when George had finished stating his case as he saw it in terms of the visible order of things, he stopped to inhale, and I jumped into the gap. I didn't want to give him a chance to rerun the miseries past me one more time. For all I knew, they could have been contagious. I told him to close his mouth and open his ears while he slurped *his* soup and gave me my turn at having the floor.

''Now then,'' I asked, ''nothing you've done to remedy your situation has helped a particle, right?''

''Right,'' he mumbled, obviously wondering what I was up to.

"It's totally hopeless, right?"

He nodded, his mouth full of noodles.

"Well then, since you've asked for my help," I went on, "I suggest we begin by applying the principle Jesus recommends—calling things that are *not* as though they *are.*"

"Whoa now!" he hollered. "Just where did you get *that?*"

"Two places, friend. I'm glad you asked. It'll keep me on my toes if you don't let anything go unchallenged. Romans 4:17 says that God 'speaks of the nonexistent things that [He has foretold and promised] as if they [already] existed' [AMPLIFIED], and Jesus tells us we are able to go and do likewise: 'I assure you, most solemnly I tell you, if anyone steadfastly believes in Me, he will himself be able to do the things that I do; and he will do even greater things than these, because I go to the Father' [John 14:12 AMPLIFIED]."

"How about that!" he exclaimed. "I never knew that!" I could see it was proof enough to suit him, so I continued. "This is not denying the existence of tough times or negative circumstances," I explained, "but is simply God's method of *overcoming* them through application of the Word of Truth. The devil is a liar [John 8:44] who tries to deceive us by getting us to focus our attention on circumstances in the natural world that are not in line with God's Word. But if we stick to our guns and insist that God's Word is true, in spite of the evidence of our physical senses, verily, verily, I say unto you, eventually the enemy will have to pack his valise and vamoose. He'll have no choice, because greater is the Word of God operating in us than the one who is in the world [1 John 4:4]."

I could see George was getting more and more interested with each spoonful as the powerful Word began sinking down into his gizzard and doing something for him then and there. Faith cometh by hearing the Word, remember? And George was hearing it.

"Notice there is a vast difference between the creative calling of things that are *not* as though they *are* and calling things that *are* as though they are *not*," I warned him. "The latter is Christian Science, denying facts by calling them 'wrong thinking,' and Jesus never recommended anything like that. But He gave us authority to use the principle of binding and loosing——binding the bad things so as to render them inoperable in our lives——and the principle of blessing and cursing. When we use these laws and principles He has given us, we're applying God's own ideas to our circumstances to cause a change for our benefit."

I could see my unemployed friend was rarin' to go to see the practical application of these principles to his own situation.

"Let's bind your present bound-up circumstances away from you," I told him, "and then we'll pray, both with the understanding and the Spirit, as God recommends through Paul [1 Corinthians 14:15]. In this case, we don't know what to pray for as we ought, but are looking to His Holy Spirit to intercede for us, according to Romans 8:26."

As we prayed together, the Spirit brought to my remembrance various Scriptures on which we could hang our faith that God was going to do something for George. We repeated together the substance of the first psalm, with its promise that as George meditated on God's Word, everything he did would begin to prosper. Then we turned to the whole catalog of promises of blessing listed in the twenty-eighth chapter of Deuteronomy. There were other passages, too, that the Spirit began to bring into focus as relevant for his situation.

As we examined these positives from God's Word, I could see in George's eyes that his faith was growing by leaps and bounds. Grabbing his hand because I could tell he was ready to agree with me—and Jesus—in prayer, we "bound" the lack of a job opening so it could no longer exert any influence on George's life. Then we blessed, literally creating a new job opportunity for him through operation of the principle of calling those things that are *not* as though they *are.*

When we had finished our lunch with a dessert of fresh fruit from the salad bar, George's outward circumstances were just the same as they had been. But inside was a brand-new man, singing an entirely different tune.

"I'll give you a call to let you in on the details of my new job," he said as he strode down the sidewalk toward the employment agency, smiling back at me over his shoulder. What new job? Why, the one we had called into being and claimed by faith, of course. Neither of us knew yet what it was or where it was, but we knew *it was,* and that George would be making connections with it very soon.

You guessed it. A few days later, one of the agencies George had contacted earlier with no results telephoned to ask if he could go to work for them in a brand-new position at once. It was a job that had been nonexistent the day we prayed, but had come into being twenty-four hours later when the board of directors of a big corporation *just happened* to decide that biophysics research would be helpful to their organization. And my friend George *just happened* to be perfectly qualified for the job.

By simply using methods that Jesus devised, we saw one element of God's perfect will come to pass in the life of a King's kid who came to the point of desperation where he dared to turn from his old unproductive ways and apply God's principles.

"Yes, but will it work for me?" someone's still wondering.

My friend Ed would have said, "You'll never know till you try."

-12-

HOW TO MAKE YOUR MONEY BEHAVE— WITH GUSTO!

Introducing God's Master Plan

It's the easiest thing in the world to make money. You just follow the right principles, and watch it happen. But making your money *behave* is an entirely different matter!

Everything you do in life takes time—sleeping, eating, bathing, driving, walking, working, talking, cooking, dressing, resting, and everything else. But the hours you spend dealing with money—on the job earning it, deciding how and where to spend, invest, or save it, in the stores buying with it, writing checks for your monthly bills, and all the rest—take an enormous amount of time. That's why making your money decisions in line with the Word of God can make a huge difference in your life.

As we have prayed about the writing of this book, we have asked God for wisdom in two specific areas:

1. How to persuade you that it is God's will for you to prosper.

2. How to show you how to do it.

189

Reading through to this point, you've probably been aware that His answer to our first concern came through loud and clear:

> *Let My Word persuade them. Faith for prosperity comes from hearing what I have to say about it. My Word will never fail to accomplish the purpose for which I've sent it. My Word from beginning to end is full of promises of prosperity for My people. Those who RECEIVE My Word and BELIEVE My Word and DO My Word will know that I want them to live like King's kids, sons of God, in all areas of their lives, including their finances. Those who judge circumstances by My Word and never make the mistake of judging My Word by circumstances will be able to see My promises fulfilled in their lives.*

That answer was totally satisfactory to us, and we have set forth God's Word to transform your mind so that you will *know* that God wants *you* to *prosper.*

Your next question is how to do it, right? Well, God's Word has a great deal to say about that too. Since Jesus said He came to preach the good news to the poor (Luke 4:18) so they would be poor no more, we can expect to find in His preaching everything we'll ever need to know to turn your poverty into prosperity. I've looked and been amazed at how much there was.

Leafing through the pages of Jesus' preaching in a red-letter edition of the *Manufacturer's Handbook,* I found all kinds of teaching designed to make prosperous the souls of His listeners, a factor tied tighter than beeswax to pocketbook prosperity. In fact, you can't have one without the other. The prosperity of a King's kid's pocketbook is linked to the prosperity of a King's kid's soul by a chain that cannot be broken.

Just look at some of the things included in the good news to the poor that jumped out at me when I glanced through the *Manufacturer's Handbook* with soul prosperity = pocketbook prosperity in mind:

Love your enemies. . . . Be merciful to those who despitefully use you. . . . Judge not that ye be not judged. . . . Make your tree healthy so it can bear good fruit. . . . Let your light shine. . . . Hear the Word and obey it. . . . Take authority over distressing situations. . . . Drive out demons. . . . Have faith for the healing of your sick situation. . . . Don't be afraid, only believe. . . . Give them something to eat. . . . Make the good confession. . . . Keep looking to Me. . . . Thank your heavenly Father. . . . Accept the Word. . . .

One day my collaborator got so carried away with the goodness and multiplicity of all His instructions to us that she compiled a bunch of them—from A to Z—into a little book called *ABCs for King's Kids: A Guide for Meditating His Word.* You'll like it. A self-addressed stamped envelope sent to the following address will bring you ordering information:

Star Books
408 Pearson Street
Wilson, NC 27893

Knowing how much I like to sum up His concepts in neat, memorable little capsules, God dropped on me one exuberant five-letter word to remind you of all you need to do, every principle you need to follow, to get His prosperity promises perking in your life.

(Hmmm! I'd never noticed *that* before. PERKING is PER + KING. Every student of language knows that PER means *through.* So how do these things work? *Through* the King of Kings!)

Now, are you ready?

GUSTO!

"GUSTO? Humph! I never saw *that* word in *my* Bible!" old diehard is snorting from his corner. But at least he's still with us, which must mean he's finally believed the good news and is hanging around for this how-to-make-it-work session.

Frankly, I didn't find the word GUSTO in my concordance either. But when I looked to see what Mr. Webster had to say about it, I struck pay dirt. GUSTO is a perfect word for how we are to do God's Word. Just look:

> gusto = enthusiastic and vigorous enjoyment or appreciation; vitality marked by an overabundance of vigor and enthusiasm.

Don't you think God would like for us to do His Word with GUSTO? I do. The word *overabundance* leaped out at me from the dictionary definition, probably because of the *superabundance* we encountered in John 10:10.

Feeling I was on the track of something big, and not wanting to miss what God might want to say to me through Mr. Webster, I checked on the concordance entries immediately above and below where GUSTO would have marched in the alphabetical arrangement, had it been included. More pay dirt!

> gush = a sudden copious outpouring of affection or enthusiasm.

192

gutter = the lowest level or condition of human life.

My reaction to all that? Hallelujah! The word *outpouring* made me think of the Malachi Scripture where God said He was going to open windows and *pour out* blessings. And *lowest level* was certainly an apt description of the financial condition of poverty-stricken folks. Then I saw that King's kids can rise from the lowest *gutter level* of poverty through GUSTO to the point where God's prosperity promises will be suddenly, enthusiastically *gushing* into fulfillment in their lives.

I was so impressed that I added GUSTO to my concordance.

"Humph! I'll bet you didn't find a single Scripture reference to back *that* up," old diehard interjects. And he's right. I didn't find a *single* Scripture, I found a whole bookful! Any time God impresses anything on my mind, no matter how trivial, He confirms it with His Word. He backed up GUSTO in many different places.

Just for G, for instance, He gave me pages and pages. For instance, G is for

> GIVING thanks for all things with a
> GRATEFUL heart. Knowing to do
> GOOD, and devoting myself to doing it, fitting in to the
> GOOD works He has designed for me to do. Pursuing
> GODLINESS, without which no man may see the Lord, because
> GODLINESS with contentment is
> GREAT GAIN. Being
> GENTLE, showing meekness to all men, whether they deserve it or not. Receiving the

193

GIFT of righteousness, and the
GIFT OF GOD which is eternal life with Him. See-
ing that I come behind in no
GIFT, but coveting earnestly the best
GIFTS.
GIVING GENEROUSLY and cheerfully to
GOD and to the poor, because
GOD loves a cheerful
GIVER.
GIVING myself to prayer.
GIVING the hungry something to eat.
GIVING a cup of cold water in the name of
Jesus. . . .
GIVING thanks to the GOD of heaven, staying
tuned to His wavelength.

That was only a beginning. There was page after page
of G, U, S, T, O. There was no way I could include them *all*
in this book. (They're all included in *ABCs for King's Kids*
mentioned above, however.) All were good, but I've sin-
gled out the ones that seemed most indispensable for
special emphasis here. Consider this overview, and then
we'll look at the supporting Scriptures and how they
operate:

G is for GOD first,
    GIVING GENEROUSLY;
U is for USING wisely what U have;
S is for SEEKING first the Kingdom,
    SAVING SOMETHING every week, and
    SPEAKING God's Word;
T is for THINKING God's Word,
    THANKING God for all THINGS;
O is for OBEYING God's Word, and
    OWING no man anything
    except to love him.

Isn't that great? Now let's look at GUSTO piece by piece:

G Is for GOD First
GIVING GENEROUSLY

Put God first, the Scripture says, and everything else you need will be given to you: "Seek ye first the kingdom of God, and his righteousness; and all these things shall be added unto you" (Matthew 6:33). How do you seek Him first? In His Word. Reread chapter 4 for how this worked out in my life.

One money-behavior principle I find throughout the *Manufacturer's Handbook* is the principle of sowing and reaping, otherwise known as GIVING and GETTING. Here are three Scriptures to put it into focus for you:

> "Judge not, and you will not be judged; condemn not, and you will not be condemned; forgive, and you will be forgiven; give, and it will be given to you; good measure, pressed down, shaken together, running over, will be put (*poured* NIV) into your lap. For the measure you give will be the measure you get back." (*Luke 6:37, 38* RSV)

Remember this: Whoever sows sparingly will also reap sparingly, and whoever sows generously will also reap generously. Each man should give what he has decided in his heart to give, not reluctantly or under compulsion, for God loves a cheerful giver. And God is able to make all grace abound to you, so that in all things at all times, having all that you need, you will abound in every good work. As it is written:

195

"He has scattered abroad his gifts to the
poor;
his righteousness endures forever."

Now he who supplies seed to the sower and
bread for food will also supply and increase
your store of seed and will enlarge the harvest of your righteousness. You will be
made rich in every way so that you can be
generous on every occasion, and through
us your generosity will result in thanksgiving
to God.   (*2 Corinthians 9:6–11* NIV)

"Bring the whole tithe into the storehouse,
that there may be food in my house. Test
me in this," says the Lord Almighty, "and
see if I will not throw open the floodgates
[*windows* KJV] of heaven and pour out so
much blessing that you will not have room
enough for it."   (*Malachi 3:10* NIV)

You get the point of what all three of these Scriptures
are saying, don't you? GIVE AND YOU WILL GET. It's as
if your GENEROUS GIVING GREASES a channel GOD
can use to GIVE MORE THAN GENEROUSLY to you in
return. As Jesus said in another place:

"Truly, I tell you, there is no one who has
given up and left house or brothers or sisters
or mother or father or children or lands, for
My sake and for the Gospel, who will not receive a hundred times as much now in this
time, houses and brothers and sisters and
mothers and children and lands, with perse-
cutions, and in the age to come eternal
life."

Mark 10:29, 30 AMPLIFIED

196

The principle of GIVING and GETTING goes into action the moment you go to work for an employer. You sow (GIVE) eight hours of labor, you reap (GET) eight hours of pay. If you begin to sow (GIVE) more than you are paid for (more than you reap or GET), you will someday begin to reap (GET) more than you sow (GIVE). That's how the principle is designed to work, and it does.

How come? That's the way God designed it. If you don't believe it, try a little experiment the way I did back in chapter 2.

"But I don't understand—" someone's sputtering.

That's all right; you don't *have* to understand how a principle works in order to benefit from its operation. You just have to *do* it. You do such things every day.

Do you understand why water comes rushing from the faucet in the kitchen sink when you turn the handle? Chances are, you don't. But when you want water, you turn the handle anyway.

Do you understand why the electric light turns on when you push the button on the wall switch? If you're not an electrical engineer, you probably answered that one with a horselaugh. But failure to understand how or why the principle works doesn't keep you in darkness. You just flip the switch and enjoy the light. How about the radio, your tape player, or the TV set? Do you understand why pictures and/or sound appear when you push the buttons or turn the dials? Does your ignorance keep you from enjoying their output? Of course not. Do you understand what goes on under the hood of your car—or your computer? Probably not, but you use them anyway.

In the same way, God's money-management principles work even when you don't understand how and why they work. Sow and you shall reap. "A man reaps what he sows" (Galatians 6:7 NIV). Simple. And that's all there is to it.

God used this Malachi Scripture about TITHING (GIV-ING a tenth to God) to begin reprogramming my financial life, transforming it according to His Word. That Word of God is where I got the inner image that worked to get me completely out of debt—out of my house mortgage, my notes due at the bank, my overdue bills. I have never been plagued by any of these icky characters since I began obeying what God says in the Malachi Scripture.

It wasn't easy for me, with all my selfish tendencies, to make myself start to tithe, but it worked when I did it. And what I had left over went so much further than ten-tenths had gone before, that I couldn't afford *not* to tithe. The Word of God always works—when we do it—simply because God has programmed Himself to make His Word work.

Where did I get that? Straight from the *Manufacturer's Handbook:* "I will hasten my word to perform it" (Jeremiah 1:12).

To me, that's the same as God's saying to me, *You just get it in gear, Hill, and I'll do what I promised.* That's how it has always worked in my life.

GIVING is an indispensable part of Jesus' preaching to the poor so they would be poor no more. "Freely you have received," He said, "freely give" (Matthew 10:8 NIV). I've learned that if you don't share what He GIVES you, you can't keep any for yourself, and there won't be any to share with others. That's God's plan for ensuring that everyone will have what he needs.

A long time ago, I decided it would be good for me if every day I looked around until I found at least one person to whom I could GIVE something—preferably without getting caught at it. The gift might be an item of clothing, kitchenware, a household item, edibles, or even money. It might be just a few minutes of time as a good listener for someone who needs to unburden himself.

This is putting the sowing-and-reaping principle to work in another way. Remember that God says we are to GIVE and it will be given back to us more abundantly. The sooner you get this sowing (GIVING) and reaping (GET-TING) principle operating in your life, the sooner you'll know how powerfully it works. Let me give you a personal illustration.

Years ago, soon after I met Jesus and began to be aware of how these money principles work, I invested a few hours of my time in talking with a wealthy client about the things of God. I told him God had delivered me from addiction to alcohol, to nicotine's three-packs-a-day stranglehold, and from a whole lot of other raunchy, second-best things. (You can read all about them in *How to Live Like a King's Kid.*)

He listened to me very politely, but the results were zero as far as I could tell with my natural senses.

Along about that time, as our AA group was praying one night, the Lord showed us that we should start a half-way house for alcoholics in Baltimore. That was before the beginning of detox programs such as we have today, and there was simply no place for a recovering alcoholic to go to get off the streets. We told the Lord we were willing to do the necessary work to get the project off the ground—if He would give us a place in which to do it.

Almost overnight, one of Baltimore's three-story row houses became available to us. God had answered our prayers, so we got busy with our part of the bargain—cleaning and renovating that dilapidated old abandoned house. In time, it became a comfortable home for many otherwise homeless drunks, giving them a chance at sobriety. Ultimately, that humble beginning blossomed into a countrywide network of rehabilitation homes for alcoholics.

Many of our residents arrived with only the clothes on

their backs—generally nothing to brag about after weeks in the gutter—no other possessions at all, and not a single nickel to buy even a toothbrush or a pair of pajamas.

One day we asked our Supplier to do something about that shortage of worldly goods. We knew He had riches in glory just waiting to be supplied to anyone who would ask for them so they could be used for His Kingdom on earth.

"Lord," we prayed, "You have put together this home. Now please bring along some personal coverings for these needy bodies. In Jesus' name. Amen."

A few days later there came a phone call from the widow of that wealthy client in whom I had invested a few hours of sharing time.

"Mr. Hill," she said, "my husband passed away quite suddenly last week, leaving a large quantity of personal effects such as clothing and shoes. I recalled your telling us about your involvement with helping alcoholics to recover from that fatal disease, and I wondered if you could use some of his things."

Thanking her for her thoughtfulness, I said I would be right over to pick up whatever she wanted to give us.

"You had better bring a large station wagon," she said. "There is quite a lot of it."

"Quite a lot" was the understatement of the year. The loot barely fit into the largest station wagon Chrysler built at that time. Dozens of shirts in their original wrappings. The same with underwear, suits, shoes, and all the personal effects a wealthy man purchases by the dozen, just for something to do on a rainy day. We had enough of the finest quality merchandise to have started a first-rate clothing store! Our people were the best-dressed men on the block.

How God honors our smallest efforts in investing time in the lives of others!

In order to get food for the men in that original alcoholic rehabilitation home when no public agency was interested in our project, Charlie, the house manager, who was himself a recovering alcoholic, visited the wholesale markets in downtown Baltimore every Saturday, when the stall operators were preparing to shut up shop for the weekend. He always came back with at least a bushel or so of slightly wilted cabbage, barely shopworn potatoes, and other less than top-grade produce, all in good shape except for appearance. Two-day-old bread and three-day-old doughnuts were quite acceptable to men who were accustomed to scrounging in garbage cans. The basics of the table needs were met in that way.

One Saturday morning, Charlie went as usual to visit the produce stalls for the weekend handouts. That day, the pickings were slim—a small basket of potatoes, a few cabbages, and several loaves of aging bread, but not much more.

"Lord, we need more than this," he prayed. "Please give us that abundance You promised to believers. And Lord, it sure would be nice if we could have some meat on the table for Sunday dinner for a change. How about it, Lord?"

As he stood there in the marketplace waiting for something to happen, suddenly a man walked up to him with an envelope in his hand. He seemed to be in a state of great agitation.

"Say, mister," he blurted to Charlie, "can you use some money?"

What a question!

"Of course I can," Charlie replied. "But if it's counterfeit or stolen, I can't use it—because I'm a Christian."

"Mister," the man continued, "that's *my* problem. I'm a Christian, too, and this here is pagan money. A friend

201

THE MONEY BOOK FOR KING'S KIDS

talked me into going to the racetrack yesterday and betting on a horse. The horse won, and I got all this money. As a Christian I can't use it, because I got it by a way I know is wrong. Can you do something with it?''

Could he! And how! Prayer answered on the spot.

Do you have qualms about how God got the money to Charlie to meet the needs of His people? You don't need to. The Bible says that when we ask God to bless whatever is coming our way, that makes it fit to eat (1 Timothy 3:3–5). And all that money represented meat on the table for those men in the halfway house. They all ate high on the hog that weekend.

If you start looking for someone to give something to—time, money, or material possessions—it will start coming back to you, pressed down, shaken together, and running over, just as Jesus promised.

Not long ago, God impressed Liz Rogers, who runs the King's Kids' Korner, to give someone a camper she didn't need. Meanwhile, we had been praying for a vehicle big enough to carry an adequate supply of King's kids' books to meetings here and there. Soon after Liz was obedient to give away her camper, God prompted someone else to give a twenty-thousand-dollar van to the King's Kids' Korner. Talk about more than a hundredfold return! We experienced it—and have been enjoying His van up and down the highways ever since.

Was there any connection between Liz's giving her camper to someone and God's putting the van into our hands? We believe the van came as a result of the law of sowing and reaping. Being available for God to use in whatever way He chooses in someone else's life opens the way for abundance to flow through us to bless others.

As often as I can, I attend AA meetings. Giving away my sobriety to a hurting person assures a fresh supply daily. That has worked for me for thirty-two alcohol-free years so far by the grace of God working through Alcoholics Anonymous.

Abundant living won't happen for everyone, because not everyone will faithfully sow something every day *now* in order to provide for a new harvest to appear every day further down the road. What are you experiencing in the way of a harvest of blessings today? Only what is in exact proportion to what you sowed yesterday or last week or last month or last year. Does the harvest seem small? Maybe you should increase your giving.

When you never let a day go by without giving away a part of yourself, the Lord of the harvest will see to it that you never miss receiving a blessing every day of your life. The blessing is always much greater than the seed sown, because God is the Lord of increase. Look at these multiplication Scriptures:

> Mercy to you and peace and love be multiplied.   (*Jude 2* wuest)

> [Sanctifying] grace to you and [tranquilizing] peace be multiplied. . . .   (*1 Peter 1:2, with 2 Peter 1:2* wuest)

> Peace be multplied unto you.   (*Daniel 4:1; 6:25*)

> "I tell you the truth, unless a kernel of wheat falls to the ground and dies, it remains only a single seed. But if it dies, it produces many seeds."   (*John 12:24* niv)

Some people call this principle SEED FAITH; some call it GIVING TO GET, but by whatever name you call it, it works because it's God's idea.

This GIVING/GETTING principle works even for folks who never consider serving God. The pagan who gives generously for the needs of others cannot fail to prosper financially. Our nation has always prospered because we have always given abundantly of our material wealth to other nations in need. Even though the motives of our politicians may not have been based on Scripture, the results showed up. Every element of God's GUSTO Master Plan always works—when you *do* it.

"But we're not supposed to expect something in return for our giving," some poor religious soul usually protests when I present these principles. His comment sounds pious—but it isn't in line with the Word of God. When Jesus said, "Give, and it shall be given unto you" (Luke 6:38), He *didn't* say that we should keep this fact a secret from ourselves.

Maybe my heckler has been misled as I was when as a new King's kid I was told, "Give, expecting nothing in return." I did just that—externally—but deep down inside, I was hoping for *a lot* in return. That stupid advice made me a hypocrite, giving with the secret motive of hoping for blessings.

And then one day I checked out the Scriptures on which folks were basing their advice. Once more, it was a case of people being so brainwashed by theologians taking verses out of context that they couldn't grasp what the words were actually saying. Hear this: "And even as you are desiring that men should be doing to you, be doing in the same way to them" (Luke 6:31 WUEST).

This is looking at the desired RESULT first, isn't it? In this case, what you want to GET determines what you sow (GIVE). This principle is no surprise to the farmer. He does it all the time.

"And assuming that you are loving those who are loving you, what sort of recompense is yours? for even sinners considered

204

as a class of individuals, also are in the habit of loving those who are loving them. In fact, if you are doing good to those who are doing good to you, what kind of recompense is yours? Even sinners considered as a class of individuals are constantly doing the same. And if you lend money at interest to those from whom you hope to receive, what kind of graciousness is yours? Even sinners are in the habit of lending money at interest to sinners in order that they may get back the equivalents.''

Luke 6:32–34 WUEST

If He is telling you *not* to love, if He is telling you *not* to do good, then He is telling you *not* to lend money at interest. Otherwise—

Doesn't it feel good to have your eyes opened? Do you wonder why you'd always thought that for Christians the lending of money at interest was taboo? Here God seems to be saying not only that it's okay in His book, but that it's *as* okay as loving others and doing good to them.

"But how about the next verse?" the devil's advocate sneers. Well, how about it? Let's look at it and see: "But be loving your enemies and be doing good and be lending money at interest, despairing of no one's ability to pay back the loan with interest . . ." (Luke 6:35 WUEST).

As I read that, I see that not only are we required to love our enemies and to do good to them, but also to loan them money at interest and not doubt their ability to repay us in full. Maybe God wants us to have a positive attitude toward the bad guys to counteract their negativity that puts them in the classification of enemies for some folks. As for me, I lost all my enemies the day I made Jesus Lord of my life.

It took me a long time to learn that GIVING with the expectation of a return is God's idea in the first place, a basic principle behind His covenants with His people. *You give Me obedience, and I will give you blessings. You give Me your tithes, and I will rebuke the devourer for your sakes.* . . . This kind of thinking may not sound very "religious" or pious, but it matches the *Manufacturer's Handbook* exactly, since it's an integral part of the principle of sowing and reaping.

Did you ever change jobs without paying any attention to what your new salary would be? You probably even negotiated it, didn't you? It's time to be set free from *all* the bondage some theologians have placed on us.

U Is for Using Wisely What U Have

Throughout the *Manufacturer's Handbook,* all the way from Genesis to Revelation——God demonstrates the effectiveness of USING wisely what U have.

In the beginning, God used what *He* had, a swirling disorganized mass of nothing, and talked it into becoming the world we live in (Genesis 1).

In Elisha's time, there was a widow who had two sons and a house full of poverty. She was so bad off, her creditors had come to take her children away as slaves. But the prophet, inspired by the Holy Spirit, asked her what she had in her house.

"Nothing but a little oil," she sniffed. Her inventory revealed basically plenty of nothing, in terms of what was needed for her household. But what did the prophet tell her? Did he say, "You're right. There isn't enough to live on, much less for you to give me a bite of anything for my lunch. I guess the four of us might just as well lie down and kick the bucket"?

No! He didn't say anything of the kind, because he

206

knew the God he served. He told the good woman to get a move on and borrow all the containers in the neighborhood, because a miracle was about to take place. Put another way, he told her to USE what she had, and it would be enough. Was God true to His Word that He would supply all of her needs? You can read the record in 2 Kings 4:1–7. Every pot, jar, kettle, and crock in the whole community was filled to the brim before the flow of oil stopped from that little pitcher. Then Elisha told her she could sell the oil, pay all her debts, and support herself and her sons on what was left over.

Where did the superabundance of oil come from? From the same place out of which He supplies *all* your needs, when you begin to USE what U have. The oil came from His riches in glory (Philippians 4:19). He has a surplus there of everything we need down here, and we can get it without paying any freight charges if we'll only BELIEVE and DO what He says to us. I like that.

Want another illustration—from the New Testament, this time—of how a situation that looked like the pits of abject poverty turned into plenty of prosperity when someone USED WISELY what was available? It's right there in Matthew 14:13–21; Mark 6:33–44; Luke 9:11–17; and John 6:1–13. Take your pick.

One evening at dinner time, Jesus and His disciples were at the beach with five thousand men and their families. Toward the end of the day, stomachs were growling, but there wasn't a cafeteria, ice-cream stand, supermarket, or McDonald's in sight. How on earth could all those famished folks be fed?

To the disciples, the hungry horde looked like a major problem, because they didn't understand that the Kingdom of God was right there in the midst of them. But Jesus told them to take inventory.

"What do you have?" He asked them.

They scouted around and found a little boy who had five barley loaves and two small fish.

"Only five loaves of bread and two fish," they replied, just as negative as before.

What did Jesus do? Did He complain, as they did, that what they had wouldn't even make an appetizer for all those people? Nope. He knew the secret—the Kingdom of abundance was right there with Him.

First He had the people sit down—you might say that He prepared them to *receive* the miracle that was about to happen. Then He took what was available, looked up to heaven, thanked God for it, broke the loaves and fish, and gave them to the disciples to share with the people. Was there enough to go around? And how! Look for yourself to see how many leftovers they took up after everyone had stuffed himself to the gills. Twelve whole baskets full! More leftovers than there was food to start with! It was a great big grocery miracle!

Did you notice that all the elements of GUSTO came into action? GIVING, USING, SAVING, THANKING, OBE- DIENCE, and OWING NO ONE ANYTHING!

Should we ever complain that we don't have enough of anything? Not if we're King's kids. We should GIVE thanks and USE whatever we have. It'll be more than enough. Sharing will make it stretch, and God will multiply it, using the same principle that goes into operation when we plant a seed into the ground. The only real difference between the usual process of food production and what happened in the feeding of the five thousand is that God didn't make the people wait for the usual planting-growing-harvesting process to take place. He just speeded things up. Since He lives at the speed of light, that was no problem for Him.

The *Manufacturer's Handbook* is packed with accounts

of how time after time God showed Himself strong to help His people when what they had didn't seem adequate. Remember how He sent manna from heaven to feed the chosen people in the wilderness? And how their shoes didn't wear out for forty years? And how often He fought their battles for them single-handedly? Perhaps you've heard, as I have, of some modern-day miracles that have happened where God's people have chosen to trust Him and He has chosen to give them a sample of what the Kingdom of God is like.

If we'll only USE whatever we have, the laws of sowing (GIVING) and reaping (GETTING) will multiply whatever into more than enough to meet our needs.

S Is for Seeking First the Kingdom, Saving Something Every Week, and Speaking God's Word

S stands for three very vital parts of the process by which God gets His financial blessings to His people. The first thing is the first thing, naturally: "Seek ye first the kingdom of God, and his righteousness; and all these things shall be added unto you" (Matthew 6:33).

Reread chapter 4 of this book if you've already forgotten how that worked out in my life—when I *did* it.

Next, S stands for SAVE—

"But SAVING SOUNDS like lack of faith to me!" the fellow with holes in his socks is howling. He's wrong though. If you're going to be a lender and not a borrower, the way God promises in Deuteronomy 28:12, you'll have to save something to lend, right? And if you're not going to be a borrower, you'll have to have something saved for the day when a major expenditure comes up—for a home, a car, tuition for your kid's college education. I mean, you can't ordinarily finance any of those things out of the receipts of a single day or out of your petty-cash pennies.

Bible backup for saving? The best. God's in the saving business Himself. He saved us, didn't He? And He GAVE to do it.

If you want more than that, check out Paul's letter to the Corinthians in which he told the folks: "On the first day of every week, each one of you should set aside a sum of money in keeping with his income, saving it up, so that when I come no collections will have to be made" (1 Corinthians 16:2 NIV).

Probably the biggest example of SAVING in the material realm is the savings plan of the patriarch Joseph. Who told him to save up the surplus of Egypt for seven dry years? Read Genesis 41 if you've forgotten.

Have we just blown down another false "religious notion" that has kept you from God's best? As you sort through the accumulation of the years in your rusty think tank, be especially leery of anything there that "sounds so religious." Chances are, it's straight from Satan, the master deceiver, and not from God.

Here's one further word for the wise about this SAVING business: Do your SAVING God's way, not granny's. Don't hide your savings in the sugar bowl or in an old sock under the mattress where thieves could break in and steal. Invest it somewhere so it can be growing while you wait. If you have any qualms about doing this because of your old, leftover religious notions, read Matthew 25:14-30, where Jesus makes it plainer than plain that He wants us to INVEST for INCREASE everything He has given us. Where and how to invest it is a long story, so we'll handle that in another chapter. But for now, mark it down that beginning today, you'll set aside something every week for SAVINGS. If you're moaning inside that you'll never be able to do it, go back and read chapter 3 for how you *can* do it.

Finally, S stands for *Speaking* God's Word. When God said, "Let there be light," He was developing a world and everything in it. And how did He put it together? By His Word. In Hebrews, God tells us through Paul how these things work:

> By means of faith we perceive that the material universe and the God-appointed ages of time were equipped and fitted by God's word for the purpose for which they were intended, and it follows therefore that that which we see did not come into being out of that which is visible.
>
> *Hebrews 11:3 WUEST*

So today, being made in the image of God, we can say, "Let it be done according to Thy Word." And when we speak that creative Word and take authority over circumstances, we can SPEAK and send storms out to sea, pray accidents off the highway, pray disastrous circumstances in airplanes into glory-to-God safe landings, and our gloppy financial circumstances into progressive prosperity. I've told about many of these things in my former books because as a King's kid, I've experienced them. I've simply taken Him at His Word, acted like a King's kid by SPEAKING His Word, and then He's performed His Word by doing what He said He would do.

"Sticks and stones may break my bones, but words will never hurt me" has the ring of authority because we learned it as children. But mature King's kids who have studied the *Manufacturer's Handbook* know that in spiritual warfare, sticks and stones are useless, while the Words of God are powerful against the power of the enemy. If any doubts are lingering in the cobwebby corners of your mind, go back and read the "it is writtens" in Luke 4, by which Jesus triumphed over all the temptations of Satan in the wilderness.

Did you notice that all this is still the sowing-and-reaping principle at work? You plant God's Word into a situation and you reap the harvest of victory, because His Word cannot fail to accomplish that for which He sent it.

Have I lost a few of you here? Do I hear you snorting your indignation at the very idea that you could SPEAK to something and cause *anything* to happen? Or maybe the thought suddenly begins to sound familiar because it's what Jesus said: "If you will SAY to this mountain, 'Go jump in the lake,' it will have no choice; it will have to do what you say" (Matthew 17:20, author's paraphrase).

That's strong stuff, isn't it? But it's just following the pattern God had already set up, making everything we can see out of what was invisible by SPEAKING it into existence. From the beginning, Jesus caused things to happen by the Words that came from His mouth. Everything was created by the Word of God, and being made in the image of God, we're equipped to cause changes in our circumstances by the same mechanism.

Our words are so important that God says we'll be called to account for every careless word we speak (Matthew 12:36 NIV). He says further that if a man is never at fault in what he *says*, he's a perfect man (James 3:2 NIV).

What words are we to speak over our finances? Not something dreamed up by our sick heads, but something completely in line with the Word of God to us.

> I am prospering and being in health as my soul prospers. My soul is prospering because I am being obedient to the Word of

God in all things. My cup is about to be running over with financial blessings because I am being faithful to GIVE. I take my tithes to the storehouse and put them in the collection plate and/or distribute them to other ministries as the Lord prompts me in my spirit. By His grace, I USE wisely what He has given me. I GIVE to the poor. I am SPEAKING to this mountain of debt, ''Go jump in the lake,'' and it will have to obey me and disappear. I am SAVING something every week, THANKING God that He is supplying all of my needs out of His riches in glory. I am being OBEDIENT to His Word and OWING no man anything except to love him.

You can go on and on forever confessing the Word of God about your finances, but even if you do it for only a few minutes every day, it will begin to make a difference in your life. The Word of God is like a laser beam——powerful, sharper than a two-edged sword (Hebrews 4:12).

Another area where SPEAKING will make a big difference is in USING the binding/loosing keys of the Kingdom that Jesus gave to Peter and to us. You can go back and review all this binding-and-loosing business in chapter 11.

Isn't it good that by the words of your mouth——in line with God's Word——you can restrict the operation in your financial affairs of all the forces of the enemy that are trying to steal and destroy your prosperity? Bill collectors, bad bargains, worse investments, dollar erosion, a leaky budget, runaway inflation——you can just bind them up and forbid them to operate by SPEAKING words out of your mouth that agree with, and exercise the authority of, God's Word.

I don't want to give you a formula about any of this, because it's far better to be led by the Spirit, who can give you perfect prayers (refresh your memory of Romans 8:26 here), but if you're stumped about how to begin, and if you weren't ready to pray back there in chapter 11, here's a slightly revised prayer that might suit you even better:

Father, I come in the name of Jesus, who has given me authority over all the bad things this side of heaven, as it is written in Matthew 16:19. I thank You for that authority, and I exercise it now so that Your Kingdom can come on earth as it has already been manifested in heaven. Thank You for giving me this way to implement the doing of Your will on earth. Help me now to have a right heart about these things, to say the right words, and to experience the results. In the name of Jesus. Amen.

Satan, it is written that I have authority over you, that I can bind you and all your army and forbid you to operate in my life, in the life of my family, and in all our financial affairs. As you are already bound away from heaven and forbidden to operate there, I bind you now by the words of my mouth in line with the perfect Word of God, and I forbid you and any of your thieving, lying, destroying minions to have any further influence on our lives or financial affairs. I command you to be gone—and it is written, you have to git!

Prosperity, I loose you to flow in my financial affairs on earth as you are already flowing in such abundance for me in heaven where the streets are paved with gold and the city walls are "gated" with humongous pearls. Since there is no end to the riches in glory of my inheritance, I loose those riches to flow in my life here, now, on earth as they are in heaven. Because I know this is the will of God, I know I can expect to see things happen, and by faith I look forward to it. Hallelujah!

And now, Lord Jesus, I turn this all over to You. In case I have missed saying something I ought to have said, or in case I have said something I ought not to have said, I trust You to redeem it and make it right forevermore. And I thank You again, Lord, that according to Your perfect Word, I shall not lack for any good thing, because You are aways supplying all of my needs. And I look for the increase of all my plantings to flow unhindered in my life from this day on.

Feel richer already? You should, because you have taken an important step in SPEAKING the will of God into your financial condition.

T Is for Thinking God's Word, Thanking God for All Things

Now we've hit an appropriate place to talk about one of my favorite subjects——the fascinating principle of meditation, brooding, incubation, or creative THINKING that is found throughout God's Word. Is it relevant to the problem of getting you out of the financial mess you're in? And how!

Incubating——or brooding upon——God's Word to hatch out God's best for us this side of heaven is given throughout the *Manufacturer's Handbook* as an important part of God's Master Plan for our success and prosperity in this world. Never heard of it? Then you haven't read *How to Live the Bible Like a King's Kid,* which shows how it works. (A defect that can be easily remedied with a trip to your local Bible bookstore, however.)

Look with me for a moment at how God does things. What was the first step in the process He used in the formation of this world? It's right there for the reading in the front end of the Book of Genesis, the same process that a hen uses to hatch her chicks out of their eggs—BROOD-ING. The same system that causes seeds to germinate when brooded over by sunlight. The same principle that, when applied to brood mares at gestation, brings forth the gangling colt in the "fullness of time." Look at it:

> In the beginning God created the heaven and the earth. And the earth was without form, and void; and darkness was upon the face of the deep. And the Spirit of God moved [*was brooding* AMERICAN STANDARD, margin] upon the face of the waters.
>
> And God said, Let there be light: and there was light.
>
> *Genesis 1:1–3*

Neat, isn't it?
The Spirit BROODED
    and God SAID
        and things HAPPENED.

Just like that. The chaos pictured in Genesis 1:2—"without form, and void"—was transformed into the "very good" created order (Genesis 1:31) by the process of BROODING or MEDITATING or THINKING, and then SPEAKING it into existence, calling "things that are not as though they were" (Romans 4:17 NIV).

In the same way that the Spirit of God "brooded" upon the face of the waters to create a universe, so we are to "BROOD"——like a mother hen——MEDITATING on or THINKING about His Word in order to establish the climate of faith in which He can bring about, through our SPEAK-ING words in line with His Word, the good things He has planned for our lives.

The THINKING has to come before the SPEAKING. As He says, "Out of the abundance of the heart the mouth speaketh" (Matthew 12:34). When the heart is full of God THOUGHTS, from meditating day and night on His Word, revealed by Psalm 1 as the avenue to total prosperity, what comes out of the mouth is God's Word, which always accomplishes what it was sent to do——in this case, to bring us prosperity, the abundant life.

"If you have FAITH as a grain of mustard seed, you will SAY to this mountain . . ." (see Matthew 17:20). If you will THINK on God's Word long enough for your faith to really grow, THEN YOU CAN SPEAK THE DESIRED RE-SULT INTO EXISTENCE, JUST AS JESUS DID.

Look again at the first psalm. It depicts a King's kid right in the middle of a world full of regular, ordinary, nor-mal, natural, unregenerate people. In the midst of all that, he is prospering because he's not conforming himself to the world around him. He's being transformed by the re-newing of his mind according to God's Word because he THINKS about it all the time:

> Blessed is the man that walketh not in the counsel of the ungodly, nor standeth in the way of sinners, nor sitteth in the seat of the scornful. But his delight is in the law of the Lord; and in his law doth he medi-tate day and night. And he shall be like a tree planted by the rivers of water, that

217

bringeth forth his fruit in his season; his leaf also shall not wither; and whatsoever he doeth shall prosper.

Psalms 1:1–3

My friend Webster says that to meditate is to focus your THOUGHTS on something. And now look at the word *law*. In case you didn't know it, a law doesn't demand that you do or not do something. It simply tells how something works, like the law of gravity, for instance. It doesn't say you can't jump off the roof; it just guarantees that if you do, you'll get lumps. And the operation of a law isn't dependent on your understanding why it works the way it does. Your well-being, however, your prosperity and health, hinge on your putting yourself in a position where God's laws can work for your benefit.

God says, *If you do this, this will happen. If you do that, that will happen.* And here He's saying that if we'll spend practically full time THINKING about how His Kingdom principles operate, and put them into practice, we'll be so prosperous we'll hardly be able to believe our eyes.

When you're meditating full time on the law of the Lord, which isn't grievous (1 John 5:3) but "sweeter also than honey and the honeycomb" (Psalms 19:9–11), you won't have time to stew about the stock market's bad news, the death of the dollar, or the funeral of your money. For myself, I quit reading that stuff. There's better news in the pages of the *Manufacturer's Handbook,* and the more you THINK on it, the better life gets.

THINKING on God's Word leads to THANKING Him for it. It's an automatic response. If you'd like to know more about the blessings that begin to flow when you thank God in all things, read any of my previous books. They're packed with case histories of what I have experienced along that line.

O Is for Obeying God's Word, and Owing No Man Anything Except to Love Him

One letter to go. Last but not least, as they say. Among the things for which the O of God's GUSTO Master Plan stands are two absolute essentials: OBEDIENCE to God's Word, and OWING no man anything except to love him.

The meaning of OWE NO MAN is clear——pay off your bills and don't borrow anything else from anybody, ever! Don't buy anything you can't pay for on the spot. Quit falling for the buy now, pay later pitch. What that really means is buy now, *pain* later. When a King's kid has a need that can't be met by the money in his pocket, he should save now, buy later. Sometimes that saves you a real bundle, because after you've saved up enough for what you thought you couldn't live without, you might decide it's no longer essential or even desirable, and you'll be on your way to a good nest egg for a respectable bank account.

The principle of owing no one anything is scattered all through the pages of the *Manufacturer's Handbook.* Why, it's even in Shakespeare! Remember when the old geezer Polonius was giving fatherly advice to Laertes in *Hamlet?* Polonius intoned some high-sounding words like, "Neither a borrower nor a lender be," and it sounded so lofty, religious folks thought it was God's advice. So much for the stupid wisdom of men. God, in fact, encourages King's kids to lend——at interest——because that's one of the avenues He seems to like to use to prosper His folks. You had gotten the impression that He didn't like people to charge interest? Well, that's because you've listened to men's foolishness instead of God's wisdom. (Go back to chapter

12 for a discussion of what the *Manufacturer's Handbook* really says about all this.)

The borrower in business expects to pay you for the use of your money, and the reason he borrows it is that he can make a tidy profit above what he's going to pay you for it. Business booms, and everyone benefits. That's always true when we're doing things God's way.

Now for the other application of the letter O——and we'll be finished with the rudiments of God's GUSTO Master Plan for your finances and can head for the laboratory for the practical application of them.

O is for OBEDIENCE to every word that comes from the mouth of God. That principle for prosperity is the very first one God ever gave His people. Way back in the Garden of Eden, God told Adam he could have everything in the whole world to enjoy if he would just leave alone the fruit of the tree of the knowledge of good and evil. Because he let the devil outsmart him, Adam was DISOBEDIENT, and fell from that idyllic existence to having to go out and work for a living without air conditioning. Tough.

Further along, in Deuteronomy 28, God spelled out in great detail the blessings of prosperity that would belong to His people who OBEYED Him, and the curses that would fall to the lot of those who were DISOBEDIENT. Reading that chapter can make you sing hallelujah or head for the wailing wall, depending on the kind of lifestyle to which you've been committed.

''Oh, but I could never obey all His laws!'' someone's crying, and he's 1000 percent right. You can't keep all His laws by yourself. Brother Paul had the same ailment, remember? ''The good that I would I do not: but the evil which I would not, that I do'' (Romans 7:19).

But even that's part of the good news. You just can't get away from it. I mean, we can't keep the law, but Jesus in us can, and we can reap the benefits. In 1 John 3:22 we read, "Whatsoever we ask, we receive of him, because we keep his commandments, and do those things that are pleasing in his sight." How can that happen? Because we're dead (Galatians 2:20), and the life we live is Jesus living in us. It is Jesus in us keeping the commandments *for* us. That's the only way we can ever do the things that are pleasing in God's sight.

What is it that pleases God the most? To hear that His children are walking in the truth of His Word (3 John 4).

No matter what your past has been in any of the GUSTO areas, you can get all scrubbed up and begin with a fresh deck if you become a King's kid. (Directions for becoming a King's kid entitled to God's benefits instead of the grim "rewards" of a child of the devil are in chapter 1. It's still not too late for you to get on the winning team.)

There you have it, then—God's GUSTO Master Plan for King's kid living in the financial realm of life on planet earth. You can begin today to sow prosperity by:

GIVING generously
USING wisely what U have
SEEKING first the Kingdom
SAVING something every week
SPEAKING God's Word
THINKING God's Word
THANKING God for all things
OBEYING God's Word
OWING no man anything
Except to love him.

And now (don't I hear three trumpets off in the distance somewhere?) you're ready to get your financial affairs in flourishing order—with GUSTO! It's a perfect plan, guaranteed to work—but only when you do it. And if you want to do it but think you can't,

the hope of glory,
Jesus inside you,
will do it for you.
Hallelujah!
Amen!

And now, let's head for the workshop to get all the goodies in gear for improving *your* financial condition "immeasurably more than all we ask or imagine, according to his power that is at work within us" (Ephesians 3:20 NIV).

Put on your working clothes,
sharpen your pencils and your wits,
dig out your financial records,
and let's begin.

-13-
WHERE DOES YOUR MONEY GO?

When you consider how much money the average wage earner will take home in his productive years, it becomes scary to leave all the results to blind chance. For best results, a plan for handling all that money becomes a necessity.

"But I can't stand budgets!" wails the man programmed for failure. Well, don't call it a budget; call it a money plan. Most people don't realize that they spend their money according to a plan whether they like it or not, and whether they know it or not. Generally, a money plan laid out in advance will work better than one that just happens haphazardly as you go along, one that you don't even *see* until it's already been *used*—much too late to fix it.

If you've been having money problems—never enough greenery to go around, the bank always calling to say you're overdrawn *again,* your landlord threatening to throw you out on your ear, the phone company showing up to cut off your gabfests, the utilities folks knocking at

223

your door to cut off your water and gas and electricity for nonpayment of bills, you need a plan for doing better. In order to make that plan, you need to look at what you're already doing, especially if you've been following one of those "it just happened" plans.

Every money plan includes two sets of statistics: WICIF and WOGOF.

"What? WICIF and WOGOF? I never heard of 'em!"

Neither did I until this minute, but I can see already they're going to be very helpful to you. Let me introduce them:

Meet WICIF—Where Income Comes In From.

Meet WOGOF—What Outgo Goes Out For.

To fix anything, you have first to find out what's wrong, right? And to know what is *wrong*, you have to know what *is*. To get out of debt and head toward prosperity you need to get to know WICIF and WOGOF. Do I have Scripture for that? Of course!

> "My people are destroyed from lack of knowledge." (*Hosea 4:6 NIV*)

> I would not have you ignorant. (Romans 1:13; 1 Corinthians 10:1; 12:1; 2 Corinthians 1:8; 1 Thessalonians 4:13)

For this step, we need to employ the services of your Educated Idiot Box, your think tank, that fantastic computer riding high above your shoulders. Yes, I remember that the whole head is sick, according to what God says in Isaiah 1:5, but even a sick head is good for a few things. Serving as a space filler between your ears to keep your hat out of your eyes is only one of 'em. Seeing where your money has been going is another thing at which your Educated Idiot Box ought to excel. It's not a matter of figuring out anything, you understand, it's just a matter of looking at the record. Any properly programmed robot could do it.

To take a real look at what *is* in the pocketbook area of your life, you need to dig out all your financial records for the last twelve months, everything having to do with your personal WICIF and WOGOF. That includes all your bank statements, your canceled checks and check records, cash receipts for anything you purchased in day-to-day spending, insurance policies, credit-card statements, charge accounts, income-tax returns, current and over-due bills, mortgages, any stocks or bonds, notes due at the bank, records of withholdings. . . . Don't forget the credit union where you work. Is the CU deducting a hefty amount from your paycheck before you ever see it—to pay back old loans you got in haste and repented at leisure?

Do you have a record of the amounts withheld from your check for other purposes—social security, retirement plans, federal and state taxes? Since this is a serious operation, it is not to be undertaken in generalities based on what your sick head remembers. Make a few phone calls to gather information, if necessary. Go for the specifics, not to make yourself feel guilty but simply to arrive at the facts of the case.

While you're doing your digging, be thinking about how much money you have earned in the past and what, if anything, you have to show for it today. A home? Appliances and furniture? A car that's paid for? Income-producing investments? Paid-up life insurance? An IRA account for your old age? A safety-deposit box full of jewelry, valuable coins, or a stamp collection? Real estate?

Or has most of it simply leaked away somewhere without a trace—except for what you spent for groceries that remain as a flabby spare tire around your middle? (My *How to Flip Your Flab—Forever* will tell you how to get rid of *that*.)

Now start thinking about the money you owe—for mortgages, installment loans, overdue taxes, credit-card purchases, current and overdue bills and charge accounts.

If I don't miss my guess, all that thinking about how little you have to show for what you've earned in the past and how much you owe today has you really down in the dumps, but deeply motivated to do something—*any-thing*—to improve the picture, right? That was the whole point of having you think on these things—to get a *before* picture in your mind, you might say, so you'll remember where you're coming from. Does it look as if you have many afflictions? Glory! Look at what God has promised *you:* "Many are the afflictions of the righteous: but the Lord delivereth him out of them all" (Psalms 34:19).

With a promise of deliverance like that, you can begin to think of the things of good report, as God recommends in Philippians 4:8—the fulfillment in your life of all His promised prosperity.

While you're in the midst of all this, it wouldn't hurt to spend another few minutes looking at your future prospects in the money department. If you are now thirty years old, earning twenty thousand dollars a year—a very conservative estimate—by the time you are sixty-five you will have earned an additional seven hundred thousand dollars at the very least (not taking inflation into account). Makes you feel rich, doesn't it? But if you don't have a money plan for making all that money *behave,* you'll come to the end of the line a shabby, penniless candidate for a bed in the old folks' home run by some charitable institution. *With* the right plan, however, it can be an entirely different story.

226

You might have been absolving yourself from responsibility for the mess you're in—and for having no plan for the future—by rationalizing that these are the end times, that the dollar is dying, that we're in an inflationary period, that everything is so expensive these days, that we're in a depression, a recession, that it's all the fault of the Federal Reserve, the IRS, the XYZ. And that, anyway, Jesus is coming soon—soon enough to rapture you out of the midst of the disastrous cumulative results of all your financial folly. You hope

But suppose God's fullness-of-time timetable calls for Him to delay His return for a few more years—not unthinkable, you know, so more folks will be ready. Financially you'll be a dead duck, six feet under, long before He gets here, if you don't do something now. The best time in all eternity to get things straightened out begins today.

Admit that none of your excuses for your head-over-heels-in-debt situation has been responsible for overspending your income—*you* have been responsible, either directly or by your tacit consent. You took a giant step toward trouble in the money department the day you opened charge accounts at every store in town. The rationalization "But it's so convenient to telephone for what I need and have it delivered to my door," didn't do away with the danger. Nor did your generous distribution of plastic money credit cards to family members—or the fact that you used them unwisely yourself. You started it, and you're the one who will have to put into operation the principles that can get you out of the mess you're in.

Facing up to facts like these is a major step to recovery—and one of the major facts is that easy credit is a slick road to the poorhouse.

Lecture's finished. Do you have your financial records together now? Sharpen a few pencils, get out some lined notebook paper, your calculator and/or adding machine if you have one, sit down at a table, take a deep breath, and prepare to be enlightened.

Warning: Don't expect to finish this part of your assignment before lunch. It may take you several days to get all the figures together and put down in an orderly fashion. The important thing is not to give up but to hang in there for as long as it takes to lay the foundation.

Now begin filling in WICIF (*see* page 229). Ask the Lord to sharpen your wits for this so you won't fail to record any "irregular" income. Sometimes people look at their last year's income-tax return, put down those figures, and think that's it. But for our present exercise, be sure to include those nontaxable items of income that don't appear on your income tax return.

WICIF wasn't too bad, was it? Does it make you feel rich to see all that income written down in cold black and white? Just think of the prosperity you can have with that much money once you get your financial affairs under God's multiplying, blessing control with GUSTO instead of the thieving, destructive control of the enemy!

Ready for WOGOF now? Take a deep breath—and remember you're to record the truth—not what you *wish* it was, but what the black-and-white record shows it to be. You may feel like closing the curtains and pulling down the blinds. That's quite all right, I don't blame you. But keep in mind that this list isn't to be used *against* you, it's to be used *for* you—to open your eyes to where your money has been sneaking off. This is the time to let it all hang out—all the truth, that is.

Don't limit yourself to acknowledging only the respectable things like housing, food, clothing, utilities, transportation, education, contributions. . . . Go on, honestly, and put down what you threw away on junk food, impulse buying, video games, the beauty parlor, the trip to Aca-

WICIF
Where Income Comes In From

	Last Year	This Year (Estimated)
Salary or Wages		
Reimbursements		
Self-Employment Income (Schedule C)		
Dividends		
Interest		
Rents or Royalties		
Social Security or Veterans Benefits		
Gifts		
Scholarships, Fellowships, Grants		
Other		
TOTAL ANNUAL INCOME		
AVERAGE MONTHLY INCOME (Divide TOTAL ANNUAL INCOME by 12)		

pulco just because the airlines were having a special fare for a limited time only and you'd always wanted to go. . . . The hefty handout to the pretty blond selling coupon books of discounts for merchandise at stores where you never shop. . . .

Don't keep secrets from yourself in this. The truth is going to set you free, remember?

You don't use checks much, never bother with keeping

receipts, and haven't the kind of mind that keeps up with these things? No problem. You can still begin today, but at a different level, starting to accumulate the information you'll need for a real analysis of your financial situation. Just get yourself a cheap pocket-size notebook to carry with you at all times and make yourself record every expenditure of any kind in it. Organize the input as you go—using one section of the book for food expenditures, another for clothing, another for rent, and so on. You won't have to do this for many weeks before you'll begin to get the picture of WOGOF. Then you can transfer the information to page 237 of this book.

The degree of honesty and accuracy with which you conduct your money inventory will affect the usefulness of the bottom-line results in getting you out of debt and into prosperity.

Here are some suggestions to get you started on the categories included in WOGOF.

GIVING

CONTRIBUTIONS of tithes and offerings to God's work—what you put in the plate on Sunday, special gifts to missions, to distributors of Bibles and other Christian literature, to the Salvation Army and other good works, to the neighbor canvassing the neighborhood for cancer, muscular dystrophy, emphysema, and fallen arches, to girl scouts when they come around peddling cookies you can't have on your diet so you give them a generous contribution instead. . . .

GIFTS for birthdays, Mother's Day, Father's Day, Children's Day, Grandparents' Day, weddings, graduations, new babies, Christmas, Easter, anniversaries, going-away parties, coming-home parties, hostess gifts, an apple for the teacher, toys for children and grandchildren, valentines, Fourth of July, Mother-in-Law's Day, Groundhog Day. . . .

TAXES

Federal, state, local real estate (except for taxes on your home, which should be included in HOUSING), and personal property taxes. . . .

HOUSING

Basic mortgage or rent, property taxes; repairs—plumbing, roof, and other; maintenance—painting, new gravel for the drive, lawn mowing, snow shoveling, leaf raking, maid service; furniture and appliances and other household items—linens, curtains and blinds, dishes, pots and pans, popcorn popper, pillows, rugs; insurance—homeowner's liability and fire insurance. . . .

UTILITIES

Electricity, gas, coal, fuel oil, wood for the fireplace, water and sewer charge, garbage or trash pickup, telephone. . . .

FOOD

SUPERMARKET FOOD AND DRINK—for convenience you may include here all supermarket purchases, such as cleaning supplies and paper goods as well as food items, beverages, toiletries, dog food, canary crackers, birdseed, kitty litter.

GARDENING AND FISHING SUPPLIES—seeds, organic fertilizer, canning and freezing supplies, repairs to the plow and posthole digger, bait, new rod and reel and travel expenses for fishing expeditions. (You'd better *catch* something this time!)

231

EATING OUT EXPENSES—restaurants, fast-food places, Gloppie Shoppes, the coin-operated soft-drink or candy bandit at the corner garage, the pizza palace you telephone to have them deliver it "free" to your door. (Did you know they pay for the gasoline and delivery boy out of what they charge *you* for the pepperoni?) Don't forget what you leave on the table for tips.

CLOTHING

You name it—someone, somewhere has looked good in it. Include shoe repair, laundry and dry cleaning, and what you paid the seamstress to make you a new blazer when the ones at the store wouldn't button over your paunch.

HEALTH AND BEAUTY

MEDICAL—doctors, dentists, clinics, orthodontists, podiatrists, osteopaths, hospitals, drugs, eyeglasses, hearing aids and batteries, crutches, bandages, vitamins, the trip to Bermuda you persuaded the doctor to prescribe for your health. . . .

PERSONAL GROOMING—barbers and beauticians, shoeshine boys, manicurists, makeup, toenail clippers, lotions and ointments guaranteed to erase your wrinkles and make you look youthful again and twenty pounds lighter, diet-club membership fees. . . .

TRANSPORTATION

Car payments, gasoline (diesel fuel for some folks), oil, new batteries, tow service, parking tickets, tires, repairs, insurance, car wash, tune-ups, parking; taxi, bus, train, helicopter, dirigible, and plane fare;

moped, trail bike, bicycle, or skateboard payments and maintenance; oats, hay, and saddle repairs for Old Dobbin.

ACTIVITIES

BUSINESS EXPENSES
Expenses for which your employer didn't see fit to reimburse you, amounts you gave to collections for office parties, lunches where everyone vanished, leaving you to pick up the tab, subways, taxicabs, uniforms, bad debts from office panhandlers. . . .

EDUCATION AND SELF-IMPROVEMENT
Books, tuition, room and board, supplies, bus fees, school lunches, records, tapes, or video cassettes, library overdue fines, horseback lessons, piano lessons, dance lessons, workshop and conference fees. . . .

ENTERTAINMENT AND VACATIONS
Motels, amusement parks, admission to museums, movies, golf courses, circuses, and zoos; video games, football games, baseball games, basketball games, handball games, racquetball games, Ping-Pong tournaments, phonograph records and tapes, TV repair. . . .

PROVIDING FOR THE FUTURE
SAVINGS in interest-bearing savings accounts, or in non-interest-bearing sugar bowls and old socks under the mattress; INVESTMENTS in stocks, bonds, real estate, and so on; LIFE INSURANCE; RETIREMENT-PLAN CONTRIBUTIONS, social security and self-employment taxes, IRA accounts, contributions to a retirement fund required in your business or profession.

MONEY LEAKS

Include here any otherwise unidentified checks made payable to cash or yourself. Some of this might be legitimate—bus fare, kids' school lunches, change for toll roads. Such items should be estimated as realistically as possible and put in the category where they belong, leaving here only the cash flow that has vanished without a trace.

WOLO

Never heard of WOLO? That's because it's another newbie—something God invented just for you who read this book. WOLO expenses are all those you justified with the ragged, timeworn excuse "We Only Live Once." WOLO expenditures include all those things too extravagant, too lavish, too expensive—the things your conscience tried to justify at the moment but later was sick about. The WOLO excuse is about as helpful as hitting yourself over the head with a hammer to cure a splitting headache.

KUWJ

Does that sound icky to your ears? It is. I couldn't figure how to pronounce it myself until I looked at the results of some KUWJ expenditures, and then I knew it had to rhyme with *sludge*. KUWJ stands for the old death trap "Keeping Up With the Joneses." What should you include here?

That cruise to Bermuda just because your feelings were hurt when your neighbor was going on vacation and you were going to have to stay at home; every Saturday night out on the town for dinner, the theater, Ye Olde Gloppie Shoppe afterward, just because everybody does it, even though in your heart of hearts, you'd rather have stayed home, played Parcheesi with the kids, and soaked your feet; the monthly blast at the country club; the new projection TV you couldn't resist after the Joneses invited you over to ogle their new layout that made your still-good-as-new nineteen-inch picture tube seem ludicrously skimpy in the shadow of their wall-size wonder; the luxury new car you just had to have after the neighbors got one—even though your old buggy was in perfect shape, paid for, and good for at least another fifty thousand miles.

DEBT REDUCTION

What you've been paying on the old balance on charge accounts, installment purchases, and bank loans. Grim, isn't it? If you think you can stand the shock, look at the small print on those monthly statements and see how much interest you've been forking over for the privilege of buying now and paying/praying later. Scary enough to cure you of the habit? It ought to be. Include here also the interest on loans you had to renew—again.

MISCELLANEOUS

It's all right to begin listing items in this category, but whenever you see that a particular kind of expenditure—baby-sitting, for instance—is hogging the show, make a separate category for it instead.

Keep remembering that this detailed listing isn't for condemnation but for rectifying what's been wrong. It's to show you what's been happening while you weren't looking.

Why write down all these things for a whole year instead of for only a month or two? Because so many expenditures are seasonal, that's why. Chances are your utility bill in subzero January or torrid July isn't comparable to what it is in a balmy April. And maybe you pay your auto insurance or your property taxes only once a year. The most accurate picture possible is what you're after. That's why we're looking at actual expenses for a dozen months and looking at them month by month. This way, next August when you think you can afford to blow your growing nest egg on a blast at the local steak house, you'll have a record to remind you that auto insurance is coming up in September.

Don't forget to break down the items on all your credit-card statements into the categories where they belong. Charge accounts too.

These suggestions are just to give you a start. You'll think of other things on your own. Maybe you're making payments on a boat, motorcycle, or time-sharing condominium. If you have expenditures that don't seem to fit anywhere on WOGOF, make a new category. There's no law against having a large number of categories. The important thing is to get it all down somewhere.

If you get bogged down in the midst of the tabulations, take a break. You didn't get head over heels in debt in a day, and it may take you more than a day's scribbling to get the raw material you need to climb out of it. For a breather, you can go back over some of those wonderful prosperity promises in chapter 5. They're sure to give you a lift.

Now, here goes:

WOGOF   What Outgo Goes Out For

JAN FEB MAR APR MAY JUN JLY AUG SEP OCT NOV DEC TOTL AV*

	JAN	FEB	MAR	APR	MAY	JUN	JLY	AUG	SEP	OCT	NOV	DEC	TOTL	AV*
GIVING														
TAXES														
HOUSING														
UTILITIES														
FOOD														
CLOTHING														
HEALTH & BEAUTY														
TRANSPORTATION														
ACTIVITIES														
PROVIDING														
FOR THE FUTURE														
MONEY LEAKS														
WOLO														
KUWJ														
DEBT REDUCTION														
MISCELLANEOUS														

GRAND TOTAL

MONTHLY AVERAGE   (GRAND TOTAL divided by 12)

* Divide total in each category by 12.

Do you have something in every category—and in a few categories I never heard of?

How about savings—stocks, bonds, savings accounts? Your total here is close to a big fat zero, right? I'm not surprised. People in money trouble are usually identical twins in that respect.

"But I can't spare a penny for savings from my already stretched-to-the-hilt budget!" someone wails. "You can if you cut down on your spending," I counter. If you're really serious about getting out of debt, you'll find ways to cut expenses to the bone. The next chapter will give you some help along that line. And when you see how it works, it won't be a drag, either. You'll be rewarded by the awareness that inch by inch, debts are becoming a thing of the past, and that the reward of a healthy bank account, being able to pay your bills on time, and the assurance of something put by for the future are coming into view.

There's no substitute for the boost to your self-image that sets in when your very own savings account begins to grow through a simple plan of self-denial. Regular and uninterrupted saving does all sorts of good things to your character.

Now it's time for a little arithmetic. No, you don't need a computer to do it. Use your head—and a piece of paper and a pencil. A cheap pocket calculator might help, but it's not essential. Maybe the information you're about to see will have greater impact if you arrive at it the hard way, chewing a few scribble sticks to nubbins as you go.

What we need is your AVERAGE MONTHLY EXPENDITURE in each category. Not that swift at math? Easy does it. To get your average expenditure for food for one month, add together the food expenditures for the year (don't forget to include in your calculations the eating-out tabs and the junk food and such forbidden inessentials as soft drinks and booze to the grocery-store items), and divide the total by twelve.

Swallow hard and follow the same procedure for expenditures in all other categories.

Now add up the averages. Be sure to do this operation sitting down, with your seat belt securely fastened so you won't fall out of the chair and crack your head when you faint. The total will be so big, you'll be sure you've added wrong. And you might have. Run the total again—bigger this time, eh? That's how it goes.

Now prepare for an even bigger surprise. On an empty sheet of paper, write down, side by side, your anticipated average monthly income, from WICIF, and your total average monthly expenditures from WOGOF.

Are you still there? Smelling salts, anyone? Does the comparison between the two figures make your hair stand on end, your fingernails curl right off your pinkies?

Your average monthly expenditures are higher than your average monthly income, right?

Get your head out of your hands! Stop moaning! This isn't the time for defeat and discouragement. It's time for a victory dance! Praise the Lord! Let out a few joyful hallelujahs.

Some of you are looking at me tongue-tied and cross-eyed, as if you think I'm crazy. But think what you've just done! You've just diagnosed the problem! Now you *know* the reason you've kept getting deeper and deeper into the sinkhole of debt while working your fingers to the bone!

You've been spending more than you earn!

Your income has been less than your outgo, making the last week or so of every month strictly on the cuff, deficit spending. Over the long haul, it's impossible to keep going that way, unless your goal is to burrow a blind mole hole to China, right?

But hold on! That's still nothing to be discouraged

about. To a King's kid, no news is good news, and bad news is good news, because we know He's always working all things together for our good (Romans 8:28), and we know that we always triumph in Christ (2 Corinthians 2:10), right? Right!

Can you guess what your next job will be? That's right! To reduce your outgo to the point where it does *not* exceed your income.

In the next chapter, we're going to take an in-depth look at several categories and see how you can cut back significantly on what you spend in some areas so you can add to the too-lean categories, especially that SAVINGS category, the DEBT-REDUCTION category, and the one for GIVING to God.

These things are not impossible; they can be accomplished as God's plan for prosperity begins to operate in your life.

Before we go on, make sure your attitude is in line with God's attitude. Maybe you need to reread chapter 11 to get all this in focus. The attitude that says, "We can't make it," won't make it. The attitude that says, "All things are possible with God," has it made already.

-14-

H☺W T☺ MAKE Y☺UR M☺NEY G☺ FURTHER

How to <u>Make</u> Money on Credit Cards

In this chapter, we're going to take a look at some of the things you can do to reduce outgo in several categories of your money plan. Which categories need reducing? I haven't seen your statistics, but if you're like most folks in debt, you could probably stand to consider reducing everything except GIVING, PROVIDING FOR THE FUTURE, and DEBT REDUCTION.

Yes, I know some financial counselors like to figure the percentage of your income you're spending on this and that, compare your statistics to the comparable percentages of some national "norm" family, and encourage you to raise or lower your expenditures in every area until you match those of the "ideal" family. But I'm not going to give you any percentages like that.

How come? I don't find Jesus recommending that we compare ourselves to others, that's why. As a matter of fact, the *Manufacturer's Handbook* is pretty plain about it. Just listen:

We do not dare to classify or compare ourselves with some who commend themselves. When they measure themselves by
themselves and compare themselves with
themselves, they are not wise.

2 Corinthians 10:12 NIV

Furthermore, when Peter was about to make a comparison—in chapter 21 of John's Gospel—Jesus
strongly advised him against it. Do you remember that
scene? Peter had Jesus all to himself, and he had to spoil
it by asking Jesus about His plan for John. Jesus' reply,
"What is that to thee? You follow me!" had a ring of
"Mind your own business," didn't it? Maybe it would be
good for us to keep our noses out of other people's finances here and just stick to the empirical (remember that
word?) principles we have learned from the *Manufacturer's Handbook.*

All those percentages for comparison never made that
much sense to me anyhow. I mean, the fact that you're in
financial trouble means that you *know* you're overspending. Where? Well, that depends on what you really want
out of life. There are no magic percentages to help you
with this, no "norms" that anyone can lay down as law to
you. Let's face it. Each of us has a life that is unique, not
exactly like that of any other persons in our own culture.

Take the matter of what you spend for pet food and vet-
erinary care, for instance. Should there be a national average to which everyone should try to conform? No way. I
mean, you might be feeding and stabling a horse while I
might have only two goldfish in a bowl. There's bound to
be a big difference in what the two of us spend for pet
food.

One person might be supporting a houseful of children;

242

another might be a career girl or bachelor type with no dependents at all.

Someone's medical expenses might reflect the fact that his bucktoothed quadruplets are all undergoing orthodontic care in the same year, while in another family, all members might have long since reached the dentures-in-the-glass-on-the-bedside-table stage with nary a cavity.

One family might have an excellent garden and cut their grocery bill by canning, freezing, or drying a significant portion of the vegetables they consume every year. Another might be in such a position that the man of the house has to eat almost all his meals on the road.

No comparisons, then, but you can look to God to give you wisdom to see what's way out of line when you look at all the figures you've compiled. Chances are, He will show you how to be a better steward in every area, so you can get out of debt *fast*.

Housing

The heftiest single chunk of your monthly income probably goes for housing, right? And this is practically an essential in our modern civilization, where it's often illegal to sleep on the city streets or on freshly painted park benches. So you probably need to continue to provide for yourself and your family a roof over your collective heads, heat in winter, water for your shower, electricity or gas for lights and appliances, insurance, taxes, and repairs.

If you're a senior citizen who bought a house so many years ago that it's paid for, you've got a real head start in this area. If you're young folks just starting out, this one may be a little tougher. Even so, there are many ways almost *anybody* can save in this area.

The first thing to do is to look at what you're already

doing. Are you renting a house or apartment or buying one? Is whatever you're doing the right choice for you? Maybe you've never thought about it. Think about it now.

There's an old saying that goes something like this:

> Whether you rent
> or whether you buy
> you pay for the house
> you occupy.

Lot of truth in that, like it or not. The difference lies in who owns the house after twenty years—you (if you've been paying for it for yourself) or your landlord (if you've been paying for it for him). It doesn't take a smart computer to figure that if you're going to stay in one place long enough to make it feasible, you'd save money in the long run by buying a house for yourself. Just look at some of the fringe benefits:

1. If you itemize your deductions on your income tax—and what King's kid doesn't, since he's giving at least 10 percent to the Lord—the interest portion of your monthly payment is deductible from your income before income tax is computed on the rest of it. Significant savings there.

2. In an inflationary economy, if you have a fixed-interest loan, your monthly house payment remains steady while rents are skyrocketing around you. Friends of mine, for instance, built a two-story, four-bedroom brick a little more than twenty years ago. No frills, but quite adequate for their half a dozen plus an extra live-in

granddaddy or guest now and then. Basic monthly house payment in 1983 was still only $107.88 a month. In their town, you can't rent a decent doghouse for that these days.

3. When the house is paid for, you have a roof over your head—free! It hasn't begun to cost you as much as rent would have cost for the same period of time. And if you'd been paying rent, the only place you could sleep for free would be the park bench—until the cop on the beat made you move on.

4. Some people like to point out that building up equity in a home through regular mortgage payments provides good collateral for borrowing money later on, through second mortgages, for instance. You *can* borrow money that way, and lots of people have done it, but we're not looking for ways to make it easier for you to borrow; we're looking for ways to make it *unnecessary* for you to borrow.

"But—but—but—" someone's sputtering, "I thought you didn't want us to go in debt for anything. To buy a house, even if I had the down payment, I'd have to go in debt thousands of dollars."

Glad you brought that up, friend. There's an important distinction to be made here. In a nutshell, it's better than merely okay to buy a house on the "installment plan." Besides, that's the only way most folks will ever have one, and home ownership has lots of advantages, financial and otherwise.

Why is buying a house "on time" different from buying a car or refrigerator or clothing "on time"? Simple. Look at what happens to the value of a new car the minute you drive it off the lot. The value plummets, doesn't it? Ask any car dealer. The moment you sign the papers for a new buggy, it becomes used merchandise. It can look and perform as good as new, but you can't get a new-car price for it again even if you've driven it only five miles.

But did you ever hear of a "used house" for sale? I didn't. "Used houses" often sell for *more* than the original purchase price, putting them in an entirely different category from "used" anything else. This means that the balance remaining on the mortgage on your house isn't like any other debt. One way of looking at it is that it isn't a debt at all. It's just a convenient "swap" arrangement by which you persuade the bank to give your money to the seller of the house ahead of time so he will let you borrow it for a dwelling place, a month at a time. If ever you get tired of the arrangement, you can sell your right to live in the house to someone else, pay off the mortgage with the money, and be out of it.

Other things you've bought "on time" aren't worth what you still owe on them, but your house is probably worth considerably more than the mortgage outstanding on it. In other words, at any time you could put the house on the market and let it pay off its own mortgage. Try that with the eating-out tab you put on your credit card. Or the school supplies you charged for the kids. See the difference?

Yes, I know that some folks aren't in a position to buy a house—maybe they don't have anything for a down payment yet because they haven't gotten into God's GUSTO Master Plan for their finances. Some others are in jobs that move them every two weeks, from a view that encompasses the grass skirts of Tahiti to one frosted over by snowdrifts in Antarctica. In a situation like that, there just isn't time to close a house-buying deal fast enough to pay the movers before hammering a new FOR SALE sign in the front yard.

But if you *can* buy a house when the price is right, go for it. Home ownership seems to be the best deal on the block. Some young folks I know, for instance, bought a first home that looked like a dog but just needed a little tender loving care in the form of hard work, paint, curtains, repairs, and a little grass seed to turn it into a cozy cottage they could sell for a tidy profit and move on to another one. More power to folks who are jack-of-all-trades enough to go that route. It's a good way to get ahead.

Or maybe you're someone already in the process of buying a home but the payments are eating you alive because you made the leap when interest rates on mortgage loans were a frog-strangling 18 percent. That can choke you to death. A little arithmetic will tell you that the monthly payment on a $60,000, thirty-year loan at 18 percent interest is a whopping $904! At 13 percent, the payment on the same loan would be $664, a difference of $240— more than enough to pay your utilities, eh? In today's wildly fluctuating money market, it might be well worth a little shopping around to see if you can better your situation. You don't have to be stuck with a bad deal for life. Get a lower rate whenever the getting's good.

Don't forget to figure the up-front costs of paying off an old mortgage and getting a new one. Your friendly banker—why shouldn't he be friendly? After all, you're his meal ticket—will be able to help you figure out what's best in your case. And even a hostile banker can give you figures you can bank on.

Or maybe your bottom line says you've bit off more than you can chew—like a ten-room mansion when what you *really* need is a cozy clapboard cottage for two with

247

enough leftover money in the bank to take a springtime trip to the Holy Land. If that's what you *really* need, go for it. Some of your friends may not think it's a wise move, but they can't give you peace of mind.

Ask the Lord to help you unload the albatross. Generally, the way He works such things out is that the house that's too much for you is exactly the right answer to someone else's prayers. With the equity money in your pocket and peace of mind in your heart, you are free to move into something that better matches your means and needs. The Joneses could care less whether you keep up with them or not. There's no reason *ever* to ask yourself, *But what will the neighbors think?* They may not even *be* thinking—they're probably watching TV. Besides, who cares what the neighbors think? They might even be waiting for you to set a sensible example *they* can follow.

Along those lines, I heard about a couple of King's kids who were struggling to get completely out of debt. Being dead serious about it, they wrote down all their expenditures for a couple of months—just as you're doing—took an honest look at their monthly outgo, and decided their house payment was the thing that was eating them alive. I don't know if they swallowed their pride or took it to the pawnshop, but they got rid of it, listed their house for sale, and went shopping for an inexpensive trailer to call home. The last I heard, their debts were wiped out, there was money in the bank, and when the Lord gave them a chance to go on a witnessing mission for Him in the Hawaiian islands, they took Him up on it.

"Oh, but my husband would never agree to selling the house!" someone's saying. Are you sure? I mean, have you ever asked him? Could be that there's something he'd rather do every weekend in the summer than ride the mowing machine all over those four acres of green stuff.

There are plenty of housing options around these days. Don't be afraid to explore them.

Eating Better—for Less

The same God who is saying to His people these days, *Put your house in order. Get out of debt. The borrower is slave to the lender,* is also saying, *Rebuild My temple— change your eating habits.* And He gives some very positive suggestions for how to start changing them. Hear this, from *The Living Bible:* "Why spend your money on foodstuffs that don't give you strength? Why pay for groceries that don't do you any good?" (Isaiah 55:2).

Pretty plain, eh? Sounds as if God—*and* Daniel (*see* Daniel 1)—knew something about vitamins, minerals, nutrition, and all that before the health-food bright boys "discovered" them. A few years ago, when the Lord directed me to get busy and write the book that turned out to be *How to Flip Your Flab—Forever,* my research showed me a lot of things of which I had been ignorant until then. It was just in time, too. I could have perished from lack of knowledge of these things.

Once I had the information I needed, I put it into practice, lost thirty-four pounds of dead weight, changed my blood pressure to 115/90—just like a teenager—got rid of my hypoglycemic sugar depression and heart attacks and started feeling—at age seventy-seven—as spry as a spring chicken. And there was another real fringe benefit with particular relevance to this book: as my body grew leaner, my wallet grew fatter. The bottom line: real food, good-for-you food, costs less than dead food that speeds you to the cemetery.

Most Americans don't know the difference. They waddle around undernourished, overfattened on devitalized, factory-produced, chemicalized food loaded with poisonous residues from additives and pesticides that can only result in bad health.

"So now you're pushing that health-food kick on us!" someone shrieks. "Without even bothering to make it subliminal!"

Not guilty. I'm simply telling you how my body benefitted when I changed my fuel supply from dead food to live food—when I started eating whole grains instead of yukky bleached ones—when I headed for broiled fish and baked chicken instead of the beefeater's paradise—when I began to regard vegetables as something more than mere plate decorations.

If you'd like to start on your own program of "temple repair" before it's too late, send a stamped, self-addressed envelope to the King's Kids' Korner, Box 8655, Baltimore, MD 21240, and ask for our free King's Kids' Recipe Sheet. Meanwhile, if you're seriously interested in getting better instead of merely getting older, start getting in gear with this simple five-step program:

1. Take an inventory of the food items in your cupboards, pantry, and refrigerator.

2. Eliminate all "white" items—sugar, salt, white flour, and all sugar and caffeine-laden cola drinks from your intake.

3. Begin to eat *real food*—whole wheat, real oats, brown rice, millet, and other whole grains and items listed on the freebie King's Kids' Recipe Sheet mentioned above.

4. Refuse to read, listen to, or fall for any advertising of the food pushers.

5. Get rid of all addictive food items you're sure you "can't live without." Any sign of compulsion is a sure sign they're bad for you.

With that beginning, you're on your way out of America's 80 million chronically ill—which automatically means that from now on you'll be spending less money in the medical department.

A local banking publication has some further advice for homemakers on saving shekels in the grocery department. One issue of *Your Money and How to Make the Most of It,* put out by the First National Bank of Maryland, has an article entitled, "How to Grocery Shop for Free a Few Weeks Every Year." Sounds so simple, even I could do it. Here's the scoop in their own words:

> Couponing and refunding have become a tax-free, moneysaving hobby for many Americans today. Seventy-six percent of all U.S. households are using coupons at least on a limited basis and saving up to 50% on their weekly grocery bills.
>
> Coupons are found in newspapers, magazines, specially marked packages and in home mailers. The Wednesday and Thursday editions of your local newspaper are your best bet for finding the bulk of local store offers. These coupons are good for a limited time only.
>
> To become a successful "couponer," your first step is to organize and file any coupons you have found in magazines, on specially marked packages, in the Sunday newspaper supplement or received through the mail. You then need to go over your

251

newspaper ads for coupons on items you need or normally purchase. To make a "double play" with your coupons, you need to match a manufacturer's coupon with a retailer's coupon. Another moneysaver is to shop at your local store on "double coupon days," and you'll double your savings. A secret, though, is to buy only the items you normally buy and not to drive miles to save a few pennies.

The products that offer the greatest savings are household goods, cleaning aids, health and beauty aids and processed foods. Meats and produce are seldom couponed. A hint for couponers is to stock up on non-perishable items because it's unlikely the item will be couponed again for at least six weeks. And, remember, the stores where you shop are benefitting too (they receive an average of 7 cents per coupon for handling), so don't be embarrassed when you approach the check-out counter.

For the more dedicated couponer who is willing to work harder to make money, refunding can become a very profitable hobby.

Refunding requires you to buy one or more of a specific product, send to the manufacturer the proof of purchase and wait for your check or premium to arrive in the mail (usually six to eight weeks). Refunding can involve saving coupons for items you don't use, filing them in an organized manner to save time and swapping them for coupons on products you can use.

Couponers and refunders are discovering that they are ending up with more coupons than they can use. To maximize their savings, they are banding together to swap coupons, [refund] forms and qualifiers.

Many more sophisticated refunders are organizing swap meets both nationally and locally, sending out newsletters and bulletins and even developing "round robins" where coupons are exchanged through the mail. Refunding has become a way of getting paid for shopping.

People all over are making a game of couponing and refunding. It has become a challenge and a hobby that can be enjoyed while watching TV, reading the newspaper or paging through a magazine. If you are committed to this hobby, it's one which will cut your expenditures drastically. In fact, you may actually save enough to shop a few weeks of the year for free.

Sound farfetched? Not at all. I've talked to some women who have gotten hooked, and they say that couponing and refunding really works to save them significant amounts of money every week, money they can put in their savings accounts or use to support some facet of God's work in the world today. I've heard of one woman who takes coupons for products she doesn't use and lays them on top of the corresponding merchandise in the grocery store so that the next shopper to come along can profit from her labors. Now, when someone else takes the hint and begins to leave coupons *she* can use, the always-dependable principle of sowing and reaping will have come full circle to benefit everybody.

Don't forget that, like almost anything else, coupon swapping can become an unthreatening way to become acquainted with persons who need to hear about the Lord of your life so they can become King's kids too.

Fasting

Another little recognized method of saving money in the food department is one recommended by Jesus in Matthew 6:16–18. You didn't know that Jesus was into showing you how to save money in the food department? As I read what the *Manufacturer's Handbook* has to say about fasting, I understand it this way:

> Fast as a regular part of your normal life-style, enabling your heavenly Father to reward you abundantly. Otherwise, if your fast is based on religious doctrines, you will look like a picklepuss in order to impress others with your holier-than-thou attitude. If you do it that way, they'll be impressed, all right, but that's the only reward you'll ever get.

Fasting the Bible way has lots of built-in benefits. Please note that Jesus didn't say, *"If* you fast," but *"When* you fast," assuming that fasting would be a normal part of our everyday life and affairs on a regularly scheduled basis. The details, He left up to us.

Why does God encourage fasting as a normal procedure for King's kids? I can think of many sound and valid reasons.

In the first place, the bodily organs of digestion need frequent rests, as do other members of the body. Fasting on a regular basis enables the inner garbage-disposal system to clean out all the leftovers and get ready for a new start.

Fasting from all food for a certain length of time places the body under a disciplined routine that shows it who's boss. Getting your body under control in this way provides a perfect opportunity for God to remove destructive habits—too much sugar consumption, nicotine addiction, and so on.

One of the areas in which Jesus came to set the captive free is all second-best habits, which include addictions to garbage and junk damaging to our body temples. (Read *How to Flip Your Flab—Forever* for how Jesus set me free from the bondage of overweight.)

Please realize that I'm not recommending fasting as a means of impressing God with our acts of holiness, nor am I talking about any legalistic refraining from food as an act of penance to earn God's favor. None of that silly business. What we're talking about is fasting the Bible way for fringe benefits in the belly and billfold departments.

I first got into fasting after reading that Moses, at age 120, was not old but merely "full of years." And he graduated to glory without having to get sick to do it. Since he was a keeper of the Jewish Law, he must have fasted regularly, I reasoned, and the results spoke for themselves. He was not weak in any part of his body, so he must have been doing something right. Was fasting a key to his well-being? "Could have been," I reasoned, as I read about his ministry that was tireless right up to the end.

If Moses can do it, so can I, I told myself. Before then, fasting had not been a part of my normal routine, and I had been unaware that Jesus not only recommended it but also took it for granted that King's kids would be fasting. "When you fast. . . ."

And so, not long ago, I began fasting one day a week

for a period of thirty-six hours at a stretch. From Monday evening until Wednesday morning, I took into my body only water, herbal teas, and some fruit juice—no sugar added, of course. Then I added a "power tea" formula which proved beneficial. (Send SASE for free details.)

The weekly fast did so much for me that I added a six-day fast once a quarter. After only a few months of following this routine, I'm seeing amazing results. Folks remark on how much younger I look, and I'm experiencing a renewal of energy and vitality in my entire body.

Before I became aware of the importance of taking good care of my physical temple, I was grossly overweight, had practically no hair, and needed strong corrective lenses full time. Now, ten years down the road from my picture on the back of *How to Be a Winner,* my hair's all there, with no sign of a hole in the middle. Weight is down to 180 pounds, which suits my six-foot, two-inch height. On top of all that, my eyes have been healed about 90 percent.

"Great! But how does that help you in the money department?" someone wants to know. Simple. When you aren't eating, you don't have to shell out any shekels for groceries. I don't know about fasting for growing youngsters—better check with your own physician about that—but I wouldn't be surprised to learn that fasting would be beneficial for them, too.

What happens when you fast? Just the thought of it makes your body protest, of course, because your body is so accustomed to telling *you* what to do that it doesn't quite know how to handle the thought of taking a subordinate position in the order-giving department, but it will learn.

You might begin by saying to it, "Stomach, *I'm* going to be the boss around here from now on. You can growl all you want to, but I'm not dumping anything except liquids down the chute for the next thirty-six hours, and that's final. So you might just as well shut up, get used to the idea, and prepare for a rest from your labors just as I'm giving my molars a rest from theirs.''

Remember, no legalistic, ''My willpower is stronger than yours, nyah, nyah, nyah.'' We're not trying to outperform anyone. We're simply embarking on a new lifestyle recommended by Jesus Himself, one that is guaranteed to end in great rewards both for our physical well-being and our pocketbooks.

I did a little speculative figuring one day and came to the conclusion that some families now living next door to poverty row could save enough from fasting one day a week that fifty or sixty years from now—if they invested the savings at compound interest—folks would be tipping their hats to them and addressing them as ''Mr. Rockefeller.''

The fasting routine works so well for me that I have to recommend it to you, even aside from the inevitable financial benefits. Do, of course, check it out with your local Dr. Sawbones first so you won't get me in any trouble with the medicos.

From following a fasting plan for myself—one day a week, one week each quarter—I can report not only a healthier bank account but the following benefits as well:

1. I feel absolutely no ill effects from abstaining from all food for one day each week, one week each quarter. Hunger pains go away after the third day, and I experience no weakness or loss of vitality.

2. My health is improving continually.

3. Joint stiffness, which I formerly experienced after driving six hundred miles in a day, has completely disappeared.

4. I have a strong sense of victory over my disciplined appetite for food not really needed by my body temple of the Holy Spirit, which formerly demanded—and received—more than its fair share of my attention.

5. I now talk to my stomach like this when it attempts to regain control of my life:

> Listen, belly, you can no longer dominate my attention, so you might just as well knock off that whining and groaning. You're going to get exactly what Jesus directs me to send your way and nothing more. I am now the head and not the tail. I'm the boss and you're my servant, as it is written, so stop bellyaching and tend to your digestive job and we'll all be a whole lot happier.

6. Remember, the *Manufacturer's Handbook* says that the glutton and the drunkard both end in poverty (Proverbs 23:20, 21). Fasting sets us free from both of these areas of failure as Jesus honors our attempts to ''clean up our acts'' and take better care of our temples of the Holy Spirit.

Utilities

Utilities can take a too hefty part of your budget before you realize what's happening. This expenditure, unlike some of the others, can trip you up because it doesn't *seem* to require a deliberate choice on your part. Recognizing that this category *does* involve deliberate choices is the first step toward knocking out some of the money leakage through this area of your spending.

Heating and Cooling

Look first at what it costs to heat and cool your house. "But I like to be warm in winter and cool in summer," someone whines. Sure you do. We can all understand that. But you might save a bundle if you'd keep warm by adding an extra layer of clothing to keep your body heat in. Sweaters and warm socks can be used for many years, and they're a whole lot cheaper than fuel oil, which is used up the first time out. As for keeping the house cool in summer, almost every household magazine—free, if you read them at the public library—has dozens of suggestions for cooling things down without expensive air conditioning. Attic fans can be a big help; so can keeping draperies closed on sunshiny days. People into the nostalgia kick might enjoy *not* turning on the air conditioning, simply because Grandpa never had such a luxury.

Telephone

How about the telephone? Are you shocked every month when that bill comes in? First you blame your teenagers and storm about their extravagance. Then you realize they don't *know* anyone to call in Hot Springs, and the fault is all yours. Try persuading yourself that Great Aunt Tillie out in Timbuktu might enjoy a letter that costs twenty cents to mail even more than a long-distance call that leads you to bankruptcy fast. The letter she can enjoy more than once. With a phone call, once you hang up, that's it. I started on a real program of economy in the telephone line when I realized how much time I was spending on it, just talking to other Christians and praising the Lord with them. Nothing wrong with what we were doing—it was good. But I could have praised the Lord just as well with folks who weren't a thousand miles away.

My strategy about the telephone these days is to practice some simple discipline. At the start of a phone call, before I ever dial the number, I make a note of the points I need to cover. Then I check my watch for the time, intending to wind the whole thing up in five minutes if I can. When five minutes have elapsed, I look at my list to see how much more has to be said on the subjects under discussion. It took a lot of practice for me to develop this time-sense awareness, but I'm benefitting in many ways. Telephone talk time has been cut to less than half, and nothing essential has been left out. A little planning worked wonders. I haven't reached perfection in this area, but with God's help I've made progress. What I have done, you can do too.

What About WOLO and KUWJ?

WOLO and KUWJ (We Only Live Once, and Keeping Up With the Joneses) are two bad birds that ought to head fast for extinction once they've been identified. You know you could cut *way* down on these two if you really tried. In fact, with a little concerted effort, you could clobber them both completely out of the picture for the next year or so if you made getting out of debt a top priority, with God's help, before you ever succumbed to the WOLO or KUWJ urge again.

Why not apply the method recommended by the *Manufacturer's Handbook* here? Instead of beating yourself because you've sinned so grandly in this area of your money management, confess to God that you've really missed the mark of His high calling, receive His forgiveness, and ask Him to set you on a new road in all your money matters. Then praise the Lord that you've found a place to get so many dollars every month to put into your get-out-of-debt fund. The worse you've fallen short by overspending in the past, the better off you're going to be in the future. See how that works? When your heart is right toward Him, He takes everything bad and turns it into something wonderful.

Debt Reduction

Now look at your DEBT REDUCTION category. That's like another horror movie, isn't it? All that money owed because you bought things you couldn't really afford at the time. Mercy! And, hallelujah, it's even worse than it looks! Have you noticed the fine print on those monthly statements that come to drain away hundreds of dollars a month? Every one of the monthly statements peeking out at you from those window envelopes is required by law to tell you how much you're paying for the privilege of instant credit. The present rate of interest and additional ''carrying charges'' on these things is 18 percent—sometimes even up to 25 percent—of the original cost of the item. That means that instead of getting items on sale for cash—where you might have saved a bundle—it's as if you bought them at an extra 25 percent markup!

Makes you wonder why you bother to waste time reading the ads and shopping the sales if you're going to wipe out all the advantage with interest charges, doesn't it?

This is as good a place as any to hammer home the truth that *any time you buy something on a ''buy now, pay later'' plan, you're borrowing money to make the pur-*

chase. Sometimes that thought will help you talk yourself out of it. As a matter of fact, *when you're in debt, any purchase you make is being made with borrowed money*— even if you have the cash in your pocket for it—because that's cash that's already owed somewhere else.

Credit buying (we ought to call it *debt* buying and steer clear) always reminds me of what my dad said when I was still a kid in knee pants. He told me there was a foolproof way to avoid money worries all my life.

"What's that?" I asked him, always curious to learn something new.

"Easy, son," he said. "Just never buy anything until you can pay cash for it." So simple, but it works.

When you look at the list of debts you owe for things you've purchased that you could have lived without—in fact, some of them have already been given to the Salvation Army or relegated to the attic before you finish paying for them—doesn't it make you wish someone had told *you* that?

It does? Well, someone has told you now, so you can begin today to apply that advice to all of the *rest* of your financial life. From now on, when faced with the temptation to buy something you can't pay for (that includes *everything* while you're still in debt, remember, because the money in your pocket and bank account is already spoken for), you'd do well to borrow a few questions from Alcoholics Anonymous and ask yourself, *Do I really need it, or with God's help can I live without it one day at a time?*

That question, honestly answered, can save you a lot of grief in the pocketbook department just as it can in the booze department.

Make up your mind right now to make no more purchases without submitting the question to a family conference. Don't go by majority vote here. It's unanimity or nothing. In other words, if even *one* member of the family unit in his/her right mind thinks you can live without whatever it is, live without it. I can practically guarantee that no one will starve, no one will go naked, if all are working together toward turning that big deficit into a plus figure. And you can practically guarantee that when you've reached the goal—whew!—the whole tribe will have a big reward for their persistence in helping each other stick to it.

Can you even imagine what it will be like to be out of debt for the first time in your life? With money set aside on a regular basis for God's work? With regular additions to a savings account for a rainy day—or for the kids' college education—or to pay cash for a new car when the old one wears out—or for that long-planned trip to help your church build a mission church in Mexico for God's glory? With money enough to pay all your bills every month without having to see those awful letters that say, "This is your final notice. If payment isn't received by such and such a date, your account will be forwarded to our attorneys for collection"?

Sounds like glory this side of heaven, doesn't it?

Credit Cards for King's Kids?
How to Make Money on Credit Cards

Somebody's sniffing over in a corner. Do I detect real tears? What's the matter, lady?

"You mean I have to carry cash all the time instead of that handy little piece of plastic?"

No, I didn't mean that. I didn't even *say* that, did I? Don't misquote me.

As a matter of fact, that little piece of plastic can be

very useful—*if* you can be trusted to use it in the right way. It can actually help you *save* money! And even *make* money for you if you're game to try it and disciplined enough to be trusted. Unbelievable? Just listen.

Suppose, for the sake of illustration, that there is a supermarket or discount store near you with good quality products at competitive prices. And suppose they will let you pay for their merchandise with a credit card at the same price you would have to pay if you were using cash. Feel free to use your credit card every time you shop there—just be certain to pay off the whole amount due on the monthly statement on or before the due date so you will incur no interest charges on the outstanding balance.

"But how does that save me money?" someone's sputtering.

Ever hear of checking accounts that earn interest? Some banks have them these days. Instead of forking over cash—or a check—every time you go to the grocery store next month, you'd be leaving your money in the bank, working for you, earning interest, while you put the grocery bill on your credit card.

Billing cycles are different for different people and different credit-card institutions, but it's possible to buy groceries on a credit card for the whole month of June, have the charges show up on your July statement, with payment due early in August. Sometimes the destination will be in your own town and you can even save twenty cents postage by dropping the check off when you're conveniently nearby on another errand.

Result? Free use of someone else's money for a period ranging from a minimum of one month to a maximum of two, an average of a whole month and a half. What interest are you earning on your bank deposits? That's how much you've *made* by making purchases on credit. Or, if you can work out the timing just right——so the bill can be paid out of a just-received paycheck——you won't need to keep the money in the bank earning a small amount of interest during that period. You can invest it in the money market for a higher rate——or, use it to pay off some of your higher-interest indebtedness.

A woman I know subtracts all her charge-account and credit-card purchases from her checkbook balance as she goes, just as if she'd written a check, so she can't be fooled into thinking she has more money uncommitted than she does. I haven't tried that, but it *sounds* foolproof. Keep your credit cards in your checkbook and give it a try. At worst, you'll still get some good practice in subtraction.

Another possible angle here: Do you ever offer to buy groceries or other items for your neighbors when you go shopping for yourself? If you have time to do it, try it. They might want to pay you something for your trouble——and they'll pay you cash on delivery for their groceries. You can put their purchases on your credit card and put their money in your bank account to be earning interest until it's needed——maybe two months down the road, to pay the credit-card folks. See how that works?

Still more savings come through using a credit card wisely, in this no-interest way, because the free credit enables you to take advantage of real bargains for something you really need in the grocery department, stocking up on specials for your freezer. Further, since most banks charge for checks, and there is often a service charge for every check cleared through your account, you'll save money by writing one grocery check a month instead of one every time you visit the store. Never, never sneeze at savings or interest earnings, however small.

But if you honestly know you can't be trusted to use a credit card only when it is to your distinct advantage, scissor all of them to pieces no later than today. And never let anyone "give" you another one.

Recycling

Kids today who start picking up the aluminum drink cans and refundable bottles with which our roadsides and parks seem to stay littered can put their recycling earnings into interest-earning savings accounts that turn into very respectable beginnings for college-education funds. If kids can do it, so can you. Just keep a strong plastic bag in the trunk of your car, and whenever you see a piece of valuable litter in the shopping-center parking lot, pick it up and throw it in. You'll be keeping your city clean, exercising your midriff, and little by little building for the future.

The Shirt on Your Back

How can you save on clothing? Many ways! There's no law that says you *have* to wear the latest styles, is there? That you *can't* learn to sew for yourself if you have the time? And have you ever tried that secondhand clothing shop in your town? The ladies tell me real haute couture bargains are to be had there. And did someone say "Dye"? Right on! A faded, but otherwise sound old dress dumped in the washing machine with a carefully dissolved dollar box of fabric dye becomes an in-vogue sensation with no one the wiser unless m'lady chooses to brag about her bargain.

How about the garage sales and yard sales? Some young marrieds of my acquaintance furnished their nursery for a song with perfectly good pieces that someone no longer needed. Then, for fifteen dollars, they bought a grab bag containing a two-year supply of originally expensive toddler clothes in excellent condition.

A fresh coat of paint on the furniture, a trip through the washing machine for the clothes, and baby never knew the difference. Sure, you do have to know your merchandise to shop the flea markets—but show me a woman who doesn't.

No, I haven't tried these things for myself, but the ladies have told me about them. Sounds like they're finding treasures in trash all over the place. And somehow, amid the financial "tough times," there's victory instead of shame connected with doing these things to save money for more important things.

In some areas young folks are pooling their "atticables" to hold neighborhoodwide yard sales where they convert castoffs into cash. Newspaper ads are full of announcements, and by dawn's early light on Saturday morning, cars are lined up for blocks to get first choice of someone's trash that is someone else's treasure. Things that have outlived their usefulness for one family meet the needs of another. Other items never used, but accumulated over the years by unsuspecting shoppers who fell for the philosophy of "Cheaper by the Dozen" and "Oh! Such a Bargain!" are the answer to someone's prayer.

CBDs and OSABs are space robbers in many homes. Do you have a bundle of them? Maybe they can turn into working capital for you, too—besides serving as an example to pass up the next temptation toward impulse buying.

Lessons From the Olden Days

The next time you visit an old-timey country farmhouse, reinforce what you've learned above with a look around the premises. Notice the abundant shortage of closet space? Those houses were built without big storage areas for the simple reason that none were needed. Folks in those days used what they had, and never dreamed of squirreling away wardrobes full of little-used clothing when it could benefit someone else. Instead, they gave it away.

Furthermore, when a garment was useful to them, they wore it until they wore it out—and then made quilts or rugs out of the pieces that couldn't be fashioned into a new garment. I mean, when you had to grow the cotton or shear the sheep before you could have something to wear, you didn't lightly trade it in for a new model of anything. We could learn a lot from their ways.

True, these people were never subjected to the "Just one more buck a month" blandishments of the TV hucksters. But you don't have to be either. There's a switch or button on the front of most TV sets I've seen. One setting is labeled OFF. Everyone ought to try it sometime.

Watch Out for TV Traps!

And while we're on the subject of TV promotional tactics, do you already know to watch out for the sneaky, illegal, and highly profitable exploitation of your personal rights known as subliminal advertising?

You never heard of it? Could be, since it does its dirty work without a label. But you've undoubtedly experienced it. Read on. Maybe you'll recognize yourself in some of what follows.

Have you ever, while watching TV, experienced an unnatural craving for something completely unrelated to the content of the program being watched? Let's say you're totally engrossed in watching your favorite soap opera, "So You Failed as a Brain Surgeon." There's a break for a message from your sponsor. In the too-loud commercial, someone's chipper old grandma is being quizzed on her knowledge of automatic transmissions.

Suddenly, without warning, an overpowering urge for a jugful of that exciting new drink Swill-Slop—"not a gripe in a gutful"—hits you amidships. At once you remember, with a sinking feeling of utter doom that rivals the feelings of the Titanic's passengers, that you guzzled the last beakerful just last night and forgot to replenish your supply. Woe is me! Your insides quiver, sweat beads form on your upper lip, your palms begin to drip, your eyeballs turn glassy.

Your nice, calm, peaceful evening in front of the boob tube is scuttled. What on earth has happened? There's a possible explanation.

Maybe you have been worked on by the boys at the studio who have simply turned on their little Subliminal Fun Machine, which has superimposed a second program on top of Granny's antics, which had you absorbed to your eyeballs. The second program didn't show up on the screen in visible form. It came in very short bursts of brief duration—too fast for your eyeballs to register but slow enough for your inner spirit to pick it up and respond. Over and over, in monotonous regularity, you have been drinking in the message "Drink Swill-Slop . . . Drink Swill-Slop . . . Drink Swill-Slop. . . ."

On and on it goes, until you receive it and are thoroughly motivated to do what the message commands. You have no choice. You drag yourself out of your comfortable easy chair, fight your way through the dark and stormy night to the car, and put the pedal to the metal to get to the all-night joint and stock up. The pop-top is off the first can before you can put your change in your pocket. Glug, glug, glug. On the way home your windshield wipers give up, and except for the grace of God, you'd never have found your own driveway in that downpour.

269

That's subliminal advertising for you. Recognize any symptoms?

Sneaky? Dishonest? Conniving? Immoral? Dirty-bird tactics? Sure. It's all of that—and more. Straight from the pit of you-know-where.

Some people have even wondered if this subliminal advertising will be part of the end-times tactics of the beast, whose mark he says you must wear in order to function as a buyer or seller in this world (Revelation 13:17). Maybe even tomorrow, as you tune in to the same time, same channel, tomorrow's episode of your favorite soap, "Dirtie Gertie at the Dishpan," you will receive in your inner being an overwhelming, irresistible compulsion to have tattooed on your chest, arms, feet, and forehead a special code number—666.

Is that how it will work? Who knows? Seems that prudent King's kids ought to be watching out for influential, invisible tricks, though, don't you think?

Medical Expenses

Let's turn to your medical expenses next. After that nocturnal adventure to buy Swill-Slop, you've probably come down with walking pneumonia, at least. And already your medical expenses are higher than you think they should be, right? Well, you'll be seeing automatic reductions once you really get started on the food plan God has designed for the human mechanism and get off modern man's perversions of it. Meanwhile, while the old temple is getting renovated, if you still need medicines or drugs, ask your doctor and druggist about generic brands instead of the fancy nationally advertised variety. They're often made by the same manufacturer and accomplish exactly the same purpose. The only difference is that they cost a whole lot less. The cheapest aspirin on the shelf contains the same active ingredients as the most expensive brand.

Once you start paying attention to things like this, all your tension headaches that have been caused by worrying how you'll ever make ends meet will begin to take a powder. And when you really get into studying the *Manufacturer's Handbook* about prosperity, you'll find it's full of "recipes" for perfect health. And when you start to put them into practice, your medical expenses will be on their way to a flat zero. The same God who has made provision for your prosperity has made more than ample provision for your perfect health (3 John 2).

To learn more about all that, read my *How to Live Like a King's Kid* to get you started. And consult *Bible Answers for King's Kids in Training* for the location of specific case histories of the healing of ailments we can live better without.

Reducing Other Expenses

Transportation to and from the job eating you up? Put a share-the-ride offer on the office bulletin board. Or ride your bicycle to work. Or succumb to a car pool or a more fuel efficient car the next time you have to trade.

Taxes *terrible?* Go to the public library and read all you can on legal tax-avoidance strategies. As you increase your giving to God, your taxes will show the benefits.

Public libraries and newsstands are full of books and magazines with more suggestions. The thing to know is that you *can* cut expenditures, freeing more money to pay off all your bills sooner than you dreamed possible, so you can get on with the program of living as a financially victorious person—even in today's economy.

-15-
WHAT ABOUT SAVINGS AND INVESTMENTS FOR KING'S KIDS?

"Why put so much emphasis on saving money?" someone asks. "Isn't that showing a lack of faith that God shall supply all your needs out of His riches in glory?" (*See* Philippians 4:19.)

Nope. Saving just happens to be one of the many ways He uses to supply my needs and the needs of others with whom I come in contact.

With today's tax rates, Benjamin Franklin's old adage "A penny saved is a penny earned" applies better than ever. Actually, today a penny saved is more like *two* pennies earned, because the saved penny is tax free. That soft-drink bottle someone else tossed away in the parking lot is worth a tax-free dime—clear profit—in your pocket if you turn it in. *Earn* a dime, on the other hand, and you have to give half of it back to Uncle Sam along with a mountain of paperwork. And think of the fringe benefits of stooping to reclaim someone else's throwaway—the bending exercise will help your waistline. Saving something wherever you can is almost invariably a good idea.

Another member of the Hill family, a man widely acclaimed as the greatest financial wizard of all time, James J. Hill, who single-handedly built the great Northern Pacific Railroad without a penny of government funds, was asked one day, "How do you go about making large sums of money?" His answer came forth as a simple four-part program:

1. Begin. Start. Do it now!

2. Begin saving a specific sum of money regularly.

3. Do it every month. Let nothing interfere.

4. Make that money work for you.

"But why put so much emphasis on saving money?" someone asks. "Isn't that showing a lack of faith? Aren't we supposed to turn it all over to Jesus and trust Him for our daily bread?"

Here again, I have no argument with the questioners. I am simply explaining how it works best for me.

Since I met Jesus back in 1954 and turned over to Him the management of my life, with the request that He help Himself to me, there has always been money in my bank account to pay my own way wherever He chose to send me.

I have to give the credit for this to my dad, who taught me to save something out of every paycheck, back when I was just a kid. The habit became the practice of a lifetime and didn't go away when I became a King's kid. In fact, the King seemed to indicate that I was to keep some of what He had entrusted to me in "liquid" form where He could call on it for special uses at a moment's notice whenever He chose.

Take, for instance, the letter that came from a mission station in Madrid, Spain, pleading with me to "come to

273

this world of complete darkness and bring the light of the glorious Gospel to these desperate people.'' The folks over there had ''no funds for paying my way,'' as they put it. But I didn't have to worry about that angle, because the money was right there in God's bank account in my name. I could afford to go and give those people the message of the Gospel without worrying about where the plane fare was coming from. But did He want me to go? I asked the Head Man: ''Lord, what do You think about such a trip?''

You go and I'll provide, He seemed to be saying. Do I hear God speak in an audible voice? Not yet, I haven't, but I'm not ruling out the possibility. Meanwhile, that still, small nudging down deep inside, where my gizzard would be if I had one, is all the assurance I need to go into action. Provided, of course, that the voiceless Voice tells me something completely in line with the Scriptures. On that occasion, ''Go ye into all the world, and preach the gospel to every creature'' (Mark 16:15) was the verse that confirmed God's instructions to me.

Now a trip of that kind required some long-range planning, especially since I was at the time president of a group of companies which required my attention. But when God is in charge, things always fall into place without strain or pain, so when an opening came several months later for me to get away for a couple of weeks, I began to make arrangements to go—plane reservations, updating my passport, getting my visa, and taking care of similar necessary details for that long and expensive trip.

When everything was in order for the trip and all systems were go, as we say, I got the news: The missionary who had invited me was no longer in the area. The folks who had replaced him knew nothing of me and my proposed trip, but since the Lord had given me clearance to go, that was not my problem, and I told Him so.

''Lord, You've gotten me into this apparent mess, so

274

it's up to You to do something about it." As far as I was concerned, that settled it. My rule of procedure in such cases is to start out, refusing to doubt, and watch the Lord set in and redeem the whole mess. So I continued according to plan.

The "mission station" turned out to be a tiny cottage overflowing with a sizable family and absolutely no income except when the folks back home remembered to send something. Talk about a "faith walk"! Those folks were living it every moment of every day. If the back-home church forgot to "send something," there was no food on the table.

This was very scary to me at first, since my own faith had never before been exposed to this kind of on-the-job training. Sure, I had given to the "work of missions" in my church back home, but it had never occurred to me that the folks on the other end were literally destitute if my faith didn't produce works.

Only eternity can ever tell the outcome of a missionary trip like that in terms of lives being changed. But the Lord did let me see a few cases of "instant fruit"—like the giant of a marine sergeant who gave his life to Jesus at the Full Gospel Business Men's Fellowship International meeting at the army base outside Madrid when we "just happened" to get there too early for the meeting but just in time to bump into that desperate soldier who was on his way to blow his brains out, as he told us later.

And why were we too early for the meeting? Because the missionary had chosen to travel the back country roads out to the army base since all the main highways were blocked by police looking for the assassins who had shot an army general on the highway the previous night. Things "just happened" to work out that way so a lone serviceman could get ushered into the Kingdom.

Then there was the Glory Group of Spirit-filled Salvation

Army workers in downtown Madrid—the only charismatic group in town. Several unsuspecting persons wandered into their meetings and gave their hearts to Jesus.

Speaking through an interpreter has never been my favorite means of proclaiming the Gospel, but on that trip God gave me an interpreter so full of the Spirit and the joy of the Lord that it was difficult at times to tell which of us was speaking, and in which language. He called me Moses, and I called him Aaron, but we got along together much better than those two ever did.

The highlight of the trip came the last Sunday morning at breakfast. We all held hands around the table, the mission family and I, praising God for His abundance and grace. After the Amen, I looked forward to a good breakfast in preparation for the trip to the airport and heading home.

In the middle of the table was a small box of dry cereal, which I was invited to share. Finding the carton closer to empty than full, I declined my share, deciding I'd wait for the ham and eggs. I was sure they would put in an appearance shortly.

But they didn't. Apparently there was nothing in the house to eat except that tiny bit of dry cereal to be divided among several hungry adults and a whole houseful of starving kids. To me, it looked worse than when Jesus faced the hungry multitudes with only a kid's lunch box of bread and fish. At first, I thought God would come on the scene and command every flake of cereal to turn into a bowlful, but it didn't happen. *Something did, however.* Something better—for them *and* for me.

As we got ready to leave for the airport, our stomachs growling at each other, the missionary passed an envelope to me, saying, ''The folks took up a love offering to help defray your expenses for this trip, Brother Hill.''

Having already learned never to deprive others of the

blessings of giving, I accepted the envelope in the name of Jesus, as I usually do. And then the nudging from the Lord came deep inside as I was hoping it would: *Give the offering to the missionary.* So I did. The family wrote me later that the envelope contained "abundantly above all they could ask or even hope."

What about me and my hefty expenses for the journey? I wasn't left out in the cold. No siree. When I got back to the office, waiting on my desk was the largest contract the company had ever received. And it turned out to be the most profitable. I was able to replenish my savings account so it would be ready the next time the Lord wanted to send me somewhere as His ambassador.

Over the years, I have had the opportunity to minister in many countries on three continents, as well as in "the islands of the sea," without charging anyone for it. Because of that "sinful" bank account, I have been available for preaching and teaching God's Word in the uttermost parts of the earth. I have been able to share with small groups as well as large ones without partiality, all because of that early training to save something out of every paycheck.

But should a King's kid ever *invest* money in things on earth?

Some people answer that question with a sanctimonious *no,* self-righteously looking down their shiny noses and saying they are laying up treasure for themselves in heaven, not on earth, thank you. But those who have read what God has to say about these things in Matthew 25:14–30 have a different answer. Some of us are in a position to support missionaries, to finance the giving of Bibles, to feed the poor, and to participate in other good works God has prepared for us to walk in (Ephesians 2:10) on our way to heaven.

You've read Matthew's account and know how it goes. A man went away on a long trip, having entrusted certain sums of money to his servants to take care of while he was away. When he came home, two of the servants returned his money with interest and earned his commendation. The third, who had buried the money instead of investing it, had no profit to offer his master, only the original grubby coin which he had to dig up out of the backyard.

Do you remember *his* reward? His master called him the equivalent of "good for nothing" and had him thrown out of the house.

You may insist on being too good to invest if you choose, but God's Word strongly recommends it. And I've tried it and found it pays off, helping to bring me into the kind of prosperity God wants for me so I can be free to do His work.

"But Hill," I hear many wailing along about now, "all you ever know about is success in your investments. What about us poor slobs who always find ourselves buying high and selling low? You just don't understand what it feels like to be a big-time loser."

I don't? That's not the way I heard it. The way I heard it was that yes, I too have had my share of goofs, though not too often, and not on a really large scale when I'm being sure to listen for the guidance of the Holy Spirit before I do anything.

I had a hard time getting started in investing money, because I was a product of the money training of my frugal and overly cautious New England dad, who warned me against "four-flushers, carpetbaggers, and stock salesmen out to sell you the Brooklyn Bridge."

When I looked at him as if I didn't know what he was talking about, he spelled it out a little more clearly.

"Never trust your hard-earned money to strangers," was the way he summed it up. "And never put your money into gold mines, oil wells, or other such fly-by-night schemes which promise a fortune but lead fast to poverty.''

It was good advice, and it kept me out of a lot of trouble I might otherwise have experienced. But it also put me in a position of sometimes settling for second best. Dad found himself in the same boat from time to time.

One day when I was about five years old, a shiny black buggy drawn by a high-spirited horse drove into our backyard in the hills of Connecticut where I grew up.

''Howdy, mister,'' shouted the stranger from his seat in that impressive rig. ''Can I talk to you for a few minutes?''

''What's on your mind, neighbor?'' Dad responded, leaning his hoe against the side of the house while my eyes nearly popped out of my head looking over the man's fancy transportation.

Waving a sheaf of important-looking papers, the stranger announced, ''I have here the means of your making a fortune in the oil business. These are shares in a brand-new oil-production company, and they are yours for only five dollars a share. It's a real steal.''

That did it. The cordiality vanished from Dad's face, and in no uncertain terms he ordered the stranger off his property.

''And don't ever come back!'' he yelled after the until-then jovial stranger. ''I'm not interested in supporting you flimflammers who are out to steal the bread off the tables of widows, orphans, and honest, hardworking folks like us. Now git.''

The stranger's face paled, his voice failed him, and he *got*. A dexterous flick of the whip sent the horse into a galloping retreat from our yard.

Did my dad lose any money that day? Not a cent. By refusing the stranger's offer, did he miss the opportunity to make a bundle that could have sent a lot of young folks to Bible school? You decide by looking at the present-day value of an original share of the oil-company stock he turned down.

Somewhere, there is the right balance between the extreme caution programmed into me in my early years and the prudence that can take a good thing and make it better. I've found that the best way to go is to mix three ingredients:

1. the educated sense of market research

2. the revelation sense of words of wisdom and knowledge from God

3. a superhefty dose of prayer to get the leading of the Holy Spirit

Even then, I've missed it sometimes. Like the day a salesman came into my office selling a new machine for making dry copies of documents on ordinary bond paper. At the time, standard office copiers used all kinds of gloppy chemicals in messy solutions and produced copies of very poor quality. I listened to the salesman's spiel with my eyebrows at topmast.

"Furthermore," the salesman said, winding up his presentation, "this newly formed company is really going places. I can get some stock for you at a few dollars a share. You'd better get in on it now and make yourself a fortune."

Remembering my dad's warning about entrusting my hard-earned money to strangers, I looked over the huckster's almost threadbare attire and declined his offer of sudden and astronomical wealth.

Did I lose any of my hard-earned money by not investing in his machine with the funny-sounding name? No, I didn't lose a cent of what I had. But did I pass up a chance to multiply my money almost astronomically?

Ever heard of Xerox?

And that wasn't the end of my goofs. Later I met a man who was selling stock in a brand-new computer company. Just in case I didn't know about computers, he added an explanation. "You know," he said "one of those machines that does all your office work for you."

The man sounded sincere enough, but once again my early training came to my rescue. "Thanks, but no thanks," I said, shook his hand firmly, and showed him to the door.

He was selling shares in the Control Data Corporation.

How much did I fail to increase my holdings by refusing to invest in that highly successful enterprise? At least a small fortune.

In each case, I made snap decisions based on my soulish reactions, rather than looking into those opportunities, studying them, and getting expert advice instead of relying solely on the "Watch out that you don't get fleeced" principle.

Have I erred in the other direction too—of making investments where prudence wouldn't have done it? And how!

This time it wasn't a stranger who took me in. It was someone I knew well, a man highly respected in the business community. One day he persuaded me to give him the use of some of my funds so he could manage them in a way that simply could not fail to produce a tidy profit.

He wasn't a stranger or a fast-talking salesman out to get his hands on my hard-earned money for some get-rich-quick scheme. He was simply a friend in need of ready cash to put over an enterprise I judged quite worthy of my participation.

281

I listened to him, prayed a little, and when all signs seemed to be go, I turned over to him the major portion of my retirement fund. I had put aside quite a comfortable nest egg for my retirement years, which were still down the road, had no immediate need for the money, and his offer would earn far more than ordinary investment interest, he said. And I believed him.

Without bothering to read carefully the fine print in the agreement his lawyer prepared for my signature, I fell for it. I didn't even take the commonsense precaution of asking my attorney to examine the contract for possible flaws. I simply signed it, sure in my own heart that my good friend couldn't fail.

But I was *wrong!*

The man's business went sour when his enterprise failed to fly right. Everything turned into disaster. The whole thing failed. My contract was full of holes any attorney would have spotted in nothing flat. The result? Woe was me. Most of my retirement fund went down the drain.

How did I get myself, with all my training in money matters, in such an unfortunate "loser" position? Simple. I failed to follow the rules for success.

Yes, I know how it feels to make a bad investment. I've been there. I can understand the frustration of having made a costly, colossal boo-boo. I know the pain of remorse for stupid actions. But I knew too what I had learned from the *Manufacturer's Handbook*—that I was to praise God with thanksgiving in the very midst of the disaster. And believe it or not, I found some good things about which I could rejoice. Just look at them!

1. The amount could have been my *entire* retirement fund instead of just most of it. I did have something left.

2. Maybe my good friend needed the money more than I did.

3. Maybe, for some reason, I needed to understand how others feel when they've gotten into deals where they've lost their shirts. Maybe God was out to help me get shed of my formerly supercilious attitude toward "those poor slobs who don't know any better than to get caught making stupid investments." Never again could I say, "How stupid can you get?" when someone goofed with his money. I too have become a member of that "poor slobs" club whose members don't hit it right *every* time.

From all the experiences, good and bad, I've learned a few things. The most important is that no matter what happens, I can rejoice that God's on His throne and all is well—whether it looks like it or not—with King's kids who dare to:

1. thank Him *for* everything (Ephesians 5:20)

2. thank Him *in* all things (1 Thessalonians 5:16–18)

3. praise Him *in spite of* everything (Hebrews 13:15)

That kind of attitude control, regularly put into action by the words of our mouths and the meditations of our hearts, is guaranteed to restore all things to better shape than ever if we keep on praying for those who have despitefully used us. So I continue to pray for my good friend and his misfortunes. Meanwhile, I can see the Lord restoring all things in great abundance, beyond anything I could ever ask or imagine.

In line with keeping my attitude in shape to receive the blessings of God, I have learned never, never, never to waste any time or energy in rehearsing life's failures. We are to go on from apparent disasters with the Word of God in our mouths:

> I can do all things through Christ who strengthens me. (*Philippians 4:13* NKJB-NT)

> I am the lender, not the borrower. (See *Deuteronomy 28:12*)

> I am the head and not the tail. (See *Deuteronomy 28:13*)

If we remember what God says about these things, and *do* them, we will keep a positive attitude, conditioned by the Word of God, and we can watch the Lord come through to the benefit of all concerned. If that's not shoutin' ground, I don't know what hallelujahs are for!

It is God's idea, not mine, that His people be lenders and not borrowers. He makes it clear, as does human experience, that the borrower is the slave of the lender. Learning to be thrifty instead of spendthrifty is highly recommended by the Lord of glory throughout the *Manufacturer's Handbook.*

How does all that work out in everyday living? Making your savings work for you as you invest it in someone else's enterprises is one way.

You can lend to a bank by paying into a "savings account," and the bank in turn will pay you interest for the use of your money. That, for most folks, is the beginning of being a lender and not a borrower. True, the interest in a savings account is not all that great in terms of percentages, but it's a beginning. And remember what "Cousin

Jim'' Hill said: your money training must always begin *now* or you will never get into it.

After you have built up a sizable savings account, you are in a position to earn a higher rate of interest by investing your funds in a Certificate of Deposit. After that, as your balance grows, there are other things you can get into. You might invest in the business ventures of others by purchasing shares in corporations with proven track records. Bankers and brokers can advise you along these lines.

The basic meaning of investing is "loaning your money to another in exchange for a fair return, or profit"—which is another way of saying that you become a lender. That's God's recommendation, remember?

During the war years of the forties, when everyday household items were often hard to find because factories were involved in producing for war, the investment group of which I was a part began to look for places to invest to meet the needs of the people. Market research revealed that more and more ladies were making their own wearing apparel. Why not invest in an industry that would take advantage of that fact? We found a little company called the Simplicity Pattern Company, which made dress patterns. I loaned them—a simple term meaning I "invested in their enterprise"—eight hundred dollars for one hundred shares of their common stock. (For beginners in things financial, *common stock* is simply the term used to refer to the receipt the company gives you in return for your loan or investment.) I stashed the shares away in my safe-deposit box and promptly forgot all about them, leaving the company alone to run its affairs the way it thought best.

Sometime later, a report came in the mail telling how those folks had prospered and were "splitting" their stock and sending me an extra hundred shares without charge. *Really nice of them,* I thought, and again forgot all about it. This forgetting all about it is an important point. If you begin to love money, letting your whole attention be concentrated on your investments to the destruction of your peace of mind, watch out! You might be falling into the treacherous syndrome the Bible labels "The love of money is the root of all evil" (1 Timothy 6:10). But if you can forget all about it, you might be surprised by joy one day, as I was.

Over the years, without my being aware of it, that company continued to prosper, and I discovered one day that my original investment of about eight hundred dollars was worth ninety-six thousand dollars, 120 times what I had loaned to that little company years before!

Does wise investing pay off? And how!

"But just how does all that serve God's work?" some jealous diehard is complaining. I have the answer. Here's how that particular high-profit transaction worked for God's glory.

A small church I began attending was planning a building program and needed funds to finance it. Where do you think the Lord directed me to place most of those Simplicity Pattern shares? Into the treasury of that little church, that's where. Instead of selling the stock for myself, which would have resulted in a hefty tax bite, the church benefited, and I received an income-tax deduction which reduced the amount I had to pay on my federal and state tax returns.

Don't you suppose God knew from the beginning that those funds would be needed to help build that church house? I do. I believe He was the One who inspired me to make that investment even before I was saved. And by giving to the little church, I sowed seeds for further returns and greater prosperity.

Truly, all things work together for good when we do it God's way.

"But Hill, do you always make such high-quality decisions?" someone less fortunate asks.

No indeed. My own record contains some colossal boo-boos. Like the time someone came to me with a thousand logical reasons to invest in "crop futures." It looked like a wise investment; all the research was showing that potato prices next year would be higher than this year.

The plan was simple enough. The catch was that no one can predict for certain what will happen in a given crop year.

Without thinking it through and realizing exactly what I was getting myself into, I invested in one carload of potatoes at this year's prices, from the crop not yet planted. I fell right into the trap of the fast-talking promoter because I was so eager to make another buck in those days. Having purchased the shares, I put them away and forgot all about them. But the folks at the other end of the deal didn't forget.

When potato-digging time rolled around the next year, there was a bumper crop. Prices dropped to their lowest level in years. And I received a call from the local railroad freight office.

"Mr. Hill, where do you want us to unload your potatoes?"

"My potatoes? What potatoes?"

Instead of answering my questions, the man at the other end of the line said, "Your carload is here in the freight yards, car number so-and-so, and if you don't come and get them within the next forty-eight hours, we'll begin charging you rental on the freight car."

"Ooohh! *Those* potatoes." With a sinking heart I recalled my investment in the potato enterprise a year ago.

Do you realize how many french fries there are in a freight carload of spuds? Mentally, I was trying to visualize

287

how many bottles of ketchup it would take to cover such a heap.

"I'll take care of them right away," I mumbled, hoping I knew what I was talking about and that I could find a place to unload them in the glutted potato market.

After a few phone calls I had discovered that when you are in a state of panic and have to sell something right away, you're at the mercy of the produce brokers and have to take what they offer unless you want to set up a stand and dispense fish 'n' chips yourself. I didn't think I was the type.

Yes, I finally found a broker who would take off my hands those thousands of beautiful chips in the raw—but at "his" price, well below my original expectation. Instead of making a bundle, I lost on that investment and considered it a cheap lesson. Next time, I promised myself, I'd do a little more research.

Since that fiasco, lending money to my local city, county, or state government has become one of my favorite areas for investment. At irregular intervals, these agencies issue tax-free bonds in exchange for cash and use the revenue to finance the building of hospitals, waterworks, and other public projects. The interest rates on such bonds vary, but there are two big advantages to investing in them. One is that in lending to your local government you feel a part of things and may be more diligent to pray for those in authority who are overseeing the spending of your money. The other big advantage is that your interest income from such bonds is tax free.

What does tax-free interest mean on your tax return? A double-barreled blessing. Income from tax-free bonds not only requires that no tax be paid, but it doesn't even have to be reported as income, keeping your tax bracket wherever it was before the interest income. If you're in the 50 percent tax bracket, for instance, every dollar you earn as interest on your tax-free investment is worth double the dollars you earn as taxable income. A tax-exempt bond paying 8 percent would net you as much as a 16 percent bond on which you had to pay taxes.

Brokers tell me that an ideal way to put your money to work in the enterprises of others is to choose a large number of successful businesses, buy a few shares in each, and wait for your share of the profits.

But it would take a lot of time for you to do that personally, and you could become a slave of the system and do nothing but sit in your broker's office and stare at the ticker tape all day. To solve the problem, someone came up with the idea of a mutual fund, which enables the lender to purchase a small slice of perhaps a hundred companies, all at one time, through shares in the fund. The managers of the fund loan your money to the hundred companies they find worthy of your support. Then they relay the profits to you at accounting time. Since your investment is spread among numerous enterprises, if one doesn't do too well during a particular year, the others can take up the slack. It's a good example of teamwork, one I have found highly beneficial over the years.

More recently, the government has made it practical and simple as well as advantageous to start your own Individual Retirement Account, better known as an IRA. Under this plan, you can invest up to two thousand dollars each year into the plan without paying any tax on that money until you withdraw it, presumably in a year when your tax bracket will be lower. Consult your broker or banker for full up-to-date details about this and other good investments.

According to the *Manufacturer's Handbook,* wise saving and investing is not just *okay* for King's kids, it's an *essential* part of good stewardship.

-16-
TRAINING YOUR KIDS IN MONEY MANAGEMENT

Before we tackle the answers to more of your money questions, let's take a quick look at how you can help your kids get a better start than you ever had at managing their money. The right beginnings might keep them from going through some of the agonies you've endured in the area of your checkbook.

One thing I tried with my daughter, Linda, might work for you. When Linda was a teenager and got her first job, a car became a real necessity for getting her to and from work. I could have GIVEN her the money to buy a car, but recalling my early training from my dad, I passed on to her the opportunity to learn how to benefit from a disciplined way of life in the money department.

"Linda," I said, "here's my proposition. I'll LOAN you the money you need for a car. I'll loan it to you without interest for as long as it takes you to pay it back. With your first paycheck, you start a joint savings account at the bank in both our names and pay something into it every week. I don't want to see a penny of it until it's all paid up. Now here's the money. Get moving."

She proved a prudent shopper and didn't buy the highest-priced merchandise Detroit was offering that year. With her own wheels, she took a major step into independence. She was responsible for gas and oil, tires and repairs. Several years later, she approached me with an envelope in her hand. In it was that long forgotten bankbook in which was entered at least a dollar a week for those hundreds of weeks. On several occasions since then, Linda has thanked me for that early training in money sense which would otherwise have been missed had I simply given her the money—or the car—as a gift.

Had you been thinking you *had* to give your teen a car as soon as he/she/it (sorry about that last, but sometimes I can't tell for sure these days) was old enough for a driver's license? Give the matter a little more thought and consider training the kid to avoid the miseries that come to spendthrifts later on in life. Teaching your kids the value of a dollar—by giving them a chance to work for what they get instead of looking for a government handout—is good insurance against their burning down colleges and otherwise throwing their lives away.

Now, because I want to give you the best information available, and because I haven't had a child at home for lo these many years, I've taken the liberty for this chapter of borrowing information from the real experts on the subject—the bankers themselves.

The following material is lifted verbatim from the Winter 1983 issue of a First National Bank publication, *Your Money and How to Make the Most of It,* and is reprinted by permission. Titled "Kids and Money: Teaching the Value of a Dollar," the article has this to say:

A common wish among parents is to have their children grow up to be financially secure. Yet millions of young adults today are having to learn the economic facts of life the hard way—through trial and error and personal financial hardship. Often with considerable cost to themselves and sometimes even their parents.

Good money management skills must begin in the home and at an early age. By teaching and encouraging healthy financial habits during early childhood, parents can help insure their children's financial well-being in the future. Most experts agree that money management education should begin around the age of five or six. Before that age, few children can judge the real value of money. It is important, however, that preschoolers are taught the basic principles behind money, what it is and how it's used. Preschoolers can grasp this idea by making small purchases of their own under parental supervision. Next time you visit the grocery store, allow your youngster to pay for a piece of fruit. This demonstrates how money is used—in exchange for goods. Once the money is used up, no more fruit can be bought.

Possibly the best money management tool a parent can utilize is the allowance. This gives a child the opportunity to plan spending, make important choices, live within a fixed income and save for large purchases. Several guidelines have been developed by experts to help parents set up an allowance program for their child:

1) Parent and child should discuss all ground rules of the allowance: how much it will be, what the child is responsible for, and what extras the parent will pay for.

2) An allowance should be given in a specific amount and paid regularly on the same day each week. As a child gets older, it's a good idea to lengthen that time to once a month. This way a child is taught to manage money over a longer period of time.

3) Allowances should not be tied to a child's behavior or manipulated as a reward or punishment for an act. Household chores should be assigned and looked upon as a contribution to the family unit. Optional jobs should be undertaken for pay, such as baby-sitting, dog-walking, car-washing, or gardening.

4) When deciding on the amount of the allowance, be sure that all of the child's needs are accurately considered. Considerations should include the child's age, activities and the economic circumstances of peers. Don't make your child the "poor kid" or the "rich kid" on the block.

5) Review allowances on a regular basis. Like the cost of living—lunches, bus fares and entertainment are all hit by inflation.

Learning when to spend and when to save money is an important but often difficult task for a child to master. Teaching children to budget their allowances is a good way for them to learn when and how to spend their money. Instruct your children as to the kind of things that money should buy:

1) Necessities first,
2) optional items next,
3) and finally, things for fun.

Once your children are old enough to grasp the idea of saving and its benefits, let them open savings accounts. Open them in their names, encourage them to make deposits, and allow them to fill out deposit slips. Don't deny access to the bank when it's requested. Let your children make their own decisions when managing their money, even if it means watching them make a mistake. A $10 mistake today is better than a $1,000 mistake later in life.

Teaching children the value of money in today's society is a challenging task. But by teaching valuable money management skills today, you could be saving your children more than just a few dollars later in life.

How about that? Simple—but it covers the subject. I couldn't have said it better myself, could you? Just one thing I'd add, and that is to make certain your children begin at an early age to set aside a minimum of 10 percent off the top to put in the collection plate at church, or to send to their favorite missionary outreach. Getting them started on tithing while they are still young will help them to understand that everything they ''have'' really belongs to God. With that understanding, they'll be on the road to a prosperous future.

-17-

WORKING WIVES
What Does God Think About Them?

How about wives who work to help the family bank account prosper? What does God have to say about them? Strictly taboo? Or right on?

Again, it's useless to try to dig answers out of our own heads, so I asked Liz Rogers, who runs the King's Kids' Korner, to do some Bible research on this one for me. What follows is largely what she came up with, based on what she found in the pages of the always reliable *Manufacturer's Handbook*. But this is not a disclaimer of responsibility on my part for the ideas in this chapter. Since they agree with God, they also agree with me. But if it doesn't *sound* like me, don't worry. It isn't Hal—it's Liz. Here she goes:

What is God's idea of a perfect woman? Is it a groveling, fear-ridden spouse who must sit in the shadows and ask her husband's permission to take her next breath? Or is she to be a real helpmate to him in every area of life?

God must have known someone was going to ask these questions, because He took the time to give a detailed, perfect answer in the last twenty-two verses of the Book of Proverbs, chapter 31.

Stop and read the whole thing right here, and let it blow your mind, especially if you've been one who's thought the little woman should be nothing but a nobody in her husband's shadow. (These verses come from the New International Version of the Bible, a translation from ancient Greek into modern American so your think tank can get hold of them without any trouble.)

A wife of noble character who can find?
She is worth far more than rubies.
Her husband has full confidence in her
and lacks nothing of value.
She brings him good, not harm,
all the days of her life.
She selects wool and flax
and works with eager hands.
She is like the merchant ships,
bringing her food from afar.
She gets up while it is still dark;
she provides food for her family
and portions for her servant girls.
She considers a field and buys it;
out of her earnings she plants a vineyard.
She sets about her work vigorously;
her arms are strong for her tasks.
She sees that her trading is profitable,
and her lamp does not go out at night
In her hand she holds the distaff
and grasps the spindle with her fingers.
She opens her arms to the poor

and extends her hands to the needy.
When it snows she has no fear for her household;
for all of them are clothed in scarlet.
She makes coverings for her bed;
she is clothed in fine linen and purple.
Her husband is respected at the city gate,
where he takes his seat among the elders of the land.
She makes linen garments and sells them,
and supplies the merchants with sashes.
She is clothed with strength and dignity;
she can laugh at the days to come.
She speaks with wisdom,
and faithful instruction is on her tongue.
She watches over the affairs of her household
and does not eat the bread of idleness.
Her children arise and call her blessed;
her husband also, and he praises her.
"Many women do noble things,
but you surpass them all."
Charm is deceptive, and beauty is fleeting;
but a woman who fears the Lord is to be praised.
Give her the reward she has earned,
and let her works bring her praise
at the city gate.

Isn't that great? I get a picture here of a woman who is in full partnership with her husband, fully cooperating with him in every detail of life. She operates her home in an efficient manner and branches out from there into the business world, where she trades in real estate and merchandise. She is skilled in sewing, knitting, and weaving, not afraid to pitch in with her hands to do anything needful. She is a good teacher, and her children admire and praise her for her ministry to them. She starts the day at an early hour, has time to help the poor and needy, and everyone praises her for her good works.

What kind of a wife is she? Not necessarily a person of outward beauty or charm, but one who reverently and worshipfully puts the Lord first in her life.

Here is a rich and prosperous household because the woman and her husband work together to make it so. She is enthusiastic in everything she does because she does it as unto the Lord. She never fears the future, because she has learned to apply God's laws of successful living, prosperity, and health.

This wife of noble character has nothing to do with gossip, discontent, and self-pity. She is forever building up her husband, never tearing him down, and in turn, her husband praises her. The whole household blesses one another.

Her clothes are expensive, costly purple garments fit for royalty.

This is a successful husband/wife team—and it is all God's idea. The husband has a gift from God whose price is far above rubies. Instead of running up debts, his wife adds to the family finances. Because of her, her husband lacks nothing of value.

Any of you women who have been feeling guilty about being working wives, rejoice! It's plain here that God highly approves of at least one of them. And to understand how much He approves of the Proverbs woman, take into your system this footnote from the *Amplified Bible:*

"Many daughters have done . . . nobly and well . . . but you excel them all." This is a very great deal to be recorded of her, a woman in private life. It means she had done more than Miriam, the leader of a nation's women in praise to God, Exod. 15:20, 21; Deborah, the patriotic military advisor, Judg. 4:4–10; Huldah, the woman who revealed God's secret message to national leaders, II Kings 22:14; Ruth, the woman of constancy, Ruth 1:16; Hannah, the ideal mother, I Sam. 1:20; 2:19; the Shunammite, the hospitable woman, II Kings 4:8–10; and even more than Queen Esther, the woman who risked sacrificing her life for her people, Esth. 4:16.

In what way did "she excel them all"? In her spiritual and practical devotion to God, which permeated every area and relationship of her life. All seven of the Christian virtues (II Pet. 1:5) are there, like colored threads in a tapestry. Her secret, which is open to every one, is the Holy Spirit's climax of the story, and of this book. In verse thirty that "reverent and worshipful fear of the Lord" which is "the beginning and principal part of Wisdom" (Prov. 1:7) is given the full responsibility for a life which is valued by God and her husband "far above rubies or pearls."

That's the secret, isn't it? Not so much whether we women work or don't work outside the home but that whatever we do, we do it as unto the Lord, with our motives those of reverence toward Him.

Thank you, Sister Liz. That covers the subject pretty well, don't you agree? God hasn't made woman to be any kind of second-class humanity but right up there beside the man to have her life fulfilled, just as he does, with hearing and doing the Word of God.

-18-

HOW TO SUCCEED IN YOUR OWN BUSINESS

If you have a *big* business, chances are that you already have CPAs, MBAs, and ABCs handling all the financial details for you. This chapter is for the small businessman who has to be a do-it-myselfer in the financial realm—someone who may be floundering without realizing why.

Is that you? And are you sometimes confused by the baffling array of percentages, markups, markdowns, discounts, escalated contingency reserves, and the rest of all that Greek? Hold on for a few pages, and let's see if we can get rid of some of the confusion.

It makes no difference whether your business is big, small, a Mom 'n' Pop enterprise, or individual self-employment incorporated only to get tax benefits. If the bottom line is sick, the whole operation will eventually tumble down.

What is the bottom line? Simply stated, it's the amount you end up with after all the numbers have been totaled. It's your reward for all that sweat and struggle. If your INCOME isn't more than your OUTGO, the OUTCOME will be a forced folding of the operation.

Furthermore, if that bottom line is less than you could earn with the money invested in other ways while you went on a permanent vacation, taking a vacation might be advisable so you could take a closer look at what you've been doing.

Let's go back to the beginning and assume that you are just now planning to start your own business with the intention of supporting yourself—wholly or partially—on your earnings. Maybe you have a family to support too. This means that your investment must produce a percentage return that is significantly better than you could obtain by investing the same amount in savings certificates, savings accounts, or other places where your money would earn a guaranteed, no-risk return. Otherwise, it would make no sense to struggle (yes, business is often a struggle) with working when you could do just as well for yourself without lifting a finger to make a living—which would leave twenty-four hours a day for King's kid laboring to bring in the harvest of souls.

Let's assume further that you've done your homework and studied the market and are persuaded you can do better on your own. Let's say you decide to open a Christian bookstore. A lot of folks seem to be doing that these days. You have prayed about it, and maybe others have told you it's really God's will for you.

How much money will you need to begin operations if you plan to quit your regular job and give this your full-time attention? Too much!

Starting your own business means you should plan on working for no income for at least a year, and probably longer than that until the thing gets off the ground. In my own case, seven days a week was barely enough to handle all the details of buying, selling, advertising, shipping, paying bills, and so on. I couldn't afford to hire an assistant.

To be on the safe side and ensure that your enterprise will not fail before it has a chance to get off the ground, you should have in reserve enough money to live on for at least two years. That's in addition to the funds you'll have to have on hand for the merchandise you plan to sell, the rent, insurance, utilities, and all the rest.

Am I trying to discourage you? No indeed. I'm just trying to make you aware of realities so you'll have a chance to succeed if you go for it. Remember, I went this route some years ago and built a few hundred dollars into a multimillion-dollar gold mine. That makes me qualified to share a few success principles with you, right?

Once you decide to go ahead, believing it's God's will for you, talk with others who have similar operations. They can warn you of possible pitfalls and things you might not have considered. They can also tell you about how much you'll need for basic inventory. For expert advice, write to the Christian Booksellers Association, 2620 Ventucci Boulevard, P.O. Box 200, Colorado Springs, Colorado 80901. That's an outfit that has helped many bookstores get started, and they're well qualified to advise you. Besides which, they have developed some helpful printed materials you can use to good advantage.

Make up a budget sheet, listing your investment, loan interest, rent, utilities, insurance, and all other costs that will be involved in your business activity. Don't forget such items as travel, a contingency fund to cover bad debts, shoplifting, and damaged merchandise.

Just to give you a little idea of what you're letting yourself in for, let's analyze your hypothetical bookstore (or other operation) a little further.

Step one might be borrowing fifty thousand dollars from a local lending institution at 12 percent interest for your basic inventory. (Substitute whatever interest rate is prevailing in your area for small-business loans at the time you're considering the big leap.) You can see at a glance that the cost to you of using their money is going to be six thousand dollars a year, or five hundred dollars a month.

Next step, for the sake of our illustration, assume that you gross one hundred thousand dollars in sales your first year. That's highly improbable in the beginning, but it will give us a working figure. One hundred thousand dollars sounds like big bucks, doesn't it? But don't plan your Florida vacation quite yet. Gross volume doesn't pay the bills; gross profit does. Assuming you buy merchandise at a 40 percent discount, more or less standard with big book jobbers and some publishers, the cost to you of the merchandise on which you've grossed one hundred thousand dollars has been sixty thousand dollars.

"Praise the Lord!" I can hear you hollering. "What are we waiting for! I'll resign my old job tomorrow! A clear profit of forty thousand dollars—why, that's more than I've been making at my present nine-to-five job, and the fringes aren't all that fancy. Let's go!"

Whoa, Nellie. That's exactly why we're going through this hypothetical case history—to call your attention to things you might otherwise miss. And you've just missed a lot. Before sticking your neck on the chopping block, you need to look a little deeper.

Where were you planning to display your sixty thousand dollars worth of merchandise, for instance? In the middle of the boulevard? There's probably a city ordinance against it—besides which, it sometimes rains, even in California. And if you were planning to sleep on top of the merchandise to prevent thievery, you'd probably find the job a little too confining, even in the open air. So you need a building, right?

And buildings cost money, and buildings need lights and water, and insurance, and bookkeeping services, and supplies—all of which lead to expenses to the tune of something like what's portrayed below:

Annual Expenses

Interest on loan	$6000
Rent at $200 a month	2400
Utilities	1200
Insurance	1200
Contingencies	2000
Bookkeeping services	600
Supplies	600
Janitorial services	000*

Total cost per year $14,000

* The asterisk means you'd better count on doing the dusting, window washing, and vacuuming yourself the first year. You can't afford maid service. Sorry about that.

Now what's happened to what you thought was clear profit? It's down to twenty-six thousand dollars.

"I'll settle for that anytime!" you shout, still high as a kite. "I don't mind doing the dusting." But wait a minute. You haven't set aside a thing for advertising. How are you going to let folks know you're in business if you don't advertise a little?

Now consider the annual volume of one hundred thousand dollars in terms of the number of books sold. Do you actually think you can sell one hundred thousand dollars worth of merchandise all by yourself without a helper?

There are many other hidden costs, but these two will serve as examples. Many new businesses fall on their faces during the first or second year simply because they overlook these "hidden costs."

If each book sold at an average price of five dollars,

you'd be handling twenty thousand books a year, or four hundred books a week. (We're letting you close two weeks for unpaid vacation, see?) In a forty-hour week, you'd need to average selling ten books per hour every hour. Knowing how retail trade is seldom spaced out evenly but has rush hours and slack hours, and a lot of folks who come in to take up your time without buying anything, it might not be feasible for you to handle the operation alone. Besides, what if you got sick, or had to go out of town? Who would mind the store? Realistically, you ought to consider having at least one full-time assistant plus a part-time helper. That gross profit of twenty-six thousand dollars doesn't look so great when you consider it might have to be divided two and a half ways, does it?

Food stamps, anyone?

And how about the IRS people with their hands out for their share, and the local sales-tax folks, the social security payments for yourself and your employees, medical benefits, and goodwill contributions to the panhandlers who may be your only "customers" on the first day of business?

Unless trouble is your hobby, starting your own bookstore business looks so gloomy, it makes you wonder why anybody ever starts anything, doesn't it?

But if you've consulted the experts and seriously considered all the factors, and *still* believe it's God's plan for your life to start a Christian bookstore, take a realistic look with me at some further percentage thinking. Look, too, if you've already begun a business and are having problems you can't quite seem to put a finger on but you see your capital leaking away without apparent reason.

Failure to do some realistic percentage thinking accounts for a big proportion of the scary rate of failure among businesses each year. Percentage thinking must be cultivated and become an automatic part of your thinking if your business is to have any chance of success.

What is percentage thinking? Simply the ability to examine a business transaction and tell in a moment whether it is a "winner" or a "loser." There's nothing mysterious about percentages. *Percentage* is just a word we use to talk about a fraction of a total situation, whether it be parts of a dollar, slices of cake, or "pieces of the action."

"But I hated fractions and percentages in school," someone whines, "and I just don't want to hear any more about them." Feel free, friend, but if that's your attitude, you'd best not start a business of your own but let a boss handle that part of your life. Unless you are willing to discipline yourself to think in terms of percentages, you are doomed to fail in your own business.

In running a business, it is necessary to stop thinking in terms of dollars per se and look at each transaction in terms of all the directions the dollars take during the process of the transaction. Dollars become secondary in our thinking and percentages take their place. A single transaction may involve a million dollars, but unless the profit percentage is healthy, bankruptcy is just around the corner.

Let's look at the sale of a single book as a microcosm of the whole operation. Suppose you sell the book for an established price of five dollars, for which you have paid your supplier three. You already know that doesn't represent a clear profit of two dollars, or 66⅔ percent (your three-dollar cost divided into the gross profit, or your gross profit divided by your cost, whichever way you like to look at it) on your investment. Many things have to come out of that two dollars—rent, heat, light, insurance, taxes, salaries—before there's anything left to put in your pocket.

The net profit, after all costs have been paid, must be at least 15 percent of the investment for a business to be practical. If you cannot earn at least that much on your investment, you'd be better off investing in someone else's business, unless your business is intended only as a hobby or for fun. How much profit must you make on an item for which you pay three dollars in order for you to have a 15 percent profit? Three dollars × 15 percent = forty-five cents. Do you have forty-five cents left after you've paid for your merchandise and everything else? If not, the ship is going to sink.

The picture is even worse if your customer isn't a cash customer. Suppose he charges the purchase on a credit card? Then you have to give the credit-card people a certain percentage (sometimes 5 percent) for them to handle the transaction for you.

Or suppose the customer pays with a check that bounces? That happens far too often. Think of the time and trouble you may have to expend in order to collect what's due.

Or perhaps the customer has a charge account at your place of business and you write the charges down for him to pay later—only he doesn't pay. Every time you send him a reminder, at today's postage rates you're cutting your profit by twenty cents plus the cost of invoice, envelope, typewriter ribbon, and so on. Some customers are slow payers and will come up with the money eventually (but maybe not until you've spent all your profit in dunning them), and there are others who will never pay.

In the case of the merchandise for which you were anticipating a forty-five-cent profit from a cash customer, having to send a bill or two before you collect could mean that all your profit is gone and that you've entered into a loss operation. At some point, you might decide not to send any more good money after bad and give up on trying to collect—or turn the whole mess over to an agency that will take a hefty chunk for their own efforts at collecting it for you. Many businesses fail every month because of such termite erosion of their profit structure.

After taking a realistic look at this side of the percentage picture, it's all right to take a peek at how percentages can work in your favor.

These days, at the bottom of many invoices for goods purchased for resale, you may find a notation something like this: "2 percent ten days, net thirty." That simply means that you can take a 2 percent discount from the amount you owe if you will pay it in ten days instead of waiting until the end of the month. On a bill for one hundred dollars, you would have to pay only ninety-eight dollars, and automatically your percentage of profit would go up a little.

What if you begin giving a discount to certain customers? You're scuttling your own ship. Put down some figures of your own and think it all through. Better to shed your tears over the paper figures than over the real thing.

You've done all that figuring and *still* come out in the black? You *still* think it's God's will for you to go into a particular business? Go for it! If it's really His plan for you, He will make it work.

Here are a few random hints that might help you along the way:

1. Pay your bills promptly, to have the advantage of the 2 percent off if paid in ten days. In a business grossing one hundred thousand dollars a year, that could amount to a tidy extra profit of twelve hundred dollars.

2. Don't give discounts to good customers—you can't afford it.

3. Strongly consider buying and selling for cash only. By paying for merchandise as soon as you receive it, you can get special discounts, and your bad-debts account will be zero if you sell for cash. Otherwise, the no-pays can eat up your time and profits.

Forewarned is forearmed, they say, and since you have the whole armor of God to protect you from the on-slaughts of the evil one, more power to you. Invite me to the tenth anniversary of the founding of your bookstore, will you? And set up a table where people can come to buy an autographed copy of my latest book—and meet Jesus while they wait. That's the whole point of starting a Christian bookstore in the first place.

The last two chapters of John's Gospel end with state-ments that could have been made by someone looking over the merchandise on the shelves of a Christian book-store, had you ever noticed?

Jesus did many other miraculous signs in the presence of his disciples, which are not recorded in this book. But these are written that you may believe that Jesus is the Christ, the Son of God, and that by believing you may have life in his name. . . . Jesus did many other things as well. If every one of them were written down, I suppose that even the whole world would not have room for the books that would be written. (*John 20:30, 31; 21:25 NIV*)

Glory!

-19-

LIFE INSURANCE AND WILLS

No-Nos or Necessities for King's Kids?

Does a Christian Need a Will?

Knowing as little about last wills and testaments as most of you, I decided to consult an expert on this subject for you. Clarke Murphy, Jr., my attorney, good friend, and fellow King's kid, consented to discuss with me the facts of life about these things.

I came away convinced that every Christian absolutely needs to have a will. Yes, even if you and your spouse own everything jointly. Even if you think you'll be leaving nothing behind. Even if there's no individual you'd like to designate as a beneficiary. Even if you have no life insurance. Even if you think there's no reason for you to have a will because you have no worldly assets to become left-overs when you leave planet earth.

Without planning it, you still might graduate to glory in such a way that someone else's insurance would leave a sizable estate either to heirs you had designated or—if you had no will—to the state, which might use the funds to improve its dog-racing track. How much better to leave a will specifying that whatever you leave behind would be used to bless your loved ones and to promote the work of the Lord.

How about a do-it-yourself will? Generally not recommended, my expert friend told me. Sure, you can buy a book of legal forms, fill in a few blanks, and *hope* for the best. But with every state having different, subject-to-change laws about these things, you'd never know whether your will would hold up in court.

There are good, honest lawyers in lots of places. Find out from one of your trusted friends the name of one of them and get your will written, signed, sealed, and delivered to a place of safekeeping before another week passes. You'll have peace of mind, and God won't be cheated of anything you might want to leave for His work on planet earth.

Reducing Estate Taxes

In addition to having a sound will to dispose of all you leave behind according to your wishes, you might like to take action to reduce the amount of your estate taxes before you go to the heavenly city. I can see some raised eyebrows at that, but let me tell you an experience of mine that will illustrate what I'm talking about.

One day as I was approaching retirement age, I took inventory of my financial affairs to see what my retirement plan looked like. Frankly, it looked too good—that was before my friend lost a big chunk of it for me. Taxes were going to be devastating to my heirs if I waited until my earthly remains were six feet under before I gave any of it away.

Stocks for which I had paid less than a thousand dollars had increased almost 120-fold and were now worth nearly

312

one hundred thousand dollars. An album filled with a complete set of shiny United States gold coins I had been accumulating over the years was worth nearly twenty thousand dollars when gold was eight hundred dollars an ounce.

Without realizing what was happening, I began to watch the fluctuations in the price of gold, mentally computing the phenomenal increase in the value of my secret hoard. I even found myself visiting the bank more frequently than usual, just to admire my little set of treasures.

In addition, certain other properties I had bought at low prices were now worth many times my original investment, and other stocks and bonds had also appreciated in value, adding up to an astounding total. I realized that I had literally "stored up treasures on earth," and began to be concerned about their value depreciating in the years ahead.

Concern about my financial security began to take my attention away from my real security, Jesus Christ. I was spending more and more time thinking about how I might protect my investments from "erosion," a term brokers use when they want to talk about the results of the double-digit inflation which has become so common in recent years. Truly, the "deceitfulness of riches" was beginning to choke the Word of God in my life, exactly as God had warned in the *Manufacturer's Handbook*. "What was sown among the thorns [of the Word of God] is the man who hears the word, but the worries of this life and the deceitfulness of wealth choke it, making it unfruitful" (Matthew 13:22 NIV).

Yes, I was spending more and more time watching the stock-market behavior and less time in the Word of God.

One day as I prayed about these things, the Lord seemed to say, *Why not give away that worldly type secu-*

rity to those in need at the moment instead of waiting to die and subjecting your leftovers to heavy inheritance taxes?

At that time, my daughter's husband had deserted her, leaving her to raise her daughter alone, and her financial needs were indeed great. Deep down, I suspected that my plan to leave her well-fixed after my graduation was really a cover-up for wanting to keep my money under my control in the meantime.

Getting out from under the bondage and deceitfulness of riches was not easy for me, but I determined to follow the leading of the Holy Spirit and go through with it. First, I looked into the laws governing gifts and giving in general, and found a provision in our tax law that permits a person to give a maximum "once in a lifetime" gift of sixty thousand dollars to any one person, tax free. I also discovered that I could also give an annual gift of six thousand dollars entirely tax free.

I went to the bank, opened the strongbox, and dumped out enough securities to total sixty thousand dollars. Then annually I began to give to my daughter and my granddaughter the maximum tax-free six thousand dollars toward the purchase of a home they could enjoy, thus disposing of more of those strongbox securities. In giving these things to them while I was still here to enjoy their joy, I received much more than I had given. And I no longer had to worry about erosion.

What the Lord led me to do set me free from the bondage of ownership of all that considerable amount of worldly wealth, enabled my daughter and her daughter to enjoy immediate relief from great lack, and enabled me to enter into a still greater dimension of joyous giving than I had already discovered. Maybe you can benefit from my experience and bless your loved ones now.

Want another example? One day as I was giving my testimony about these things in a small country church, the pastor told me of the great need to expand the church's facilities in order to accommodate the flood of folks who couldn't all get in to enjoy the teaching of God's Word because of the lack of space.

The pastor didn't ask me to do anything about the need, but the Lord did.

What about that valuable coin collection? He seemed to be saying. I pretended not to hear Him, but He kept seeming to say the same thing again and again.

When I finally presented the collection to the church, it was an occasion of great rejoicing for them and for me. All that "gold, silver, and precious stones" had been weighting down the box at the bank, but now it would be used to the glory of God.

What about the high-value stock certificate? Another local church needed funds to build a larger church building, and those thousands of dollars answered their prayers.

Fringe benefits to me included a fat refund from the Internal Revenue Service. When you begin to give abundantly, you will receive in like manner. It's impossible to avoid God's blessings when you put yourself in the way of them by doing what His Word requires.

The Lord chose to get me out of bondage to the deceitfulness of riches by having me give them away.

What About Insurance for King's Kids?

What about insurance for King's kids? Is it a no-no or a necessity? First, let's take a look at a definition to make sure we all understand what insurance really is.

In the ordinary sense of the word, insurance is a system

of protection from accidental happenings, where the insurer, in exchange for premium payments, agrees to foot the bill for whatever happens from then on, according to the terms of the policy.

Back in 1954, when I met Jesus Christ as my personal Savior and Lord and decided to live by faith, whatever that was, I was thinking about this very subject one day when a new Christian stood up in a meeting and made an announcement: "I'm going out and cancel all of my insurance policies and trust God alone for everything from now on. No more of this pagan practice of depending on insurance coverage for my security. I'm going to put my trust totally in the Lord." He didn't say it out loud, but the implication was that if the rest of us didn't rush right out and do likewise, we were second-class citizens—maybe even infidels.

That all sounded so religious that the rest of us embarked on a guilt trip. Momentarily, I really felt like a low-grade King's kid for not jumping up and saying, "Amen, brother! Preach it! I'm going out and do the same thing!" That would have made me a hero along with him, and the other folks could shoulder all the guilt.

But the Lord checked me before it was too late. He seemed to be saying, *Why not check My Word before jumping half-baked into the fire of stupidity by using common sense instead of My revelation sense?*

Among the Scriptures to which He led me that day was Mark 12:17, where Jesus said, "Render unto Caesar the things that belong to Caesar, and to God the things that belong to God" (author's paraphrase). In that verse, He seemed to be telling me that I was not to be conformed to the world but that I was to take advantage of the world's system when it was not in conflict with God's plans. Other Scriptures confirming what I was to do were those having

316

to do with obeying those in authority over me——I knew that some states require insurance of all licensed drivers——and praying for government leaders so that I might dwell in peace on the earth.

The Scriptures satisfied me that I was to keep my insurance, so I did, and have derived great financial benefit from this area of the world's way of doing business. Meanwhile, I have learned that there is a proper balance between the world's system and that of the heavenly Kingdom during our sojourn here on planet earth. Want to see the bottom line of what insurance coverage has paid for me in recent years, freeing my own funds for Kingdom purposes?

1. Three trips to the cardiac intensive-care unit of a local hospital caused by putting garbage food into my body temple. Those trips would have cost me several thousand dollars had I not been covered by insurance.

2. One trip to the hospital with a broken leg caused by my stubborn refusal to get on with working on a manuscript for a new book. (See *How to Be a Winner* for details.)

3. One new trunk for my Mercedes, needed to replace the one smashed by a truckload of beans. Cost: One thousand dollars. (See *God's in Charge Here* for full report.)

4. One new roof for my home needed to replace one blown apart by a violent storm. Including the cost of repairing water damage done to my home, I would have had to fork over three thousand dollars if I hadn't had insurance.

5. My wallet stolen from my hotel room in New

York City had five hundred and fifty dollars in it, reimbursed to me by my friendly insurance company.

6. Numerous other incidentals over the years, the whole list, including the above, totaling many thousands of dollars. Who paid it all? Various insurance carriers who never quibbled or argued about their responsibility but just sent me their check to cover each "accidental happening," as agreed in each policy.

My cost? Only a small part of the payments received.

But what about my life-insurance policy? I'll never benefit from that because it's designed to pay off after I'm gone. The brother who was putting the rest of us on a guilt trip said he had canceled his. Was that wisdom——or folly? Was that love for those who would be left behind at his passing? Or was it the height of selfishness? Let's look at what that means, and I'll let you be the judge.

The brother who canceled all his policies and trusted the Lord for his lifetime needs truly did prosper, and his ministry was indeed fruitful for the Kingdom. But he died not long ago and his widow was left with no resources to handle the funeral expenses. Someone will one day be faced with a bill for funeral expenses for me——and even bargain funerals are anything but cheap these days, I understand. Unless I make provision in advance for such an event, I saddle a loved one with the financial burden.

Suppose I canceled all my insurance——life, hospital, automobile, homeowners, and all the rest. And then suppose I suddenly graduated to glory to live with Jesus there instead of here. I'd be in heaven, but what about my surviving loved ones faced with the problem of disposing of my mortal remains, for which I no longer had any need? As I look at it, here are their options:

1. They could simply ignore what's left of me and kick it under the shrubbery. But that solution happens to be illegal in Maryland and otherwise impractical because of our hot summers. Admittedly, it might conceivably work in Antarctica, where the ground is too hard to dig anyhow and the whole outdoors has been frozen solid as a turkey in a frozen-food locker for longer than anyone can remember. But I'm not planning to move that far away just to get a bargain funeral.

2. They could choose a more conventional method of carcass disposal and be stuck with the bill for it. These days, there is no low-cost method.

In other words, a superreligious attitude toward life insurance could mean that someone close to me would be stuck with the expense of getting rid of the earthly leftovers of Harold Hill.

Get the message? It all sounded so religious and highly spiritual that day when the brother derided us for not canceling all our insurance. But I have never regretted consulting Jesus about it and am highly gratified with the results. Seems to me it's simply good etiquette and thoughtful consideration of the well-being of your loved ones for you to carry sufficient life insurance to take care of the last rites procedures instead of burdening someone else with the bill.

I'll say it again: Don't be hung up with someone's dead doctrine about any of these things. Jesus set you free so you would be *free,* not so you would be in bondage to anyone else's ideas, ever.

So there you have it, folks, my personal report on how God's Master Money Plan works for me. Begin today to apply these principles from the *Manufacturer's Handbook* to your own life and affairs and report back to me. For best results, start a King's Kids' Money Training Club and help your friends along the road to a life that's free from financial worries—the Bible way.

Send a self-addressed stamped envelope for details to get you started.

King's Kids' Korner
P.O. Box 8655
Baltimore, MD 21240